REVOLUCIÓN TO ROXY

From dodging bullets in '50s Cuba
to Roxy's 50th anniversary,
and a whole lot more in between

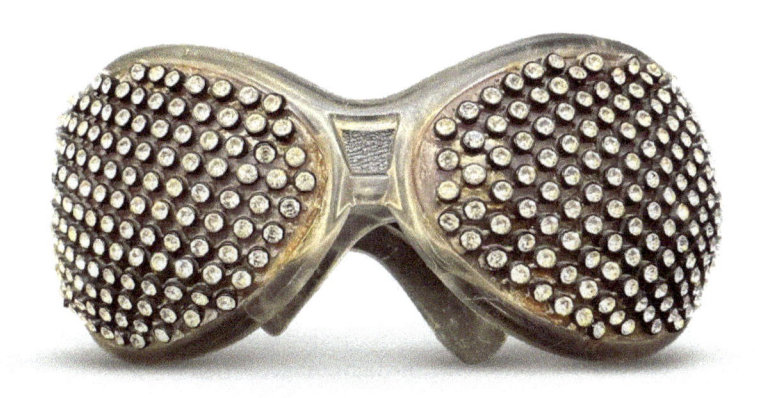

Phil Manzanera

*To my parents, Duncan and Magola,
forever grateful for a life "sin fronteras."*

Revolución To Roxy

Copyright © 2023 Phil Manzanera

First published in Great Britain

expression

ISBN: 978-1-78324-281-8

www.manzanera.com

Artwork by Simon Ryan
Book design by Wordzworth

The moral right of the authors has been asserted

All rights reserved. Without limiting the rights under copyright reserved above, no part of this publication may be reproduced, stored or introduced into a retrieval system, recording or otherwise, without the prior written permission of both the copyright owner and publisher of this book

A CIP catalogue record for this book is available from the British library.

"

Soaring like an angel one minute and stumbling like a sleepwalker the next.

-Ian MacDonald

CONTENTS

Preface		vii
Chapter 1	"You Say You Want a Revolution…"	1
Chapter 2	We Don't Need No Education…	27
Chapter 3	Roxy – Take One	47
Chapter 4	Recording	59
Chapter 5	On Tour	83
Chapter 6	Roxy – Take Two	99
Chapter 7	The Beat Goes On…	113
Chapter 8	In Search of Roots	125
Chapter 9	Serendipity	137
Chapter 10	The Things You Do	149
Chapter 11	Family Revelations	157
Chapter 12	Producer	167
Chapter 13	Have Guitar Will Travel…	177
Chapter 14	Roxy – Take Three	187
Chapter 15	The Gilmour Years	199
Chapter 16	Going Solo	209

Chapter 17	Endless River	215
Chapter 18	A Rainbow With a Pot of Gold	221
Chapter 19	Pizzica in Puglia	227
Chapter 20	Pirates of the Caribbean	239
Chapter 21	Return to Cuba and Other Adventures	243
Chapter 22	It's Only Rock n' Roll But We Like It …	251
Chapter 23	The Seventies	265
Addendum		275
Thanks		285
Photo Credits		287
Index		289
Discography		303

PREFACE

The question you may be asking is, does the world really need another 'rock-star memoir?' And to be honest, it's a question I've sometimes asked myself. The answer in my case is that, having recently researched my mum and dad's rich family history, there have been countless times when I've thought, "I wish I could have asked them that – I wish they'd written down some of their stories." Also, over the years, when I've given talks or interviews about various episodes from my life, kind people have often said, "Phil, you really should write all this down in a book." Usually when that happens, I nod appreciatively and think "yes, but all my time is taken up by music, so how will I ever get around to it?" Then came the 2020-21 global pandemic, we were locked down in our homes, and I wondered whether I could turn adversity into creativity and make this the perfect opportunity to begin writing down some of my stories. And never having been someone content to have just one project on the go, I also have lockdown to thank for the twenty-five songs I co-wrote with my friend Tim Finn.

So here they are. Some of the stories from my life. I've written them down for my children, my grandchildren, and for my wider family including my numerous cousins in Colombia. And of course, they're also for the fans who have followed my musical twists and turns over the last half century, and to whom I am forever grateful.

I hope you'll find my family's history every bit as fascinating as anything in my fifty-year career in music. Of course, it's no problem if you want to skip straight to Roxy, but I think you'll be missing out on some cracking stories if you do.

ONE

"You Say You Want a Revolution…"

It's not by chance that rock and roll got itself grouped in the cliché alongside sex and drugs. Nothing for me will ever quite match the thrill of striking the first ear-splitting guitar chords and projecting a fusillade of sound into the eardrums of 200,000 happy people, all of them ready to clap their hands and stamp their feet in the blazing Italian sunshine. Or of jamming with duelling guitars alongside some of the world's most legendary rock heroes whose music has provided the soundtracks to our lives. It's something like sex or drugs, or maybe it's more like leaping off a cliff-edge and feeling the warm wind beneath your wings. No drug drink-induced rush could ever quite match it and you just can't wait to do it all again.

But any lifetime in rock and roll with so many highs will have some lows too; sometimes involving amazing talents who've left us far too soon, and some occasioned by friends who made the classic mistake of believing their own publicity. Through it all, I feel I've had less than my share of bad luck, more than my share of good luck, and I count myself extremely fortunate to be here to tell some of the tales.

I'm under no illusion that any fame or celebrity I may enjoy arises mostly from my fifty years as the guitarist in Roxy Music. I'm proud of everything we achieved in all those years. However, I do have quite a few of my own stories, many of which took place alongside the Roxy experience or during the years when the band was "resting". At the time of writing I'm also celebrating fifty years of continuous work as a professional musician. For some of those years I've stood center stage, and for quite a lot of them I've stood right alongside some of the finest musicians of the last half century. And I've loved every minute of it. More or less.

In the first ten years of doing interviews with Roxy Music, no one ever asked me about my Latino roots, and I don't suppose anyone even knew I was fluent in Spanish. You might have thought that using a Latin stage name would have been a clue – I always used my mother's family name Manzanera rather than my very British father's surname Targett-Adams. Interviewers would assume I'd been an art school student like Brian Eno, or even better a Fine Arts man like Bryan Ferry: Roxy was labelled an Art Rock band. I would apologetically say in press interviews that my trajectory was a million miles from theirs, but that wasn't what they wanted to hear. So, I just stuck to talking about the Velvet Underground or Terry Riley or systems music, Motown, or Miles Davis.

The lack of interest among the music press in my South American roots was understandable because the common perception in Britain in the 60s and 70s was that Latin music was of the Edmundo Ross variety. Latin music as played on the television show *Come Dancing* and generally just kitsch stuff. The reality was far from it. The reason the 'British invasion' of pop music took decades to take off in South America was that they already had a very sexy form of music to dance and party to. Carlos Santana was really the first exploration into Latin rock and that was West Coast USA. Os Mutantes from Brazil would only be discovered by Kurt Cobain and David Byrne in the 90s. Pretty much all Latin dance music had a strong groove which made what was coming out of the UK seem lightweight. They had no need for wimpy music sung in English by 'melenudos' (moptops).

Looking back on my recordings with Roxy there was no scope for injecting any salsa, cumbia or mambo, but my constant attempts to inject my cumbia 6/8 feel with the use of repeat echo is there to be deciphered. My real musical journey started in Cuba in 1957 but New Year's Eve in Havana, Cuba, 1958, was the momentous occasion of my childhood and the reverberations of that night are still with me today.

Brother Eugen, sister Rosemary and one year old me, Clapham London, 1952

The Cuban revolution was all a very long way from my earliest childhood years growing up with my mum, dad and my older brother Eugen and sister Rosemary in a four bedroom semi- in the leafy south London suburb of Clapham. Our house was attached on one side to the Salvation Army Hall, and I have a distant recall of hearing the distinctive music of the brass band striking up on Sunday mornings and echoing through my bedroom walls. "Abide with me."

In those days we felt safe playing together on the Common, so I'm not quite sure why my first memory is of a uniformed constable of the *Dixon of Dock Green* variety bringing me back home to my worried parents. Maybe I'd wandered off somewhere. The bobby had a big black moustache, which reminded me of a scary cartoon character who I think was called Hank, and so I hid behind the sofa.

I attended the local primary school, rode my bike, drew numbers on the paving stones in chalk, played hopscotch, and generally did everything a happy south London kid would. We had a black and white telly with a tiny ten-inch screen in a walnut cabinet, and I loved all those shows like *Robin Hood*, *The Scarlet Pimpernel*, *Hopalong Cassidy*, and *The Lone Ranger*. In those days no-one saw any problem with the masked man calling his native-American sidekick "Tonto", and even I didn't know at the time that "Tonto" means "stupid" in Spanish. It was all a long time ago. We devoured comics like the Dandy, Beano, and the Eagle, and I was drawn to anything vaguely scientific. My best friend Steven lived in a block of flats nearby, and he and I produced an ingenious walkie-talkie communication device consisting of two tin-cans connected together with a long piece of string. He'd be in his bedroom window speaking into one end, and I'd be outside trying to receive the message. Not a great success.

There was a corner shop and for a treat I'd get a bottle of Tizer, and in those days the milkman delivered in an electric-powered float which would glide along almost silently save for the rattling of glass bottles in their crates. He sold all sorts of treats like chocolate milk, and there was a frozen orange drink in a solid triangular shape called a Jubbly, which was a favourite. I remember going to Brighton with my dad on a steam train

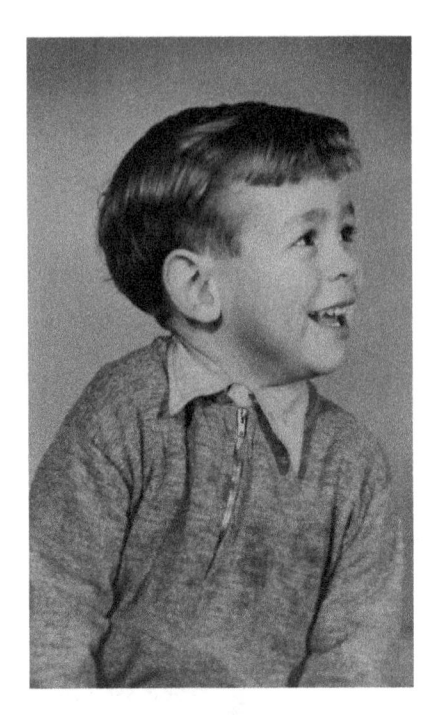

Me aged four, Clapham, London

and holding his hand on the walk down that long hill from the railway station. I recall him being very big alongside me, and the special smell of the ozone-filled air and the crunch of beach pebbles underfoot. That must have been the first time I ever went to the seaside.

Our dad worked for the airline BOAC, which much later merged with BEA and became British Airways. Tall and slim, he was always smartly dressed, heading out to work every day wearing a stylish long overcoat and trilby hat. He'd had a promising career as a film extra in his earlier days and looked a bit like Errol Flynn. He'd first met Mum when he was working for the British Council and had been posted overseas in Colombia. It was against the rules to fraternize with the locals, but he was 29, handsome and a long way from home. Magdalena Manzanera was 20, pretty and there.

Tío Alfonso, Mamá, Eugen, Me, Rosemary, and cousins, Carmenza and Elsa outside our family road, West Road, Clapham

When they found out she was pregnant, they married quickly and moved to a new posting in Argentina, fixed by dad's mentor, Sir Eugen Millington Drake, head of the British Council in South America. My brother Eugen was born in Tucumán, but by the time my sister Rosemary was born four years later they had returned to England, which Mum must have found very disorientating. A Colombian woman speaking hardly any English was like a fish out of water in 1950s London.

To all appearances we were a very normal family in which young children were to be seen and not heard, and so I neither asked nor was offered any explanation when, one day in February 1957, I was taken with mum, dad and sister to London airport at Heath Row (as it was known since the Second World War). We were boarding a plane to the tropical island of Cuba, where the Gulf of Mexico meets the Atlantic and the Caribbean. Dad was being sent to open the first BOAC office in Havana, with a mission to recruit the necessary staff and prepare for the inaugural flight. Recent advances in jet propeller planes and pure jet aircraft meant more adventurous possibilities, and new intercontinental routes were being opened all around the world. Offices, infrastructure and logistics all needed to be set.

BOAC Stratocruiser

The first passenger terminals at Heath Row were ex-military marquees which formed a tented village along the Bath Road. They were primitive but comfortable, equipped with floral-patterned armchairs, sofas and small tables containing vases of fresh flowers. There was no heating in the marquees, which meant that during winter it could be bitterly cold. To reach aircraft parked on the apron, passengers had to walk over wooden duckboards to protect their shoes from the muddy airfield.

There on the tarmac was the luxurious and elegant BOAC Stratocruiser, which was one of the new propeller planes capable of flying long distances. A thing of elegant beauty. My memory of it is in black and white, and as I think about it, everything I remember in London from my early life is in monochrome. Maybe it's through the prism of passing time, but whenever I think about that day, my mind goes to those final scenes of Casablanca, complete with my dad as Bogie. We walked into the dark foggy night towards the plane, climbed up the steps and settled into the small first-class compartment. I was six years old and about to take my first ever flight, first class. Travelling as part of 'the firm' had its rewards.

The interior of First Class on a Stratocruiser was based on the great tradition of British railway trains. There were couchettes above the seats that pulled down for sleeping, but the stand-out novelty feature was a spiral staircase leading down to a cocktail bar. This was 50s living VIP style. The privileged treatment included membership of the Junior Jet Club, which came with a smart lapel badge and a little book which was signed by the captain.

We made two stops on our transatlantic crossing, both US air force bases, one in Shannon and the other in Newfoundland, Nova Scotia. Then on to Nassau in the Bahamas where we transferred to a Cubana de Aviación flight to José Martí airport in Havana. It was the start of my lifelong keen interest in planes.

Everything about Cuba was about as far removed from Clapham as my young mind could take in. The people were noisy and boisterous, and everywhere you looked

Couchette in first class

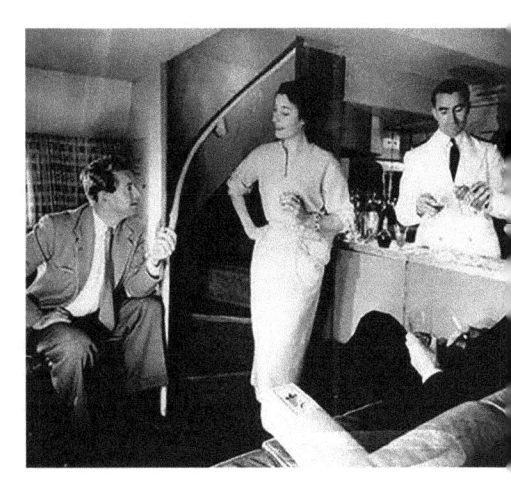

Bar downstairs

there was sunshine and bright colour. This was Cuba before the revolution, before Fidel Castro and Che Guevara, when decades of instability and military coups had culminated in a tropical paradise for rich American tourists, playboys, and high rollers. The government run by President Batista was corrupt from top to bottom, and the vast gap between rich and poor was a crucible for dissent and eventual revolution.

But all that was still a couple of years away, and when our family landed after our epic journey, we went straight from the airport to the pink iconic Hotel Naciónal situated by the Malecón, a seafront promenade leading to old Havana.

Built in the 1920s, the hotel was a magnet for the rich, the glamorous, and the famous including Winston Churchill, The Duke and Duchess of Windsor and later Frank Sinatra, Rita Hayworth, and Ava Gardner.

It's worth recalling a bit of the history because it gives some context to the music, and anyway it's entertaining. So much so that part

Hotel Naciónal, Havana, Cuba

of it was depicted by Francis Ford Coppola in memorable scenes from *Godfather 2*. By the time we were guests there, Hotel Naciónal was the home of the largest grossing casino in the world, which had been sub-let to the well-known mobster Meyer Lansky. In December 1946 the hotel had hosted the so-called Havana Conference, which was a summit of the most notorious gang bosses from the American mob. Run by Lansky and 'Lucky' Luciano, it was attended by Santo Trafficante Jr and Vito Genovese amongst others. The unholy alliances between mobsters and politicians made sure that Cuba in this period was a kleptocracy, and its tawdry glitter proved irrestible to some of the world's most famous musicians and movie-stars.

A vivid insight into the atmosphere of the times is provided by Rosa Lowinger in her book *Tropicana Nights*. "In early 1956, Marlon Brando took off for Cuba on the spur of the moment. On the flight, Brando ran into Gary Cooper, who was on his way to visit Ernest Hemingway at his finca on the outskirts of Havana

Me age six, poolside, Hotel Naciónal Havana, March 1957

… Brando loved to drum, so he tried to buy the tumbadora, the biggest of the conga drums, from the congero in the Tropicana's orchestra, but the guy refused, saying, 'I'm using it'. The dancers were all going crazy seeing Brando in the audience, and after the show ended, he took off with the two most statuesque of the showgirls, to explore the underground clubs."

Film producer Carola Ash, who left Cuba with her family after the revolution, elaborates: "Back in the 50s, if a star like Alec Guinness or

Marlene Dietrich, came to town, my father, (the well-known film critic Guillermo Cabrera Infante), may have spent time with them," probably partying hard in some very racy nightclubs.

I guess you could say it was colourful, but anything like that was of course going on in a parallel universe way above my six year old head and moving out of the Naciónal to a rented apartment within a month meant that I could now go to the American school on a US-style yellow school bus. It was exciting being picked up outside the apartment with my tin lunch box filled with egg sandwiches made by my mum. Quite a difference from the Glenbrook primary school in Clapham. I exchanged *Bill and Ben*, *Robin Hood* and *Quatermass* for *Tom and Jerry*, *Zorro* and *I Love Lucy*. Instead of fish and chips, roast beef, and Yorkshire pudding, I was eating caraotas negras con arroz, congrí, plátanos fritos, tostones, ropa vieja and lechón asado, washed down with proper American Coca-Cola in real glass bottles. However, asthma struck in that first year, maybe an allergic reaction to pollen from tropical plants, and I have vivid memories of looking upwards from the confines of an oxygen tent in a local hospital, at the worried faces of parents and doctors.

Living in an apartment opposite the British ambassador's residence should have been a clue when years later I began wondering why my parents invariably ended up in countries on the brink of revolutions. Everywhere we went we seemed to have close connections with the British Consul or Ambassador. There appears to have been a reason, but I wouldn't learn much more about it for the best part of half a century.

Within a year we moved again, and this time it was to a spacious house with a large garden in the affluent residential area of Miramar. The house was rented by BOAC and was a white two-storey modernist building in the style of Max Borges Jr, who was the famous Cuban architect who built the Tropicana club. Number 521, Quinta Avenida, Miramar was a light and airy building with balconies looking out over exotic tropical flowers. The best bit for me, though, was that it had a proper bar-type room, like a mini nightclub, complete with cocktail tables, leather benches and a large, illuminated fish tank. This was where my parents entertained, frequently hosting lively parties of ex-pats and exuberant Latinos. Mostly there was lively Latin-American music, but my dad also liked to

"YOU SAY YOU WANT A REVOLUTION…"

Our home in Miramar, Havana 1958

play showtunes like *My Fair Lady*, because he'd known Rex Harrison during his acting days and had a soft spot for anything quintessentially British. The house backed onto another large, rather ugly pink house that we could clearly see from the first-floor landing window, and right next door was the house of General Tabernilla who was the chief of staff of the dictator Batista. Again, at the time, it seemed like nothing more than coincidence, and I suppose the main attraction of the house for Tabernilla was its proximity to the military airfield and army camp at

Me as Zorro in garden of Miramar house, Havana 1958

Dad with Mum and Franca in front of Ford Zodiac car, Havana 1958

Campo Colombia. He had armed guards permanently stationed outside, and the soldiers were friendly to the little English boy who ran around his garden dressed as Zorro. Putting on those flamboyant stage clothes in early Roxy was never a problem after having dressed up with hat and cape, aged seven, in our Miramar Garden.

Dad had a British manufactured car, a Ford Zodiac, imported especially for him, and we'd go for family outings and buy all sorts of street food from vendors on the side of the road. We had a maid who would help with the cooking, and a special treat would be *bacalao frito*, which is a bit like fish and chips Cuban style.

Living in a new home in a new area meant I was sent to an all-Spanish speaking Cuban school. I was the only English kid in the class, and so within three months I was fluent, much to the delight of my Colombian mum. My school was just a short walk away, further along the same road we lived in, and my new ex-pat life made me happy and more confident.

There were frequent trips to the British Club for swimming, and on one occasion I thrillingly played my first game of cricket in a 'fathers and sons' match. Life was good for this excitable youngster, and I have lots of photos and super 8 footage to prove it.

My brother and sister, both older, were at boarding schools in England but would visit for holidays. Music was everywhere but trips to the famous Tropicana Club to see shows featuring fantastic musicians and exotic semi-naked dancers were wasted on a boy of that age, who mercifully would be falling asleep at the table by the time the show reached its steamy climax.

Many of the musicians who ended up 40 years later in the Buena Vista Social Club were in their prime, and often playing at the Tropicana Club and the Sans-Souci club. Though I might often be dozing through the shows, the sounds and rhythms swirling around me were no doubt seeping in and taking root, helping to form my musical DNA. However, the most significant part of my early musical life occurred in that white house in Miramar the day my mum came home with a Spanish guitar made in Havana. Mum had an Italian lady friend called Franca who was married to the British Consul, and they used to love singing together, so they decided to have guitar lessons to provide accompaniment to their classic Spanish and Latin songs. It's incredible that it's taken writing this book to make the connection that my music career started at that moment, and I have my mother to thank for it: my first and only guitar teacher. I inherited that guitar and see it every day in my music room.

Listening to my mum and Franca practicing their music, I came to realize

Franca and Gladys, her daughter, with that guitar, 1958

that there is a canon of songs sung in Spanish that you can hear in almost every Spanish speaking restaurant even today. I guess they're what we call evergreens. Being an inquisitive and annoying seven year old, I wanted to touch the instrument that made such a sweet sound and my mum succumbed to the inevitable and said, "if you are going to be such a pain about touching my guitar, I'll have to teach you some chords." So began my musical career.

Mum's Cuban guitar in my music room

Songs such as *Paloma* and *Cielito Lindo* are imprinted on my brain, and even now, if I drink enough margaritas, they are likely to come out spontaneously.

Although the island of Cuba was filled with music, in January 1958 everyone in Cuba was listening to Radio Rebelde, the rebels' mouthpiece, which was reporting that Fidel Castro and Che Guevara, the Fidelistas, were making progress through the island, winning battles, and attacking the dictator Batista's troops. The Sierra Maestra mountains had been their base and a number of American journalists had embedded themselves with the rebels, writing articles about these charismatic characters who wanted to bring their own brand of Marxism to the region.

Among the rebels' objectives was to attract international attention to their struggle, and their opportunity came in February 1958. The Cuban Grand Prix had been established the previous year by the Batista Government which wanted to create an event to attract wealthy tourists, particularly from the United States. A street circuit was established on the seafront of Havana, on the Malecón. The first competition had been won by the Argentinian world champion, Juan Manuel Fangio, driving a Maserati 300S, and had been a huge success.

Mum at Miramar house, 1958

In this second year the official Maserati team arrived in force in their fleet of 300S cars, with Fangio and the British ace Stirling Moss as drivers. In an interview for the newspaper *Diario de la Marina* on Saturday 22 February, Moss said he had a great car this year and was

> **DIARIO DE LA MARINA.—Sábado, 22 de Febrero de 1958**
>
> STIRLING MOSS y señora aparecen rodeados de Ducan Targett y Mr. Simon con sus respectivas esposas, todos ellos miembros de la Embajada británica así como nuestro compañero Antonio Meizoso. — (Foto Bernard).
>
> ## STIRLING MOSS MUY CONFIADO
> ### LLEGO A LAS 9:00 DE LA NOCHE. TIENE BUENA MAQUINA
>
> Ayer a las 9 en punto de la noche llegó a La Habana el subcampeón mundial de automovilismo Stirling Moss acompañado de su Sra. esposa. Moss, que está considerado el más peligroso rival de Fangio actualmente, está sumamente confiado en que podrá obtener una gran victoria tripulando su Ferrari de 4,100 c.c.
>
> El gran corredor británico que es capitán de la mundialmente famosa escudería Vanwall va al frente de la puntuación este año con ocho puntos a su favor.
>
> El año pasado Moss no pudo demostrar ante el público cubano todo lo que vale como volante ya que la máquina que tripuló además de ser antigua era de pequeño cilindraje. Comentando sobre la carrera del día 24 el británico manifestó lo siguiente: "Estoy muy contento con estar de nuevo en Cuba y espero que tendré más suerte que el año pasado. Sé que la carrera será muy disputada ya que sólo vasta con echar una ojeada a la lista de pilotos para comprobar la clase de la misma. Creo que Fangio y Behra serán los rivales más peligrosos ya que disponen de máquinas muy modernas y veloces".
>
> Moss confía en que hoy podrá hacer el mejor tiempo en las primeras pruebas de clasificación y así alcanzar un lugar bueno en la arrancada. Stirling declaró también que tripulará en las 12 horas de Sebring una máquina Aston-Martin que compartirá con Tony Brooks que también pertenece a la Vanwall.

Newspaper article, L to R : Tommy Simon, Mum, Dad, Stirling Moss, British Embassy staff and Franca Simon, 22 Feb 1958

looking forward to winning against Fangio. The article is accompanied by a picture showing Stirling Moss and his wife, along with the British Consul Tommy Simon with his wife Franca, and with them are my mum and dad. They all look very glamorous.

By the morning of the race, we were in a frenzy of excitement and we positioned ourselves on the grassy knoll of the Hotel Naciónal, facing the Malecón, to watch the qualifying heat. If I close my eyes, I can still vividly recall the sight, sound and smell of those Formula One Ferraris and Maseratis with their open cockpits, their engines roaring like the approach of Armageddon.

Starting grid of F1 race

All was going according to plan until, on the eve of the race, a band of armed men burst into his hotel and kidnapped Fangio. They were members of the 26th of July Movement, so-named to commemorate an attack five years before on the army barracks on Santiago de Cuba in an earlier attempt to overthrow the Batista regime. The rebels' plan to create an international news event to publicize the troubles in Cuba was working. Suddenly the eyes of the world were on the island.

The kidnappers never intended to cause any harm to Fangio; the idea was just to make him miss the race and then let him go. The Cuban government, frustrated at not finding his captors and fearing the bad publicity, panicked and ordered the race to continue. Moss and Masten Gregory led the race, which was red flagged after just six laps because the Cuban driver Armando Garcia Cifuentes horrifically crashed his Ferrari into the crowd, killing seven. We watched it all unfold live before our eyes, and we learned later that Fangio also watched the coverage on the television in his captors' rooms while tucking into a steak dinner. Stirling Moss was declared the winner, but it must have been a hollow victory.

In the course of the rest of the year, Fidel and the guerillas of the 26th of July Movement made more progress, especially in winning over the hearts and minds of the Cuban people. At the beginning of 1958 United States companies owned about forty percent of the Cuban sugar lands, almost all the cattle ranches, ninety percent of the mines and mineral concessions, eighty percent of the utilities, practically all the oil industry, and they supplied two-thirds of Cuba's imports. The conspicuous disparity between the vast wealth and hedonistic lifestyle of the rich, especially foreigners, versus the extreme poverty of ordinary local people, proved a fertile breeding ground for what was to come.

Gradually the Batista regime was also losing international support, and when the U.S. declared the elections in November as invalid and stopped sending weapons, the dictator realized the game was up. On 11 December, the U.S. Ambassador Earl Smith visited Batista at his hacienda and informed him that America could no longer support his government. Two weeks later, on 28 December Che Guevara attacked and seized Santa Clara, which is halfway up the country from Santiago de Cuba and near the capital. Then on the 30 December Camilo Cienfuegos led a victory in Yaguajay and finally Batista realized he had run out of time and needed to make a fast getaway.

Marta Rojas, a journalist at the time for Bohemia Magazine, was able to reconstruct Batista's last night in Cuba, "… which he spent at his Campamento Colombia residence, hosting a New Year's Eve reception with his wife, Marta. Late that night, he convened his military elite to declare, in the third person, that Batista was resigning from the presidency and departing immediately. His closest allies quickly led their wives, still in their evening gowns, and pyjama'd children to the awaiting planes on the base's airstrip. One of the passengers on Batista's plane envisioned the DC-4 as 'a huge casket carrying a cargo of live corpses.'

The dictator took along a personal fortune reported to be more than $300 million that he'd amassed through bribery and corruption. Batista and his supporters were later accused of taking as much as $700 million in fine art and cash with them as they fled into exile. Batista had hoped to return to his estate in Daytona Beach, but Ambassador Smith informed him that he was not presently welcome in the U.S., so the dictator was forced to announce that his plane was changing course and heading to the Dominican Republic.

Once again, the resulting mayhem out in the streets was vividly represented by Coppola in *Godfather 2*. Everywhere there was unseemly panic as whole coteries of assorted gangsters and conmen abandoned their gambling chips and women and bolted for the airport. What was left of the army attempted to keep order, and there were random shootings by both sides.

Victorious 'Barbudos" enter Havana, 1 January 1959

One week later Fidel Castro made his glorious entry into Havana, where he was greeted like a saviour. This was 8 January, but for some reason he didn't officially declare himself president for another six weeks. By the end of Batista's rule, later described by President Kennedy as "one of the most bloody and repressive dictatorships in the long history of Latin American repression" up to 20,000 Cubans had been killed.

The way all this was experienced by my family was recalled by my dad in an interview with the Honolulu Star Bulletin, given shortly after he arrived there three months later to take up a new post in Hawaii. The article, written by an Alton Slagle, is dated Wednesday 18 February, 1959, and headlined, 'Briton Watched the Fall of Batista, Sees No Rising Castro Dictatorship'.

Dad's optimistic view of Castro establishing a democratic Cuba was widely held by the West but of course as events unfolded this was not to be.

"Duncan Targett-Adams was confident he lived in the safest place in Cuba. Because next door resided a general named Tabernilla – chief of the Cuban Army under President Fulgencio Batista. Then, less than three hours after New Year's Eve revelers had begun their horn-tooting last month, a bearded 32-year-old rebel lawyer named Fidel Castro ended a month-long siege of Batista's quaking dictatorship, and the Targett-Adams family was suddenly in a very unsafe spot. 'I saw twenty soldiers – Tabernilla's guards – arrested', Targett-Adams said yesterday. 'The General himself escaped, but his home was looted'."

The article continues: "Targett-Adams ... is an old hand at South American revolutions. He lived in Argentina when President Juan Perón was ousted, and in Paraguay when rebel forces fought President Higinio Morinigo. Added the mild-mannered Briton of his Cuban adventure: 'They took quite a lot of our things away, too. The second night we neighbours formed a security patrol. I had no gun, but my companion did. However, the revolution was remarkable for its self-control. There were many cases of looting, but not, I think, by Castro's men. They only attacked the houses of Batista's associates. Most who came to Castro were simple mountain people. Their conduct was very good. We slept on the bathroom floor; it was the safest place in the house. The television kept

Briton Watched the Fall of Batista, Sees No Rising Castro Dictatorship

HONOLULU STAR-BULLETIN, WEDNESDAY, FEBRUARY 18, 1959

By ALTON SLAGLE

Duncan Targett-Adams was confident he lived in the safest place in Cuba.

Because next door resided a general named Tabernilla —chief of the Cuban army under President Fulgencio Batista.

Then, less than three hours after New Year's revelers had begun their horn-tooting last month, a bearded 32-year-old rebel lawyer named Fidel Castro ended a months-long seige of Batista's quaking dictatorship, and the Targett-Adams family was suddenly in a very unsafe spot.

"I saw 20 soldiers—Tabernilla's guards — arrested," Targett-Adams said yesterday. "The General himself escaped, but his home was looted."

ASSIGNED HERE

Targett-Adams, who arrived Saturday to head a new Honolulu district office of the British Overseas Airways Corporation, is an old hand at South American revolutions.

He lived in Argentina when President Juan Peron was ousted, and in Paraguay when rebel forces fought President Higinio Morinigo.

Added the mild-mannered Briton of his Cuban adventure:

"They took quite a lot of our things away, too. The second night we neighbors formed a security patrol. I had no gun, but my companion did.

"However, the revolution was remarkable for its self control. There were many cases of looting, but not, I think, by Castro's men. They only attacked houses of Batista's associates.

"Most who came to Castro were simple mountain people. Their conduct was very good.

"We slept on the bathroom floor; it was the safest place in the house. The television kept warning which houses would be looted next.

"There was no police force, and there are nearly two million people in Havana."

PEOPLES' REVOLT

It was a peoples' revolt for which an underground movement had been planning for 18 months, said Targett-Adams. It completely upset the economic life of Cuba, which, thanks to sugar production, is a very prosperous country, he added.

"Castro is making enormous efforts to get everything back to normal," he said. "After a period of problems and anxieties, Cuba should be a better country."

Castro has the full support of 90 per cent of Cuba's population, said Targett-Adams.

NO DICTATOR

"It will be a surprise to everybody if he emerges a dictator. His policy is against dictatorship."

Mass executions of Batista's henchmen were necessary to prevent the return of his regime, Targett-Adams believes.

"We saw the first tribunal trial," he said. "It was the general feeling that the people on trial did what they were accused of doing. The Batista torture stories were apparently true.

"These men got what they deserved."

Duncan Targett-Adams

Dad's interview in the Star Bulletin, Honolulu, Hawaii, Feb 18 1959

warning which houses would be looted next. There was no police force, and there are nearly two million people in Havana'."

All that was no doubt recalled by my dad after some time and opportunity for calm reflection. My own memory as a seven year old is more emotional. I recall that the New Year's Eve parties were over and by 2am we were fearing for our lives. We were all crouched on the bathroom floor, heads pressed down by my shrieking mother, and our hearts pounding. Bullets were flying all over the place, lighting up the darkness outside, and a gun battle was taking place from our back garden towards General Tabernilla's house. With every rifle shot my mum screamed and was praying out loud. It was terrifying. Hours later in the daylight, around midday and now watching from the window on the landing, we saw two green canvas-topped 26th July Movement military trucks, with their distinctive red and black logos, pull up from either end of the street. 'Barbudos' (so called because of their 'rock star' black beards) in green fatigues and with black and red armbands jumped out from the back of the trucks. The Batista guards standing outside the house, dressed in blue police uniforms, were waiting for their pay, planning to disband, discard their uniforms, and run away. It was not to be.

Instead, they were lined up against the garage doors and made to put their hands in the air. One did a runner over a nearby fence, and we heard shots. I could only suppose he didn't get away but by now my mum was hysterical and telling my brother to stop taking photos. The strange thing is that, even though I've rewound the scenes in my head countless times, I have no recollection of my dad being there. The prisoners were then carted off either to 'el paredón' (the wall for executions) or to the prison on the Isla de los Pinos, which was an infamous heavy-duty jail that had previously been used by Batista for incarcerating the insurgents. Months later, a letter arrived from one of those guards called Santana who had befriended us at our house, asking for help to get him out of jail and out of Cuba. By then we were off the island and of course there was nothing we could do for him, and we never heard from him again.

Mass looting broke out over the next week and Castro put guards on a lot of key houses to try to stop the chaos. We would watch as cars pulled up and people went into the house opposite us, coming out later with booty of all descriptions. They'd stash whatever they'd grabbed in the trunks of their 50s Chevrolets and Oldsmobile cars and drive off. Eventually a soldier was stationed outside the front door of Tabernilla's house to stop the free for all.

We used to look at the guard from the landing window, that same window where we had witnessed the events of the previous week. One day my mum said, 'He looks so bored and probably would love a cafecito. Why don't you take him one?" I was duly dispatched with a tray carrying coffee and cake. I approached nervously and asked him whether he would like the coffee. A broad smile appeared. He had a green uniform with a bandolier slung over each shoulder with .303 shells. He undid one, emptied the gunpowder and put a match to it. *Whoosh*! followed by that distinctive smell of cordite. I was impressed, but my mum would have been horrified. I loved his green combat cap with the black and red flag with '26th July' on the front.

Me with Barbudo in garden, Miramar

One day a truck came down the street handing out caps and armbands for us kids – even they had merchandise. We chatted and he pointed to the door behind his chair. "Quieres entrar?" "Si por

Me with Barbudo

supuesto," I replied. What I saw has stayed with me. It was full of rubbish up to a height of about eighteen inches. Just loads of 'stuff'. The looters had strewn everything around the floor. Piles of it. Picking my way through the debris, I went from room to room collecting whatever caught my eye into a bag. What kind of things does a seven year old pick up? Empty .303 rifle shells, the gold encrusted epaulettes of the General's white dinner jacket and a photo album. That photo album with pictures of Cuban air

View from Britannia plane leaving Havana

force officers with British RAF officers have made me think over the years; why was the British government selling planes and bolstering Batista? Though of course I could not have known it, we were just four years away from events which would take the world to the very edge of nuclear war.

For the moment our lives went on as before, until one night we came back to our house and discovered it had been burgled. All of us were shaken up, and when it was suggested that foreigners should move to a guarded apartment block, my parents agreed. The new apartment was on the coast, just down the road from the Teatro Karl Marx. Swimming there, I had my first encounter with a

The plane we left Cuba on (Bristol Britannia 175 - 318, Cubana de Aviacion 1959)

black sea urchin, and the excruciating pain of treading on it has left me very wary of entering the sea without rubber shoes to this day.

It was just six weeks before we were due to leave and on 14th February we were evacuated from Cuba to New York. Ironically, we were flown out on a Bristol Brittania jet prop plane purchased by the state airline, Cubana, from Britain.

The plane, fondly known as the Whispering Giant, trundled down the runway, and the moment the wheels left the ground there was spontaneous applause in the cabin. The sudden noise terrified our chihuahua Winnie, which we'd somehow managed to finagle onto the plane. The release of tension was palpable, and I joined in and started laughing. Four hours later we were in New York.

TWO

We Don't Need No Education …

My sister and I were watching a TV show about Honolulu and Waikiki and just getting used to the delights of hotel room-service when our dad returned from visiting the BOAC office in New York. "Where are we off to next?" we shouted. Dad said nothing, and just pointed at the screen. "Hawaii? Wow!" We were thrilled.

It's difficult to think of anything more exciting for an 8 year old kid at that time than to be heading to the island of Oahu, Hawaii. All the while we'd lived in Cuba, we'd been watching American TV, and now we were off there at exactly the moment when it was transitioning to become the 50th state of the USA. Dad moved us into a lovely bungalow-type house about twenty minutes' drive from Waikiki beach, which then was about as beautiful a stretch of sand as anyone could imagine. All the houses in the district had well-manicured and unnaturally green lawns, with those American post-boxes on a pole at the front. There were no fences dividing the front gardens, and the newspaper delivery boy hardly paused on his bike as he lobbed the daily news somewhere in the direction of the front door.

Eugen, me and Mum, New York City, Feb 1958

Suddenly, for the first time ever, we got to go to something called "the steakhouse", which was incredible, and where you could also get things like fries and a milkshake. I used to love all that American stuff. Dad even bought an American car, a Chevy, and we took our Chevy to the Hawaiian levee at the beach with picnics near to the famous blow-hole and generally got into the 50s Hawaiian American lifestyle.

By now my brother Eugen and sister Rosemary had returned to boarding school in England and I was on my own with Mum and Dad, once again speaking English. I was sent to a Catholic school; not that we were religious, but South American Catholicism is like a series of, "how can we work the system so that we don't have to go to church on Sunday morning?" We might have to go to the service at six o'clock in the evening and then we could party after that.

My school finished for the day about 3pm, and then I'd get on a bus and meet my mum at Waikiki beach. We'd have some sort of Asian noodles, which always tasted delicious. One day I decided to try to hire

WE DON'T NEED NO EDUCATION...

Rose arriving in Honolulu with Dad and us at post box Aina Haina, then us all at beach Feb 1959

a surfboard, which I was able to do from the Royal Hawaiian Hotel. I paddled out and managed to climb onto the thing, and then there was a huge wave which rose on the surf, flipping the board into the vertical and struck a hard blow on my head on the way down. It was one of those heavy, proper big boards and it nearly knocked me out cold. But notwithstanding the odd head injury, here I was surfing the waves on the Pacific coast, living the dream, against a backdrop of Diamond Head, which is the big volcanic bluff visible in the far distance at the end of Waikiki Beach. Of which more later.

These days the tourist hotels fill every inch of space behind the beach, but in 1958 there were only two seaside hotels, and my mum and dad were very friendly with the manager of another one a bit further back. We used to go there often, and they would settle me down in a bedroom upstairs while they'd socialise and party with my father's work colleagues and other ex-pats. I vividly remember being in the room one time when a noisy altercation in the corridor broke into a full-on fight, and there were grunts and screams and the sound of fists connecting with flesh. I was still inside the room, hearing all this going on outside. After everything that had happened so recently in Cuba, I didn't know what was happening and felt a bit traumatised.

Me on Waikiki beach with Diamond Head in the background, 1958

The reason we were in Hawaii was so my dad could oversee the inaugural BOAC flights between San Francisco, Honolulu, Tahiti, New Zealand, and Australia. Everything must have gone to plan, because there were joyous celebrations to mark the arrival of the first 707, including a traditional island greeting complete with beautiful dancing hula-hula girls, wearing pretty leis and grass skirts.

No sooner had I begun to settle into my new version of paradise than Dad's bosses decided that he'd done what they needed him to do in Hawaii. By now he was fluent in Spanish, he had a Spanish-speaking wife, and so he was the obvious person to be sent to open a new office in Venezuela. From the capital, Caracas, he'd be able run the services between Colombia, Venezuela,

WE DON'T NEED NO EDUCATION...

Trinidad, Barbados, and Antigua. So once again we were plunged straight into the privileged and rarefied lifestyle of a new ex-pat community, whose main preoccupation seemed to be drinking fruit cocktails and sunbathing around a swimming pool. Picture a scene from the TV series *Mad Men* and you've got it.

Family life in Caracas Venezuela, 1959-1965

Our first house in Caracas had a huge mamoncillo tree outside, otherwise known as Spanish lime, which was laden down with small green fruit tasting a bit like lychees and absolutely delicious. My dad was a keen golfer, and I used to love going around as his caddy. I picked up the rudiments, and still have his clubs to this day.

By this time, I was getting used to starting at new schools where I knew no-one, and when I learned that I was going to the British school I thought I'd meet some boys my own age from back home. In the event I found there were very few British kids in the school, but at least this one was mixed and there were a lot of birthday parties where it was possible to meet and talk to girls. Maybe we were a bit young to be interested in girls, and possibly it's a South American thing, but we really were. I was infatuated with a girl with the unlikely name of Rosita McDonald, and then later with my best friend's sister called Nena. We'd be dancing in Latin style, which at the time I could do properly. Young love.

Framus Lorelei guitar with Hofner pick up

One day I was sitting in the garden with some girls and another English boy called Charlie Lindsell. He had an acoustic guitar and suddenly he started to play some Chuck Berry riffs. I'd never heard anything like it before and the sound had an immediate effect on me; like it literally struck a chord somewhere deep inside, and I remember asking him straight away to show me how to play it. He did, and that was it. I'd already got the Latin influence, and now I started to put it all together in my head and with my fingertips on the fretboard. That was really the beginning of me being able to play.

At the same time, my friend Michael Sanchez Vegas and I noticed that the girls were gravitating towards these American boys who had arrived for the summer, and that's when I said to Michael, "we've got to get tooled up … we've got to get electric guitars."

Michael's father was a doctor who loved sea-fishing, and he'd take us out on his boat at five in the morning and we'd all get terribly seasick. Then at some point when we were far out to sea, he'd throw us in the water. God knows how we didn't drown. He was married to an American lady who, thinking about it now, seemed to be having an affair with the chauffeur, he drove us everywhere and even drove the boat.

Gradually I'm beginning to hear rock and roll music for the first time, there are lots of American kids arriving on vacation and I'd developed a yearning to listen to anything and everything I could find. My dad had these incredible Zenith radios with huge aerials which allowed us to pick up stations from Europe. I remember hearing Chuck Berry, Buddy Holly and then The Shadows playing *Apache*. While it was undoubtedly fabulous growing up in Caracas, I was increasingly aware that I was a million miles away from the centre of everything that was happening in the big wide world. My determination to progress from acoustic to electric guitar, coupled with a growing desperation to exchange my diet of black beans to baked beans, meant that I started thinking it was time for me to join my older brother and sister back in London.

Michael Sanchez Vegas's flash Italian guitar Caracas, 1960

My Dad's Zenith radio for listening to the BBC World Service from Caracas

The same thought must have been occurring at the same time to my mum and dad, but for different reasons. The frequent changes of school meant I'd fallen way behind in my studies, and if they waited two more years until I was 11, I'd be likely to struggle to get into a decent school. My older brother was boarding at Dulwich College, and maybe I could go there, with the hope that I'd catch up before the 11+ exams. So that became the plan.

Throughout my life I have been a bit accident prone, with a tendency to trip over things, usually in the dark. One evening, just about a month before starting at Dulwich, my mate Michael and I were larking around in the nearby country club's pool when I fell and broke my arm. Luckily Michael's dad was a doctor and was able to set the thing in a plaster. A few years later Dr Sanchez Vegas would treat another member of my family, but this time with catastrophic results.

I characterised my earlier expedition from London to Cuba as going from black and white to colour and returning in the other direction felt like the same process in reverse. My first impressions as I got off the plane was that it was freezing cold, the days were short, and everything was shrouded in dense fog. Nobody seemed to have any central heating, and if they did, it certainly wasn't turned on.

I was going to be a full-time boarder, so for the first time in my life I was facing being apart from my parents for an extended period. The shock of the change of environment was compounded when I realised that instead

The Alleynian, Dulwich school magazine, 2005

of going to school wearing shorts and a T-shirt, I was now expected to wear a very formal uniform, which included a cap, a black jacket, long flannel trousers and, almost unbelievably, a white shirt complete with starched detachable collars and a tie. I didn't even know how to tie a tie and had to be shown. Though it was all new and strange, I can't say I found it all too awful – after all, I was well used to dressing up as Zorro. What was unfortunate though, was I started my Dulwich school days with an arm in plaster.

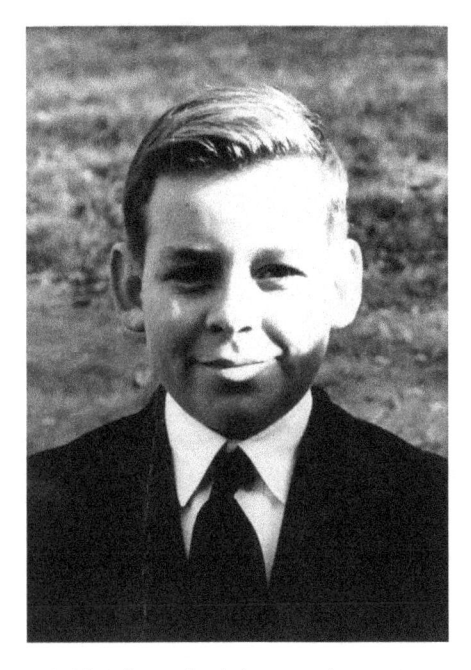

Dulwich College school photo, aged ten, 1961

I joined a class of thirty boys, all starting at Dulwich at the same time; some were day pupils and others were boarders like me. Before and during the Second World War Dulwich College had struggled with its academic reputation and the depletion of pupils. With the Education Act of 1944 threatening its very existence as a non-state school they increased the number of pupils from 700 to 1200 by taking in a wide range of pupils paid for by local councils and based on the Common Entrance Exam. This was called 'The Dulwich Experiment' and led to boys coming to the College from a wide range of socio-economic backgrounds. Having been brought up abroad I was oblivious to the British class system anyway and I'm extremely glad that it stayed that way, thanks to 'The Dulwich Experiment'.

From the start I slept in a dormitory with five others, which was a new experience, having grown up effectively as an only child, and so suddenly I had lots of friends. The best thing about school was the food. Soggy chips, spam fritters, lumpy custard, and they had a place called the Buttery where you could buy cream buns and crisps. Heaven.

Orchard boarding house Dulwich College, 1961

What I didn't know at the time was that my arrival at Dulwich had been accompanied by an assessment from my previous school in Caracas, which made me sound like a character out of a Rudyard Kipling story and must have made the teachers think they had their work cut out. I'd been at the Venezuelan school for only six months, it reported, but "when he arrived, we found him to be very far behind his age level in the basic principles of numbers, and his English was very much confused with Spanish which is his mother's first language. Prior to entering our school,

Eugen, Dad and me at Dulwich College, 1961

he had attended three other schools in various parts of the world which explains many of his difficulties." On the plus side I was also reported to be "tall, well-mannered and popular with my classmates," so not entirely feral.

I have to say I enjoyed it all from the start, but it very quickly became clear that I was bottom of the class academically, which was a bit worrying because if I wanted to stay in the school, I had only a year to make up enough ground to pass the exam.

The only thing better than the food at the school was the sport, but for that first term I had to watch from the touchline with my arm in plaster as the rules of this alien British combat sport called rugby football were explained to this bemused nine year old. We'd play football with a tennis ball in the schoolyard during breaks, but then more formally we'd do rugby, tennis, hockey, athletics, and swimming. I loved them all and ended up as captain of the swimming team. There was even boxing, but the novelty of jumping around while being punched in the face wore off quickly.

Music was always buzzing around in my head, and I was keen to have piano lessons, but then it was unfortunate that the piano-teacher turned out to be a sadist. During one of my lessons, he slammed down the piano lid, narrowly missing crushing my fingers, and said, "some people have got it, other people haven't, and you ain't got it." After that I was a bit afraid of him and didn't want to go to lessons, but then I'd see him approaching through these round windows they had in the classrooms. "Why haven't you turned up for your piano lesson?" It was a story I enjoyed telling when I was invited back to talk to kids at the school thirty years later to formally open an exhibition of Dulwich's music making from 1617 to the present day. I told the audience of teachers and boys that they had perhaps asked the wrong person as I had been very much *persona non grata* in the music department.

Twice or three times a year I'd be back and forth to see my parents in Caracas. It was always nerve-wracking because families of airline staff could only fly free if there was a spare seat. Often I'd have to wait until the very last minute to know if I was going or not, and then I'd be whisked onto the plane and straight into First Class. That would have been fine, except that one or two of my friends would be having fun in tourist class and I'd be sitting on my own for hours on end.

Like every other teenager at that time, I was obsessed with the Beatles, so much so that I'd bought one of their distinctive collarless jackets and a black wig cut in their trademark hairstyles. Looking back on it, I must have seemed a bizarre figure wearing this ridiculous outfit in the intense heat of the Venezuelan summer. It was lovely to see my family, but I was always ready to get back to my new life in swinging London.

Of course, I missed my mum and dad during term-time, and the sunshine of the tropics, but what I was missing most of all was my guitar, and so I set about trying to work out how I could lay my hands on one. Somehow, I managed to get hold of a catalogue from a shop in Surbiton called Bells Musical Instruments, and instantly my eye was caught by a picture of a Hofner Galaxy, in gleaming red. It was a thing of beauty, and straight away my obsessive desire took over from common sense.

The only communication from my parents in those days were occasional letters written on flimsy blue airmail notepaper, and in one recent envelope they'd enclosed my 10th birthday present, which was a postal order for £5. That was a good start, but unfortunately the Hofner was priced at £55, (£1,300 in today's money) and so there was a significant funding gap between me and my holy grail. That's when I discovered something called hire-purchase.

Incredibly, aged just 10, I took out an HP agreement with my £5 deposit and a few days later the guitar duly arrived complete with an

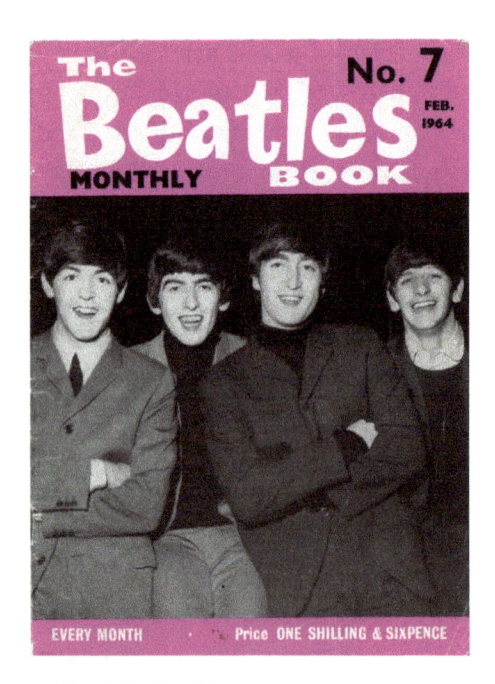

Beatles fanbook, 1964

imitation snakeskin case. But my joy was to be short-lived because straight away my 'peculiar' house-master intervened and, discovering that I'd bought an electric guitar, he confiscated it and put it in his study. Unbelievable cruelty. Tantalisingly I was occasionally allowed to go to look at it, but I couldn't actually play it until the end of term. If something like that happened these days you'd contact Childline.

It wasn't until later that I learned the drawback of a hire-purchase agreement, which was that after a few weeks a letter arrived saying, "you haven't paid the next instalment." Needless to say, I had no means to do so, and by the time I got on the plane back to South America with my suitcase and my gleaming red beautiful guitar, I was also carrying a solicitor's letter threatening to take me to court for non-payment. So now I'm panicking the whole way there and as we get closer to landing, I'm becoming more and more wound up and thinking, 'what's my dad going to say?' When I eventually arrived at Caracas airport, my dad came onto the plane to meet me, and straight away I showed him the snakeskin case, showed him the letter, and burst into tears.

Dad was first of all confused, then angry, but I have to say that once he'd worked out what had happened, he was pretty understanding about it. When we got back into the house, I opened up the guitar-case, and he said, "ok right, plug it in," and I realised he thought you had to plug it into the electric socket in the wall. When I explained that I also needed

Bells catalogue, Hofner Galaxie guitar, 1962

an amplifier, he no doubt thought I was even crazier than he had before. Nonetheless, to my enormous relief, he very generously paid off the rest of my debt and even bought a small amp from the local music store.

So now I was off. Back at school I was allowed to keep the guitar with me, and straight away I got together with four other boys to form our first pop group. It consisted of drums, bass, two of us on guitars, and we called ourselves the Drag Alley Beach Mob. Don't ask. It was all happening, new bands were emerging, and every day someone would turn up with a new record by The Beatles, The Stones or The Who and we'd sit down in the old gymnasium (which was well away from the rest of the school), and try to pick out the riffs.

Good fun though it was, it wasn't too long before I started thinking that the Drag Alley Beach Mob didn't have a great future, so by the time we got to aged thirteen and into the next boarding house, it felt like the right time to form a real band. With my friend Bill MacCormick signed up we heard about a drummer from the lower school called Charles Hayward. When we discovered that he was the proud owner of a huge, red glitter,

Drag Alley Beach Mob rehearsal in the old gym, Dulwich College, 1964

WE DON'T NEED NO EDUCATION…

double bass drum Premier kit, he was immediately invited to join the band. Bill had an older brother called Ian who was smart and knowledgeable and as cool as could be and began to introduce us to all the most interesting bands of the time like Velvet Underground, Soft Machine, and Cream. Ian would later change his surname to MacDonald and became assistant editor of the New Musical Express, also writing a seminal book about the Beatles entitled *Revolution in the Head*. Sadly, he suffered severely from depression which eventually led to his suicide.

It was Ian who gave our band the name Pooh and the Ostrich Feather, I have no idea why and it says a lot for the esteem I held Ian in that I never questioned him on it. However that didn't really matter because it was all about the music. We'd listen carefully to all the new bands, and then sit for hours picking out our own freeform jam sessions based on songs like *Interstellar Overdrive, Crossroads,* and *Rolling and Tumbling*. Two of our friends got hold of an epidiascope and we soon had our own psychedelic light show. We played our first public performance at an event called the *Summer Miscellany* which was a general arts show put on by the boys in the Great Hall at Dulwich. We played three songs including, for the first time, an original called *Marcel My Dada* which I'd written with Charles. Sometimes we'd take over the swimming baths hall, which was drained during the winter, and played to what seemed like hundreds of boys from the school.

Some of the detail has become blurred through the passage of time, but I recall that Bill was also a drummer, so rather bizarrely we had two. Inspired also by John Cale in Velvet Undergound, we experimented for a while with an electric violin, but it was all very "make it up as you go along".

Pooh and the Ostrich Feather gig, 1968

Right from the start I was drawn to music which allowed me to improvise. I found I had a natural aptitude for the fretboard and was quickly able to rely on a kind of instinct to let me know where my fingers should go next. I'd study individual riffs played by people like Eric Clapton and Peter Green, but what I liked best about it was the freedom. When I was playing guitar, my mind and hands could go where they liked. I wasn't under anyone else's control. Mostly I wasn't afraid that it would all go wrong. Playing music meant being free to fail – something might go off key for a moment, but then straight away you could pick it up and make it all fly again.

Quite often I'd spend an hour or so trying to perfect a particular riff which had caught my attention, at the end of which some smart-Alec would comment, "sure but you're playing it wrong." I knew it was wrong but that didn't seem to matter all that much to me so long as it sounded good, and eventually I told myself that maybe I could make a career out of getting things wrong. Many years later my friend Ian MacCormick/ MacDonald would describe me as "soaring like an angel one minute

Ostrich feather gig at St.Barnabas Church. Bill, Charles, and me

and stumbling like a sleepwalker the next", which I'm happy to settle for.

Much has been written about the sense of freedom we all felt in the sixties, and I don't plan to add to it, but there's no doubt that a newly found liberation and wider social revolution filled the air, permeating every aspect of our young lives. It was heady and intoxicating and living in London felt like living at the centre of the universe.

And sometimes it's just exactly when you're flying high that you can be tempted to believe that your life is charmed and that nothing can go wrong, and then it does.

It was a Saturday in May 1966. My brother Eugen was a student in Cambridge, but he and I were alone in the house in Clapham when there was a ring on the doorbell and we answered to find our next door neighbour, Mrs. Pattson, on the step. We didn't have a phone, but she did and she'd just received a phone call from Mum in Caracas, and had come to tell us that our dad had died.

More than fifty years later, I still can't find adequate words to describe how that felt. The closest I can come is that it was like I'd been hit over the head with a cricket bat. My brother and I were stunned. The last time I'd seen my dad he was fit and well, and only just 54 years of age. The thought of his dying had never even crossed my mind, and in that instant my world collapsed.

Over the following hours and days, we learned that Dad had suffered what had been thought to be a minor heart attack but had been recovering. Normal communications were slow at that time, and it hadn't even been serious enough for us to be informed by telegram. But then a few days later our family doctor, Sanchez Vegas, who was also my best friend Michael's father, had given him an injection of some kind and the allergic reaction had killed him.

Much of what followed is a blur, but I remember being sent to stay with my two English aunts, Gigi and Gerts, my dad's beloved sisters. They lived in Gravesend and having no children of their own, had always been my *in locus parentis*. Thinking back they too must have been devastated but had to put on brave faces for their nephew. Eugen set off to Caracas to help pack up and accompany home my mother and sister, along with my dad's body.

Dad's OBE citation

Later there was a service at Brompton Oratory which was attended by lots of smartly dressed colleagues of my dad's. I was surprised by the number of people who came to pay their respects. We then drove in the funeral cars all the way to Hastings, my dad's birthplace, to a cemetery high on a hill above the town looking out to the sea. Among the many aspects of this tragedy was that Dad had been due, one month later, to return to London to go to Buckingham Palace to receive an OBE (Order of the British Empire). The award of the medal was a huge honour in recognition of services 'given to her majesty's government'. I feel very proud of him but also felt so sad that he missed the opportunity to receive it from the Queen.

I didn't go back to school for the rest of that term. Watching England beat West Germany in the World Cup Final proved a welcome distraction, even though seeing it on a 12 inch black and white TV wasn't ideal. We then spent the rest of the summer in Bogotá and Girardot, Colombia, staying with my mum's family and returned to London in time to start the autumn term in September.

Any child who suddenly loses a parent finds their world shifting on its axis. All of us were shocked and traumatised, and of course it must have been especially appalling for my poor mum. Aside from finding herself a widow in a strange country, with three children all pursuing their own paths, she was also very concerned about making ends meet. She would receive a modest pension from dad's former employer, BOAC, and she owned the house, but there was certainly no inheritance coming her way.

I was attending a private fee-paying school and although I had passed the 11+ exams which meant that my tuition fees were paid by the Inner London Education Authority (I.L.E.A) I was still boarding at the school. Unbeknownst to me there was now no prospect that those fees could be paid. Nothing was ever said on the subject in my hearing, and for many years I have wondered which good angels gathered to allow me to continue at Dulwich without further worry. I'd always assumed that the Board of School Governors had waived the fees or given me a bursary. It was only a year ago, after making enquiries via the school's archivist Calista Lucy, that I finally discovered a letter from the Headmaster and Bursar at Dulwich to Sir William Houghton at the Inner London Education Authority which says, 'I'm very glad to know that your Authority has agreed to maintain this boy's boarding costs at Dulwich ... I am most grateful to you for reconsidering this matter.' The wording implies that an earlier request to pick up the tab for my education had been turned down, but at that time I had no idea how close I'd come to my path taking a dramatic turn, with who knows what consequences for my future.

With Dad gone and Mum reeling from shock, I felt a strong personal survival instinct kicking in. It seemed to me that the worst thing that could happen had already happened, so I experienced a renewed confidence and determination that I was going to succeed. I don't remember ever talking about my dad's death to anyone: the surrounding public school culture was very much of the stiff upper lip variety, and I think I was expected just to carry on as normal. Today, thankfully we know much more about how to handle bereavement and how and when to get counselling support. It wasn't until I was aged forty-five that I finally did so.

THREE

Roxy – Take One

In the wider world, tens of thousands of American boys just a little older than me were being sent to fight in the war in Vietnam and Harold Wilson was the UK's Prime Minister. These were tumultuous times, but more important in my young life was that pirate radio was bringing all kinds of new music to our ears, the Beatles had just performed their last live concert, and someone had shouted "Judas" at a Bob Dylan concert because he'd picked up an electric guitar.

I was probably never going to be an outstanding scholar, but by now I was doing fine with my schoolwork and had caught up with the other boys in the class. I spent as much time as I could doing every kind of sport but, more importantly, playing with my mates in the band. Seven months after my dad died, at Christmas 1966, I casually mentioned to my mum that I wanted to be a rock guitarist and to be in a band.

I can only imagine what this suggestion triggered in the mind of this woman from Barranquilla on the Caribbean coast of Colombia. She asked what must to her have seemed the very reasonable question, "Que es eso, I know about cumbia, salsa and boleros, but what is this rock music?" Overhearing her from the kitchen, my brother Eugen interjected, "Okay, I know this guy from Cambridge who's just joined a band as a professional musician. Let's go and see him and ask what you have to do to become one."

I was all for it, and so Eugen made a couple of phone calls and we set off to Earl's Court, to meet at a restaurant opposite Wetherby Mansions where the founder member of Pink Floyd Syd Barrett shared a flat with the pop-artist Dougie Fields. My brother's friend turned out to be none other than David Gilmour. Neither David nor I can remember what advice he gave me that day, but he now jokes that it must have been good because five years later I joined Roxy Music. After lunch we went up to David's flat, he packed his Stratocaster into its case and off he went to Abbey Road to continue recording *A Saucerful of Secrets*, the first Pink Floyd album he played on, and which turned out to be Syd Barrett's final recording for the band.

I decided to stay on studying at Dulwich with a view to going to university but also pursuing my musical ambitions and to see what this might lead to. I continued to take my schoolwork seriously and my new-found determination to succeed, bearing in mind that there was no safety net, seemed to be working because I went on to pass 13 O-levels, and now I embarked on A-levels in English and History. Later I'd also work on my own to take the A-level in Spanish. Quite naturally, all of us boys were wondering what might be coming next, and one day the Careers Master asked everyone in the class 'what do you want to be when you leave school.' He went down the aisles between the rows of desks asking each of us one by one, and nodding approvingly as he heard the answers, "lawyer", "accountant", "doctor", "chemist", "teacher". Eventually he got to me, and I said, 'rock guitarist sir'. He rolled his eyes, said "next" and moved on.

Apart from David, the other inspirational musician I met at that time was Robert Wyatt, who was the drummer and vocalist of Soft Machine. Robert lived with his mum in a house not far from the school, and the band used to rehearse in their living room. My friend Bill's mum knew Robert's mum, so he and his brother Ian would go round on their way home from school and watch them rehearsing. Full of excitement, they'd tell me all about it on the following day. The music from the so-called Canterbury scene was weird and experimental, and we absolutely loved it. When they released a single *Love Makes Sweet Music,* we thought that was about as cool as it was possible to be, and meeting David and Robert redoubled my determination to make my way in the world as a musician.

Soft Machine were one of the hippest and coolest bands of the era and I noticed that Pink Floyd often played on the same bill. I'd followed their progress and when their first album, *The Piper at the Gates of Dawn* came out in 1967 it was an exciting moment in the new evolving, British music scene. I had a French girlfriend at the time and she and I went together to see Jimi Hendrix at the *Christmas on Earth Continued* event at London Olympia. Also on the bill were Soft Machine and Pink Floyd, and what turned out to be the last ever gig with Syd Barrett. The poster's sub-heading said, 'All Night Christmas Dream Party.' It was during a severe winter freeze and badly publicized, so this event in the vast Olympia Hall was not only a disaster for the organisers but also for my French girlfriend who was subsequently sacked from her au-pair job for stopping out all night.

I kept my promise to my mum and applied to my brother's college, Emmanuel, in Cambridge to study history. I made a total hash of the interview, at the end of which I distinguished myself by saying goodbye, turning to go, and walking into a cupboard. Possibly this was something to do with the fact that not only was I very short-sighted but I was in the early stages of what would shortly be diagnosed as glandular fever: it just wasn't meant to be.

After leaving Dulwich College in December 1969, I felt as though I was attending the university of the brothers MacCormick, Bill and Ian, who were constantly introducing me to a wide and eclectic mix of music: Stravinsky, Miles Davis, Cecil Taylor, Terry Riley and a Scandinavian band called Burnin' Red Ivanhoe. It was great fun to make these musical discoveries.

Listening to this range of music made us want to experiment with different sounds and textures. Ian nudged us towards bringing in saxophone and keyboards, so we placed an ad. in Melody Maker and held some auditions. I remember we saw a saxophonist who'd been in the army for six years, and then a good keyboard player who'd also been to

Dulwich College and was 6 years older than us, named Dave Jarrett. We didn't have a bass player as Bill was still insisting on playing drums but we told him to learn to play the bass. Little did we know what a virtuoso on the four strings he would become, as many people who've heard the 801 Live album will testify. At the same time we exchanged the band's school name for the rather more interstellar Quiet Sun.

Every spare moment I had would be spent scouring all the music equipment stores in the Charing Cross road, and one day I went into a tiny shop called Orange where my eye was caught by a Gibson SG guitar hanging on the wall. Once again, I could only buy it with a hire purchase agreement, so I left a deposit of £5 and took the forms home to be signed by my mum. She duly did so, but when I went back to collect the SG the shop-owner said he'd sold it. Instead he tried to palm me off with a

Gibson 335 guitar

Gibson Les Paul Junior. I didn't like the look or the sound of it, so I took it back the next day and pointed to a Sunburst Gibson 335 with a Bigsby tremolo arm. It wasn't the Fender Stratocaster that most of the rock and rollers were using, but it seemed to suit the kind of music I was playing, so I took it home and got stuck in.

While I loved to play guitar with my bandmates, in those days I felt nervous about the prospect of appearing on stage, so when I knew we had our first real gigs coming, I raided the medicine cabinet and found some of my mum's temazepam. They did the trick, and after about three months I found I didn't need them any more. We were probably paid a few pounds for our occasional performances, but certainly not enough to enable me to pay any bills, so I got a series of jobs to tide me over until I could apply again for university the following year. Included among them was delivering for the Sunlight laundry, a spell working for a travel agent, and then a much more enjoyable job as a tourist guide for groups of American high school girls visiting the UK. It was strictly against the rules to date any of the girls, but the temptation was far too great, and inevitably I was sacked for doing so.

My mum was delighted when I received offers of university places from Kings College, London, and Southampton, and now I was in a race to make progress in my music career to avoid having to go. We were starting to do well with Quiet Sun, supporting bands like Caravan and Robert Wyatt's Symbiosis at various gigs. We hired a studio in Clerkenwell to record a demo, splitting the £15 it cost for three hours, and recorded a track called *Years of the Quiet Sun* which we sent to Richard Williams at Melody Maker, the most read weekly music paper, accompanied by some promotional blurb written by Ian. We read Richard's column avidly every week, so were

Quiet Sun, Clapham Common, London, 1971

disappointed when his response came back: "the best thing about this recording is the press release accompanying it." Undeterred, we also sent the demo to every record company we could think of. Each one of them sent back letters of rejection, and the words "absolutely no commercial potential" are imprinted on my mind.

I was 19 years old, and this was 1970 – the year the Beatles released *Let it Be*. Paul had announced that it would be their last album, and approximately 600,000 'heads' had turned up on the Isle of Wight to see Hendrix and The Doors. Having wanted to be in a professional band since the age of 9 or 10, I felt I was making some headway at last. Warners paid for us to do a week-long residential session in a recording studio, and we were beginning to gig regularly. But then, just when it all seemed to be happening for us, came a bombshell. Our friend Robert Wyatt announced that he'd been asked to leave Soft Machine and was forming a new band called Matching Mole, (a play on the French translation of Soft Machine, Machine Molle). Very Robert, very pataphysical. Bill MacCormick was leaving us and going to join him. My plan for rock stardom had taken three steps forward and now it was two steps back.

"That's great for you," I told Bill, and then rather sullenly said: "but what am I going to do?"

That was when Bill told me that the band Roxy Music was looking for a guitarist and pointed to an ad. in Melody Maker. "Wanted" it read; "The perfect guitarist for avant rock group: original, creative, adaptable, melodic, fast, slow, elegant, witty, scary, stable, tricky. Quality musicians only."

> **"The Perfect Guitarist"**
> for AVANT-ROCK GROUP
> Original, creative, adaptable, melodic, fast, slow, elegant, witty, scary, stable, tricky
> QUALITY MUSICIANS ONLY
> "ROXY" 223 0296

Melody Maker ad, 1971

Up to that point, Roxy had been only on the periphery of my musical radar. The same Richard Williams who'd been so lukewarm about the Quiet Sun demo tape had written glowing reviews of their work, but I knew little more about them. But it was a job with a band which was gigging so I applied and was invited along the following week to an audition. The band was called simply Roxy at this point. I learned later that Bryan and Andy had originally named the band Roxy, but had then discovered that there was an American band recording under the same name, so it was changed to Roxy Music.

Bryan Ferry and Andy Mackay were both employed as teachers at the time and were sharing a cottage in Latchmere Road, Battersea. I was still living with my mum in the family house in West Road, Clapham, so it was an easy bus-ride with my Gibson 335. The cottage had a small living room with a bed in it, one bedroom upstairs, and a little kitchen and eating area in the back. Brian Eno and Graham Simpson were there with Bryan and Andy, and so we all sat together in this back room. First, they played me the Roxy demo tape, which I thought was great; then I played them the Quiet Sun demo tape, which they thought was terrible. Eventually we sorted ourselves out and started to have a jam. I can't remember what we played – maybe a Carole King song – but I recall it was a very simple tune with probably only two chords. Having recently been playing a lot of esoteric jazz improvisations with very complicated time signatures, I felt this was all very liberating and reminded me of the Velvet Underground, which I loved. My enjoyment was only slightly impaired by the fact that I had an awful cold and kept sneezing throughout.

We played for a while and then Bryan and I went upstairs for a chat, which was mostly about our mutual interest in films, and I think I must have told him about my history growing up in South America. Even then I knew there was a significant gap between their experience and mine. For one thing they were five or six years older than me, they'd also been to university, had things like bank accounts and cars, and they seemed to know all about art and the avant-garde. Meanwhile photographs of me at the time show a very hairy bloke with long beard and thick glasses. I also think they didn't like the look of my Gibson 335 and wanted their guitarist to play a Strat'.

I thought it was fair enough when I heard that Dave O'List had got the gig. I'd heard Dave play on the first album by the band The Nice, and even seen them at the Royal Albert Hall. He was a terrific guitarist, and he also played a white Strat'. However Dave's relatively exalted status caused some friction from the outset.

An early hint of the problems came when Roxy was scheduled to audition with EG Management. EG was a highly successful management company run by David Enthoven, who went on to manage Robbie Williams, and Mark Fenwick who was a member of the Fenwick's Newcastle department store family and who later became Roger Waters' manager. At the time they looked after King Crimson, T.Rex and Emerson, Lake and Palmer. The audition was held at a theatre/ bingo hall in Wandsworth. I'd continued to see members of the band, out and about, and for some strange reason, of which I have no recollection, found myself there alongside Richard Williams from Melody Maker. We became aware of an altercation on stage between Dave and Roxy's new drummer Paul Thompson. It was all a bit uncomfortable and when the lights went down, I was under the impression that the row developed into a minor fistfight. Years later I asked Paul what the fight was about, and in that wonderful Geordie accent, he said, "I was fed up with him always turning up late for everything. This was an important break for us with a top management company, so I guess my frustration had been building up." Notwithstanding the fracas, the audition seemed to go well, except that as he left the hall, Mark Fenwick was overheard to say, "get rid of the guitarist."

Not long afterwards, Roxy were due to play at a Friends of the Tate Christmas party off the Tottenham Court Road, in the centre of London. I attended because Dave Price, my friend from school, was doing the lights with the epidiascope. It was a tiny gig and the band turned up in a Ford transit van with Bryan Ferry driving, and Brian Eno slotted into a tiny space between the gear at the back. All of the band with the noted exception of Dave O'List started carrying the gear into the hall. Since Dave wasn't helping, I grabbed a few amps and speakers and helped them to set up. The party was small with an audience of maybe only twenty or so, but Eno was standing to one side mixing the band's sound live, and I thought they were terrific.

I remember standing there feeling a rising panic and thinking, "what about me? I've got to get into a band," so after Christmas, and with my 21st birthday fast approaching, I scoured the 'musicians wanted' page of Melody Maker again. I spotted an advertisement for auditions with a band which was not in the same league as Roxy, but at least were playing some paid gigs. Full of nerves, I lined up with the other hopefuls in an outer room of a small rehearsal in Bromley, and within ten minutes I'd failed my second audition.

By the time I celebrated my 21st birthday with a party on 29 January 1972, I thought my morale couldn't't sink much lower. But then my best friend and erstwhile band buddy Bill MacCormick told me that he was about to go on a month-long tour of Europe with Robert Wyatt and Matching Mole supporting John Mayall. To make things even more painful for me, he looked every inch a rock star in a blue velvet coat and matching boots, and I wasn't even in a band. I tried very hard to be pleased for him, but despair won out. That was the first birthday party I'd had since I was 8, having always been at boarding school for my birthdays, and it's one I always remember for the wrong reasons.

On my actual birthday, two days later, I was back at the day job in a room in Stratford in London's East End, with thirty other temps making

Me onstage before recording the first album, Bristol 1972

paper planes out of invoices for a travel company called Clarksons, who were trying to work out why they'd lost a million quid. What I didn't know on that day was that Bryan Ferry had rung and left a message with my mum asking me to ring him. When I eventually called him back he said, "would you like to come and mix our sound because Eno needs to get on the stage and not be mixing it in the middle of the audience?" I told him that I didn't know the first thing about a mixing desk, but he was undeterred. "Don't worry," he said, "Eno will show you what to do." This sounded a bit weird to me but hey, it seemed like an opportunity.

In those days I used to record John Peel's radio shows on my dad's old Telefunken reel-to-reel recorder, and among my tapes was a session Roxy had recorded just a few weeks earlier. I spent an evening listening carefully to it. Most of their songs were played on only two or three chords and were hardly difficult, so I got the hang of them quickly.

I was told to turn up at a house in Notting Hill, but when I got there the place seemed to be more or less derelict. It turned out that a friendly property developer was letting Roxy use the house for band practice. The place was a total shambles but did at least have an electricity supply. There was no sign of Dave O'List, but Bryan Ferry, Andy MacKay, Brian Eno, Graham Simpson and Paul Thompson were all there. One of them said something like "Dave's not coming but he seems to have left a guitar – why don't you have a go?" So, I picked up the guitar and, lo and behold, I could play every one of their songs straight off. They were impressed and the next day they offered me the job.

Every long career in the music business has its highs and its lows, and for me the day I was offered the gig in Roxy as a full member of the band was one of the most memorable highs of my life. A turning point, especially as just a week before I was staring into the abyss. It was 1972, the sixties were over, the Beatles were no more, the psychedelic dream had become a heroin-fuelled nightmare, and pop music was ready for the new wave and new sounds. Here was I, 21 years old and in an innovative band, with a unique sound and style which seemed to be going places: we were ready to ride the wave. Christmas was only just behind us, but now I thought it was Christmas every day.

Ten days later I joined the band. On 14 February 1972, Valentine's Day, Roxy signed an agreement with EG management. It was a so-called "tape lease" deal, in which the company funded the recordings, but then owned the tapes. This arrangement was to cause huge problems later on, but at last I could call myself a professional musician. I was earning £15 a week.

Early Roxy Music gig after the release of the album. Andy, me and Eno, 1972

FOUR

Recording

My first instruction from the band? "Ditch the Gibson 335 and get a Fender Strat'."

My mum had learned to be resilient in handling disappointments, and I don't think she was surprised when she heard the news that I wasn't going to university. I kept the two offers of places open until August 1972, when I sent letters to both thanking them but letting them know that I'd joined a rock and roll band instead. There's a part of me that regrets missing out on the chance of reading Latin American studies for three years, but if I'd done so, I wouldn't be here writing this book. Mum gamely accompanied me to the St James Square branch of National and Grindlays, the historic bank established in London in 1828, which was the bank my dad had used for many years: they somewhat surprisingly agreed to lend mum £120 to buy the required Strat'.

The first gig I played with Roxy was in front of a crowd of American college kids at the Hand and Flowers pub opposite Olympia. The second was in Leicester where I'm embarrassed to admit that my stage outfit consisted of 'double denim'. I can only say in my defence that the others

Roxy Music, April 1972

didn't look much better. The third was in Bristol at the university, where a photo taken on the night shows me wearing my school cricket pullover, but I'm also the proud owner of a Fender Strat' in glorious Sunburst.

After these three live performances, and even though we didn't have a record deal, our management stumped up £5,000 to book time in on old BBC studio called Command Studios, which was close to Piccadilly Circus. It had a recording area below the control room which was just like the Abbey Road studio 2 where the Beatles had recorded. The album was to be produced by the King Crimson lyricist Pete Sinfield, who was also managed by EG.

This was something I had dreamt about since my first sight of all those great pictures of the Beatles recording in Abbey Road. I don't remember any photos being taken of us during that first recording in Command Studios, and in fact there seems to be only one picture of us from the the making of the next four albums at Air Studios. This was the first of many oversights and missed opportunities by our management team.

Of course, we knew all the songs well, but even so it was daunting for me to be in a proper recording studio for the first time. I was also still to learn that recording is not just about playing your part, but that your sound has to fit in with everyone else's. This was especially true for a band like Roxy whose signature sound was based on its unique soundscapes. We wanted to find ways to create a musical landscape which would perfectly complement and be the context for Bryan's particular voice and style, which in turn would distinguish us from everyone else playing at the time. All this would only be made possible by a mix of our own individual skills and musical influences, combined with the way we used the technology, which was limited at that time to a VCS 3 synth and readapted Revox quarter inch tape recorders. The only other people doing the same things at that time were The Beatles and Pink Floyd. The lack of more sophisticated equipment meant we had to be original and inventive with whatever tools we had – necessity was the mother of our inventions.

I approached the whole thing with nervous excitement, but also a strong feeling that this was the moment I'd been preparing for since I first heard Charlie Lindsell play those Chuck Berry riffs half my lifetime ago. I knew the sound I wanted to make, I knew my guitars, and I felt ready to go. Every time we would climb up to the control room to listen back, I just prayed that my parts would sound ok. Luckily they did, and naturally I didn't feel any need to let anyone else know about my anxiety. That's chutzpah for you.

We wanted our sound to feel live and raw, a bit like the Velvet Underground on some tracks while others needed space but their own distinctive soundscapes. This was where my Gibson 335 with its whammy bar and tendency to produce feedback came into its own. In *Chance Meeting* I used the feedback of the hollow body guitar and its tremolo arm to create an other-worldly sound with echo that to this day some people think was produced by Eno on the synth. One of the great 'treatments' of our instruments by Eno that contributed to our unique sound is really evident on the track *Ladytron*. It has Andy Mackay's oboe going through Eno's VCS3 synth with Revox echo and then, at the end of the song after

Bryan has finished singing, it turns into something quite different. Paul Thompson's drums play an up-tempo hoof beat rhythm and then it all heads off to unknown territory, ending up with an almost sonic battle between Eno and me, which eventually became a staple of our live show. One by one the band would drop out, leaving the two of us duelling with our instruments. Gradually I would drop to my knees and lie prostrate on the stage floor with feedback echoing around the audience. There was a lot of humour and generally hamming it up in the early days.

We did manage to record the entire first album within the two-week deadline, at the end of which we celebrated by heading down to the far end of Piccadilly where the Hard Rock Cafe was the current "in" place to be, and where we set about large platefuls of American-style hamburgers. It was the first Hard Rock Cafe in the world and was founded by Americans Peter Morton and Isaac Tigrett. It's hard to believe now, but it was the only place in the whole of the UK where you could get a genuine US burger. (I didn't mention that I spent my time in Hawaii consuming vast quantities.)

The Hard Rock Café was not the tourist destination it is today, back then it was part of the American zeitgeist in the UK, along with the film 'The Last Picture Show' directed by Peter Bogdanovich, and the band Sha Na Na which all harked back to 1950's America.

Most LP covers in those days showed pictures of the band, usually trying to look cool or mysterious in some back-street, and I had no idea what to expect when I was told to turn up for the photo-shoot for ours. The extent of my ability to look the part consisted of asking my mum to sew some diamante patterns onto an otherwise plain white shirt, and so I was feeling quite some distance out of my comfort zone as I boarded the 137 bus to Knightsbridge. My discomfort was scarcely eased when I first met Antony Price, who was an up-and-coming fashion designer at Stirling Cooper and was in charge of styling the album. I was desperately naïve in those days, and Antony was the first overtly gay person I'd ever met. Certainly, he wasn't too impressed by my feeble attempt to look stylish.

"What on earth is this?" he said, holding up my mother's handiwork. He shook his head with incredulity, "No, no, nooooo," he said, and then cast it aside and handed me a leather jacket. Next, he rootled around in what looked like a bag of odds and ends, and came up holding a pair of wrap-around sun-glasses, onto the lenses of which he'd glued a lot of diamante studs. "Take these," he said, handing them to me. "You're done," and he was off to sort out the next person. The whole process took five minutes and thus my trademark look was born.

All of which would have been fine had it not been for the fact that I couldn't see a thing. I was short sighted anyway, but peering forward, the bug-eyed glasses were completely opaque, and the only direction I could see was downwards towards my feet. I was just about able to see bits of the fretboard, so any song with more than two chords was a no-go, and no wonder critics thought my solo guitar playing was abstract and even 'wonderfully avante garde.' It's an everlasting wonder to me that I didn't ever fall off the bloody stage.

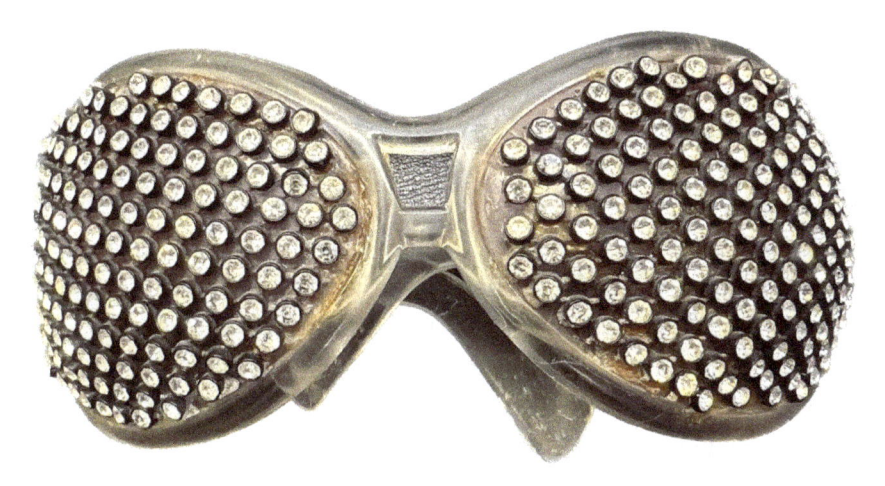

Bug eyes

The creation of the first album cover was left in the expert hands of a team headed by Bryan, along with art director Nick de Ville. Nick and Bryan had both been students of Fine Art at Newcastle University where they studied under the great Richard Hamilton who is widely acknowledged as the father of British pop art. Also in Team Roxy was the aforementioned Antony Price, along with a selection of the top photographers of the day. The front cover ended up as an eye-catching and brilliant 1950s style fashion-shoot of the model Kari-Ann Muller who later went on to marry Mick Jagger's brother Chris. I was delighted with the cover and gatefold design because it perfectly captured the visual tone of the band. The team had done a great job and we thought it was emblematic of Roxy as an 'art rock band', and set a new standard.

Our eponymously named first LP was released on Chris Blackwell's Island Records on 16th of June 1972, which was the same day as *Ziggy Stardust* by Bowie. It was incredibly well received by fans and critics alike, reaching number 10 in the UK charts, and it's gratifying that over the years it has often been cited as one of the best debut albums ever made. This may partly be because, while many artists take a few albums to get going, we seemed to have appeared out of nowhere, apparently fully formed. This in turn led some other bands around at the time to feel resentful that we hadn't 'paid our dues.' Even the legendary "Whispering" Bob Harris introduced us on The Old Grey Whistle Test with the words "style over substance," though the critics later said that our live performance had forced him to eat his words. None of this mattered to me though – I was just over the moon about our instant success. I had no expectations about a long-term career or anything similar. All I had wanted was to play gigs, make real albums, and see the world. To get good reviews, especially from critics we respected like the BBC's John Peel and The Melody Maker's Richard Williams, made us feel as though we had the blessing of the most important opinion formers of the day. Some artists say they don't care about reviews, but I don't believe them. Good ones can help a lot, and bad ones hurt and can seriously damage a nascent career.

What I didn't realise at the time, and only learned from his recent biography *The Islander*, was that Chris Blackwell was initially 'indifferent' to Roxy. "At first," he writes, "I didn't know what to make of Roxy's music. I listened to it in a meeting wearing a fur hat, probably to keep out of the cold or to hide from Tim's hopeful face and just stared into space, not sure what to say about it'." The "Tim" he's referring to is Tim Clark, who worked at Island, later went on to manage Robbie Williams, and was mad keen to sign Roxy. Chris continues 'what I didn't know was that Tim had already offered their manager – and Tim's future business partner – David Enthoven, a deal, assuming it was obvious I and Muff (Winwood and brother of Stevie) would give it the green light. I changed my mind when I saw some fabulous Roxy Music artwork in the Island office a couple of days later. Enthoven was bringing it in to show Tim, oblivious to the fact that the deal hadn't yet been approved … It was the oddly flirtatious sleeve for the first Roxy record, very bright and appealing but slightly sinister … it was unlike anything around at the time which always gets my interest. I casually asked Tim Clark if we had managed to get them signed."

My mother, who just a few months earlier had no idea what a rock star was, began to see the benefits of having an embryonic one as her son. I heard that she was soon telling the Manzanera clan back in Colombia that 'mi hijo es una Estrella!' The band was off on a mission to win over new audiences to Roxy Music world, and everyone was welcome.

There had been one casualty since the recording of this album. Graham Simpson had been in a band with Bryan called The Gas Board, while Bryan was studying fine art at Newcastle University. Graham was an accomplished bass guitarist, but sadly things went spectacularly wrong shortly after the release of the first album. We were due to do an audition for Kenny Bell from the Chrysalis booking agency in some rehearsal rooms underneath the old Covent Garden. At that time we used to start the set with a little number called *Memphis Soul Stew*, in which the instruments came in one by one. It started with a very funky bass riff and then Bryan would say, "give me a little bit of funky guitar," and then "give me a little bit of sax." I'm not sure now why we thought that was cool, but that's what we did.

On this occasion the lights went down, and we waited for the bass to start. Nothing happened. We waited a bit longer, and still nothing happened. A bit longer, still nothing. Eventually someone turned the lights back on and poor Graham was found cowering behind the bass stack. We learned later that his mother had recently died, and he'd had a kind of a breakdown. Being mere "'lads" none of us had known. So, the audition was cancelled, but then sometime later Graham was seen running barefoot down the King's Road, where our management had an office

Rehearsal room, Covent Garden, March 1972

above a hairdressers. He threw a brick through their upstairs window. I'd only known him for 4 months and I never saw him again. Suddenly we found ourselves without a bass player so had to audition for a new one. It was a pattern that repeated itself time and time again, the revolving door of the Roxy bass player syndrome. At the time of writing, we have notched up fifteen.

It was about that time that Bryan and Andy turned up at rehearsals one day after seeing a gig by David Bowie, and it had clearly been a moment of epiphany. The musicians had all been wearing spaceman-like outfits and make-up, they had proper theatrical lighting, and the impact had been sensational. We realised we needed to do something radical about the way we looked and presented ourselves on stage, and so began what became its own art form. Antony Price remained largely responsible for our overall look and brand, but each of us employed our own friends who were recent fashion design graduates to create ever more outlandish and eccentric stage outfits with virtually no budget. None of us ever used the same people, except that Wendy Dagworthy designed mine and Bryan's outfits for the next few years. Wendy went on to run her own fashion label and eventually was made Head of Fashion at both St. Martin's and the Royal College of Art.

Stage Clothes

The band would never collaborate or compare notes on what we were going to wear for a particular gig or TV appearance. A few minutes before we were due to go on, one of us would ask, "what are you going to wear?" "I don't know, what are you going to wear?" "Ok you show me yours and I'll show you mine" "No you show me yours …" and then time ran out and we just would leave the dressing room to the stage howling with laughter.

Eno was usually dressed by his girlfriend Carol McNichol who went on to become a famous potter. Between them they used to favour costumes featuring all sorts of feathers, and he usually looked the most "out there" of all of us. In fact, it was a constant source of amazement to us that he seemed to have an extraordinary power to attract girls. We were all tall with lots of hair, while he was short and going thin on top, and yet he had this hypnotic stare and the ability to chat to women, which was a skill the rest of us lacked. "Trust in me," he seemed to say, and frequently they did.

One Sunday we were due to play at the Greyhound pub in Croydon as the support act to David Bowie. The Greyhound was quite a famous

REVOLUCIÓN TO ROXY

Roxy Music outfits

venue at the time, variously featuring performances by bands like The Faces, Status Quo, Mott the Hoople, Yes, and many others. My busy music life meant that I had very little time for a long-term girlfriend, but I'd been seeing a girl called Sharon Potter since my last year at school. In fact, such was one of the downsides of being a boarder at an all-boys' public school, that she was my first serious girlfriend.

Sharon's parents ran the Golden Grove pub in Bromley near Croydon, so I'd spent the afternoon with her and turned up early for the gig. I remember walking up the stairs and there, sitting on four upright chairs in the corridor, was David Bowie and his band, The Spiders from Mars, all dressed up in their make-up and stage outfits. Meanwhile I was wearing my cricket jumper and jeans and thinking, 'wow they must dress like that on and off stage!" There were headlines in the newspapers next day about the queues of hundreds of kids snaking all around the block but unable to get in because of the limited capacity of the hall. Many years later I reminded David of the evening, and his reply was, "if I had a pound for everyone who claimed they were at that gig, I'd be a millionaire." I took the opportunity to remind him that he was indeed a millionaire several times over, but it was a running gag over the years that made us both laugh.

The promoter at the Greyhound was Steve Mason, who later went on to look after and distribute a clutch of indie labels, including my own. Steve has a good memory for these things, and claims that on that evening he paid us £5, which would have been shared between six.

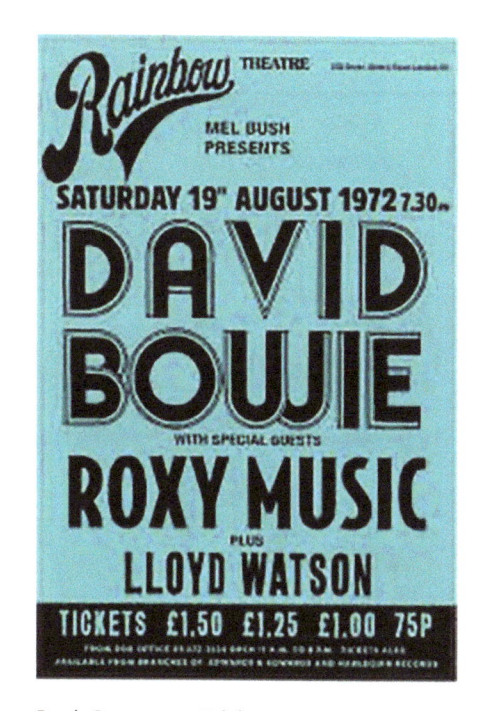

Bowie Roxy poster Rainbow

In those days, for some reason which now eludes me, it wasn't thought cool to have a single on your album. This was obviously crazy because, apart from anything else, we didn't have anything to play on Top of the Pops, which was the only chart-show on British television. So, within a very short time we went back into the same studio and recorded *Virginia Plain*, which quickly got to number 4 in the singles charts, and sure enough our Top of The Pops appearance on 24 August 1972 started to propel us directly into the living rooms of a whole new audience.

It's been a great source of pride to me that Roxy Music has always had such a diverse and appreciative fan base; it's a community where everyone is welcome. Over the years many people have said to me that when they saw Roxy Music on our first Top of The Pops appearance, they felt inspired by how we looked, dressed, and sounded. It gave them permission to be who they wanted to be. When I re-watch this TOTP performance fifty years later, I totally get how it made them feel. If you look at our costumes and make up, and then look at the audience dancing around us, it does seem as if we have just landed from the Planet Zog.

Sheffield University gig poster

Straight away we got going on a frenzied round of gigs, travelling up and down the country from pubs and clubs and lots of students' unions. I still have a poster advertising a typical gig at Ranmoor Hall at Sheffield University in November '72. "Admission 50p," it says, "advance payment or 60p at the door." We were very happy to be playing these various gigs, and most appealing for me was that travelling up and down the UK was an entirely new experience.

Maybe it was ironic that as a small boy I'd been lucky enough to travel to many parts of the world, but the furthest north I'd been since I returned to London in 1960 was the guitar shops in Tottenham Court Road. Now we were regularly screaming up and down motorways in our transit van, driving through the night, often in thick fog on roads covered in black ice. It was a real eye opener to see cities like Sheffield, Nottingham, Manchester and Glasgow, parts of which seemed to be still recovering from bomb damage caused in World War Two. Sometimes we'd be the support act, sometimes the headline act, and often the only act. Audiences usually consisted of a few hundred people, but sometimes it was more. Occasionally on our journeys between venues we'd stop at the Blue Boar service station on the M1 and meet other bands doing the same thing. We'd all have an unwise breakfast, exchange chat about audiences and venues, and get on our way.

In December the same year we embarked on a three-week tour in the US. Returning to New York for my first fleeting visit after fleeing Havana in 1959 was incredibly exciting. Anyone who has watched Spinal Tap and seen the band arriving for the first time, driving into Manhattan in a limo, will get the idea. That's exactly how it was for us. The bullshit-o-meter was set at ten for the reception by the record company, assuring us that we were going to be the next big thing. The following night we supported Jethro Tull at Madison Square Gardens and straight away the wave that we had been riding since the release of the album and single came crashing down. We found ourselves in a vast and cavernous building, with only our tiny amps, stage set-up and stagecraft appropriate for small British venues. We beat ourselves up at the time for not having won over the audience, but on reflection I realise they never even heard us because the sound coming out of the PA was virtually non-existent. This kind of experience is like a rite of passage for any support band, most of whom are oblivious to the fact that the headline band will do everything possible to scupper them for fear of being overshadowed. Welcome to the dark arts, especially as they were practiced in the USA.

Years later we discovered that the coolest critics in New York had been alerted to the idea that we were the next big British export and had turned up to see us. They were sitting in the first two rows and were probably the only ones who were able to hear our act. They had no interest in seeing Jethro Tull, and so had promptly left as soon as we'd played. This was another example of our management's lack of experience, particularly when it came to breaking through in America.

We came away from that show shell-shocked and realising that this was America and a totally different ball game. Jethro Tull had an all-singing, all-dancing show with loads of big amps and a lighting rig which the audience lapped up. We went on to support bands like Ten Years After, the Edgar Winter Blues Band and even Steve Miller in Chicago on New Year's Eve. Supporting Carlos Santana's brother in Fresno (red neck country alert) we had water bombs thrown at us accompanied by shouts of "get off you faggots!" We ploughed on undeterred through *The Bob Medley* ... (otherwise known as the Battle of Britain medley), which was our closest thing to prog. It was a steep learning curve and a great adventure, and everywhere we went we attracted all the freakiest people in the city, many of whom ended up at our hotel after the gig.

On returning to the UK, we quickly had to get ready to record another album. It's accepted pop-music folklore that the second album is always difficult, but none of us felt that way.

Our approach to it could scarcely have been more different from the way we'd addressed the first. This time we were scheduled to record at Air Studios, which had been set up by George Martin after he'd left Abbey Road. He'd brought with him a lot of the best engineers and technicians who'd worked with him producing the Beatles albums, and all the experience of working with the new technology which was facilitating a revolution in the pop music-making industry. The studios were just down the road from the BBC in Portland Place, high up above the shops and looking out on Oxford Circus. A few hundred yards away was Carnaby Street, which was the flower-power capital of the world.

Our friend John Cale from the Velvet Underground was working as a staff producer at our label Warner Brothers in LA, and he recommended Chris Thomas as our producer. However, Chris was otherwise engaged in the studio next door mixing Floyd's *Dark Side of the Moon*, so we got underway with John Anthony who'd produced successful albums by Queen, Genesis, Lindisfarne, and Van der Graaf Generator. John was great but it wasn't an ideal fit, so when Chris became available we brought him in to team up with Bill Price and John Punter as engineers.

The great thing about Chris Thomas was that he had been George Martin's assistant with The Beatles from *The White Album* onwards. Whereas on the first album with Pete Sinfield producing we had just recorded our live set, now we were learning about part-playing, which was a direct result of the George Martin/Abbey Road method of recording and production as used by the Beatles. We learned how to listen to the other band members and to complement their playing so that one sound didn't eclipse another. Two-track recording had gone to four, then eight and then sixteen, opening seemingly endless possibilities for making new sounds and the way the instruments worked together. We'd record a take, then listen back and decide that the tone of Andy's oboe from take 24 was better, but the bass sounded better on take 36. Out would come the razor blade and sticky tape, and 24 and 36 could become seamless. The whole thing was a revelation. Needless to say, the advent of computers and digital recording has long since done away with the need for razor blades and tape.

It was still accepted at this early stage that Bryan was going to write all the songs, and if there was a grand plan or design of some sort, no-one ever told me about it. There were no long discussions about direction or what we were doing, but we simply had a shared energy and enthusiasm that drove us here and there as we adapted to the changing circumstances. Half of the tracks would be numbers from our existing stage set which we hadn't yet recorded, so really there was only a need for five new ones, and we embarked on a song-writing process which continued throughout our entire career as Roxy.

This was not conventional song-writing where a writer sits at a piano or strums a guitar, sings a melody, tries out a few words and eventually completes the song, which he then plays to the other members of the band; a way of going about things which was so beautifully exemplified by Paul McCartney and John Lennon in the *Get Back* documentaries.

Whether Bryan could or couldn't write a song the conventional way wasn't discussed. He would come up with a series of simple chord sequences that we would play endlessly, adding whatever parts we felt were appropriate, so that the combined sound would create a musical context for the track. Then Bryan would take the tape away and write a top line melody and lyrics. None of us had any idea what the song would be about at that stage, including Bryan. Probably this unusual way of working was part of the reason why Roxy sounded so different from everyone else.

My use of the Revox tape recorder at home enabled me to come up with my own process for recording at Air Studios. Once the initial backing track of drums, bass and guide piano were put down, I would go home with a mix and come up with some ideas for the guitar parts. This in turn meant that we could save time in the studio, and for the next five albums I would spend hours at home coming up with three or four alternative parts for each number. Then I'd arrive at the studio and tell Chris Thomas and the others that I had several options we could all choose from. Sometimes we would select one and sometimes more. Chris would then help me to perfect the sound, making me play it many times until I got the feel, the sound, and the part just right. Occasionally over the years I'd feel frustrated when someone would comment that they couldn't hear my guitar riffs, but that was only because they'd been so treated by Chris or Brian that they sounded more like they were coming out of a synth. I was sometimes tempted to make my part more overt, but I was always able to resist the urge. This is how we were all learning and benefiting from the George Martin production legacy.

As I look back with the benefit of hindsight on the way Bryan developed the lyrics, I realise it was all incredibly risky. We were always working against a deadline, tours were booked, release dates set, and follow up hits were expected. The lyrics he came up with were pure joy and a great testament to his skills and craftmanship. The moment when he came into the studio ready to lay them down was always exciting, and over the years became more and more important to the continuation of the band.

Roxy Music photo shoot, April 1973

Imagine for a moment what it was like to hear for the very first time the words of songs like *Do the Strand, Editions of You, Song for Europe, Love is the Drug* and *More Than This*. The list goes on. Then imagine that moment in the studio when we heard his voice singing those lyrics on top of a completed musical track with solos mixed in. Often we would just cheer, clap and laugh with relief.

I'm not saying all tracks were like that, but this was how the vast majority came together. Bryan wrote some great lyrics, inspired by his pop art education and his love of both the music and imagery of Americana. He was also lucky to have Dr Simon Puxley, a friend of Andy's from Reading Uni and an English literature PhD, to bounce his metaphors off. Simon became Roxy's publicist, by default, and wrote the brilliant sleeve notes for the first album.

We realised that we would need a new single to follow up *Virginia Plain* and we were still thinking that it was not cool to have the track on the album. Bryan wanted to be able to play guitar, so I devised a special tuning for him which only required him to play with one finger in four positions. *Pyjamarama* was thus created out of virtually nothing and turned out to be another hit.

Four Musketeers, 1973

In the course of that first year after joining Roxy I'd become especially friendly with Brian Eno, and we would spend hours round at his place in Maida Vale experimenting with the Revox tape recorders which we both used on stage and for recording. In those early days we quite often had to share rooms on tour to save money, and so he and I would be thrown in together. Given Eno's legendary success with women, it was not unusual to wake up in the middle of the night to find that the room was being shared by three rather than just us two.

Thinking about it now, I reckon we were lucky that Eno lasted as long as he did in Roxy.

Brian (with an i) Eno was a different kind of artist from Bryan (with a y) Ferry. Right from the get-go Brian described himself as an 'independent mobile unit' and a committed 'non-musician'. His Ipswich and Winchester art-school education was quite different from Bryan's Fine Art education under Richard Hamilton.

Trouble soon started brewing during those first two years, with potential conflict arising even from the unusual line-up of the band itself. Just about every other successful group at the time, with the obvious exception of The Beatles, had a single front man, and we didn't. On stage we'd have Bryan Ferry on one side, Brian Eno on the other, with Andy and I spaced out in between. Critics at the time tended to focus more on Eno, probably because he was the most flamboyant of all of us, which I'm sure Bryan didn't much enjoy.

Some of the creative differences between them started coming to the surface recording *For Your Pleasure*, in which our producer Chris Thomas was possibly more focused on the song and singing parts rather than the musical context which was what Eno was so good at. I'm not sure how on-board Chris was with what Brian was trying to achieve, and side one of the album turned out to have little scope for his special treatment and tape-loop adventures. Side two consisted of songs left over from the first album where there was more opportunity to appreciate Eno's work at its best.

There were other issues too. While Brian Eno was gregarious and likely to share, Bryan Ferry tended to be very secretive, and their two personalities were the reverse of each other. There was a fairly acrimonious falling out, for example, when the rest of us discovered that Bryan had been making plans for the cover of *For Your Pleasure* which were already well-advanced. None of the rest of us had been consulted, and we gradually became aware that various people were heading off for secret photo-shoots. The eventual cover would feature the transgender model Amanda Lear holding a black panther on a leash, and on the reverse, there was a photo of Bryan dressed as a chauffeur. The rest of us took the opportunity to make very clear to Bryan that it wasn't okay to make decisions like this on his own, and for the moment he appeared to take the point.

Roxy have Tea with Dalí, 1973

Amanda was a close friend of Bryan's, and in fact he developed a habit of involving whomever he was friendly with at the time for our album covers. She had previously had a long relationship with Salvador Dali, as a result of which we found ourselves with an invitation to meet the artist at Le Meurice Hotel in Paris. Dali was already quite old by this point, and needless to say he was looking very 'Daliesque' with his familiar twirly moustache, a bow-tie, formal black jacket and pinstripe trousers. He lived in a huge permanent suite at the hotel and had set up these separate screens in the middle of the room. He offered us tea, and then insisted that we all enter this cramped semi-circle. In the main room he had fabric snakes drapped over all the sofas and chairs so it was impossible to sit down. I have a photograph of us with our little pinkies extended, drinking tea from dainty cups. It was literally a surreal experience, but such a privilege to meet this unique and legendary character.

In those days the Melody Maker was regarded very much as the bible of our industry, and we'd buy it religiously every week and scan its columns for the latest gossip, news of who else was playing where, reviews, the charts and stuff for sale. It was some time in 1973 that I spotted an ad which read "Red Gibson for sale." There was no further description or indication of the model, but I made a call and was invited to a very posh house in Regents Park. I knocked on the door, which was eventually answered by an American kid aged about 16. He told me his parents had bought him the guitar, but he hadn't played it and wasn't likely to. I waited while he went back into the house and a few minutes later he re-appeared, this time holding a 1964 Gibson Firebird VII in that classic cardinal red they used for 1950s American cars. It's a bit like the Hofner Galaxy, but with bolder and more pronounced contours

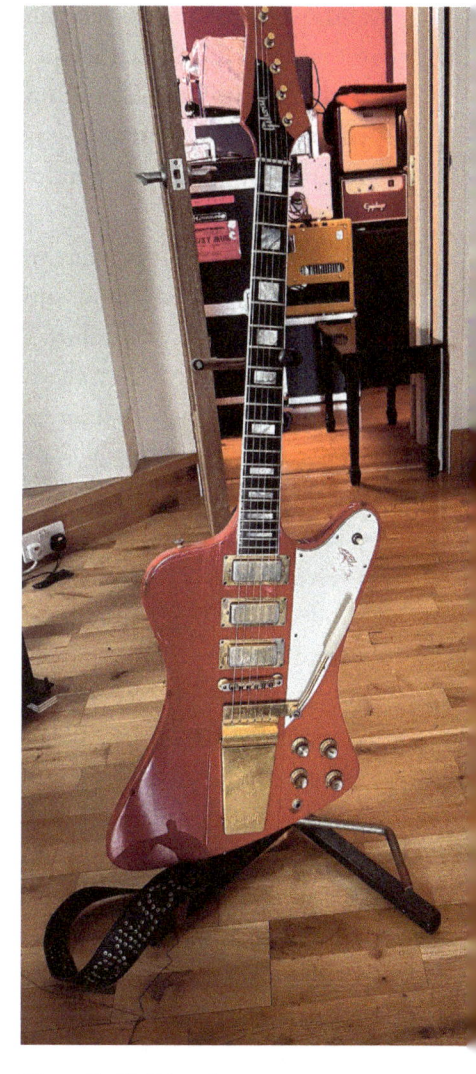

Gibson Firebird VII 1964

and curves. I'd never seen one in red before, and I've never seen another one since. I didn't hesitate or even ask to play it. Instantly I parted with (I think it was) £120, and now I had my signature weird guitar. It has ended up being part of my musical trademark from that day to this, a reliable and constant friend which sits happily within a few feet of me even as I write.

Over the next two years we toured all over Britain, and then went out to conquer the rest of the world with albums produced by Chris Thomas and recorded at Air Studios. We had enthusiastic crowds and receptions in Germany, Italy, Australia, and New Zealand among others. America, though, was a much harder nut to crack, and the way I'd put it is that we were too strong a flavour for the US market at that moment. Almost all the successful UK bands which had broken into the American scene were playing their brand of rock and roll, much of it based on recognisable twelve bar blues patterns which had originated in black music. And just about all of them had also paid off a certain man based in Philadelphia who would guarantee that their records were played on the radio, then they'd start to appear on TV shows, and their music would feature in the American charts. Most bands at that time accepted that this was necessary, but our management declined to follow suit, and so for the time being we made very little headway in the States.

In June 1973, Sharon and I were married at the chapel in my old school in Dulwich, and the wedding photos show all the band turned out in their finery. Sharon continued working for a property company in Shepherds Bush and we rented a tiny flat in Notting Hill. We didn't need much space because of course the schedule meant I was very seldom at home.

I've said that every day after I joined Roxy Music was like Christmas day, and truly it seemed that we could do no wrong. We had our own distinctive look and style which was just a bit different from so many of the other bands. We rushed from one gig to the next, having a great time everywhere we went, and never stopping to think. Our albums and singles were all big hits and well-reviewed, and our fanbase was enthusiastic and growing. As so often though, everything was not entirely harmonious behind the scenes. I've heard a lot of stories about the circumstances which finally led to Brian Eno leaving Roxy, some of which I recognise and some I don't. His relationship with Bryan remained difficult, and I had a suspicion that the ongoing dispute had an undercurrent involving someone's girlfriend at the time. That wasn't my business and I didn't enquire, but what was my business, as it was also Andy's and Paul's, was that a split was coming which would have bigger consequences for all of us.

The last gig Brian Eno played with us was on the 2 July 1973 in York. Eno and I remained on good terms, and sometimes I'd leave a recording session for Roxy's third album and head off down to another studio where he was recording his solo album, so I could play some guitar parts to help him out. Later he and I

Eno waves goodbye after his last gig, 1973

would go on to collaborate on a variety of projects and he remains a great friend to this day. I'm delighted that Brian has gone on to become a creative force in the arts: a veritable 'unique mobile unit'.

When Eno eventually decided to go his own way, Andy and I had to think hard about what to do next in relation to Bryan. We could blow up the whole thing, abandon the band and go our separate ways, or we could agree a new way forward in which each of us contributed more to the whole, which would give us more satisfaction in the music and more of a stake in the income from publishing. There was a moment where it could have gone either way, but eventually we agreed to try out a new approach. The most immediate result was that on the next album, called *Stranded*, I co-wrote *Amazona* and Andy co-wrote *A Song for Europe*. We had secured peace in our time – for the moment at least.

FIVE

On Tour

In those early days our gigs always felt like great occasions and our audiences were always very lively and appreciative. It seemed that everywhere we went, Roxy concerts attracted the freakiest people from miles around. When a concert was over, we'd always find crowds of revellers at the stage door, and getting from the venue to the tour bus and away became more and more of a challenge. Usually it was all good fun, but as our popularity continued to grow, occasionally things could get a bit out of hand and inevitably we needed to take more care that everyone stayed safe.

One time we were playing in Glasgow where, for some unexplained reason, Roxy always had an especially raucous following: could it be that a few wee drams were had before, during and after the gig? We were staying at the Station Hotel, only a few hundred yards away from the legendary Greens Playhouse, every rock band known to man had played there from Chuck Berry to Pink Floyd. Not everyone emerged from there unscathed. Word of our destination, post-gig, must have spread because a large crowd accompanied the bus all the way along the street, and when we reached the hotel, we found that just about everyone who'd been at the stage door was alongside, and we were mobbed. The next question was how to get us from the coach into the back door of the hotel. The decision was made to place a protective phalanx of roadies around each of us in turn, and that we'd run the gauntlet one at a time.

I can't remember who went first, or where I was in the queue, but all was going fine until it came to my turn. I don't know whether it was because I was wearing those mad high-heeled platform boots that we all sported at the time or what, but one way or another I fell out of the bus and landed heavily on the ground. Instantly I felt an excruciating pain in my left leg, there was utter chaos and confusion, and the next thing I knew I was being dragged off to the local hospital where, much to my horror, they declared that the leg was broken.

Not only was this painful and inconvenient, it was also terrible timing because we were about to set off on a major European tour. There was obviously no question of me being able to stand on stage for hours, let alone all the dancing and prancing about that characterized our performance. Reluctantly it was decided that we'd place a stool on the side of the stage, and I'd be perched uncomfortably with my guitar. Bryan would make a big thing about how "the doctors said he must not tour, but despite all that, he's battled against adversity and is here tonight to play for you!" and I'd get a huge cheer, which was some consolation for my discomfort and embarrassment.

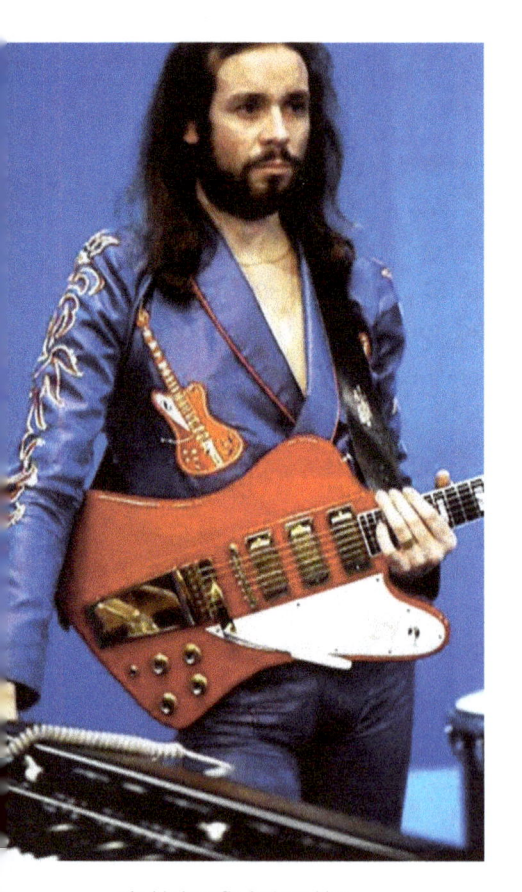

Firebird outfit designed by Wendy Dagworthy, 1974

Everything was so full-on at the time, with the relentless schedule of recording and touring, that one album tends to blur into the next. We'd scarcely finished putting *Stranded* to bed when work started on our fourth, which would be called *Country Life*. We thought we'd produce it ourselves with the engineer John Punter but it didn't work out so once again asked Chris Thomas to produce. Usually we'd start the working day at noon and spend as long as necessary getting down a strong backing track of bass and drums. We'd work until midnight and then go home via a few drinks at the Speakeasy club. I had my Revox tape recorder at home, and I'd get up early and spend the next morning working out various alternatives for the guitar parts, so that when we resumed at lunchtime, I'd usually offer three or four alternatives for everyone else to choose from. I got the chance to contribute some songs of my own and wrote both *Out of the Blue* and *Prairie Rose*.

There was no track called Country Life on the album, just as there had been no song called Stranded on *Stranded*, and there would be nothing called Siren on *Siren*. It was another of those little things which made us just a bit different and which I rather liked.

The album did well for us in the UK and was the first of ours to get into the top 40 in the US. However once again, many people remember it almost as much for the cover as for the music.

What happened was that Bryan had taken a holiday in Portugal with our stylist Antony Price. Staying in the house next door was a girl called Constanze who was the sister of Michael Karoli of the huge German band Can. With her was Michael's girlfriend, Eveline Grunwald. Bryan and Antony no doubt found them eye-catching, and the next thing was that they'd hired Eric Boman to do a photo-shoot. The first I knew of it was when I went round to David Enthoven's house to see the artwork and couldn't quite believe my eyes.

It's probably not surprising that using a picture of two incredibly sexy looking young women, one in see-through underwear and the other holding her breasts in her hands, on the cover of an album by an all-male band, might cause some concern. So controversial was it in the US, Spain, and the Netherlands in particular, that each chose different approaches to disguising or hiding the image. Early releases in the States were covered

REVOLUCIÓN TO ROXY

in brown paper, rather reminiscent of an old-fashioned top shelf magazine.

Still relatively young and naïve as I was, all I remember thinking was, "what's my mother going to say?" The two girls are credited on the lyric sheet for their German translation work. We should probably draw a discreet veil over any other contributions they may have made.

The *Country Life* tour took us on what would be my first visit to Australia, and mostly I remember what seemed like an endless plane journey, at the end of which all I wanted to do was to check into my hotel room in Sydney and sleep for England. While unpacking my stuff, I switched on the TV to see if I could discover what the Australian music scene sounded like, and I came across this amazing band who looked freaky and sounded terrific. I was just about awake enough to make a note of their name, which was Split Enz. Then when I arrived at our first gig, at the Horden Pavilion, I discovered that the very same band was our support act. I popped in after their set to say hello and let them know how much I'd enjoyed their stuff. They seemed to be really nice guys and we got on well, so when it was time for Roxy to go on stage I said, "if ever I can do anything for you …". I was surprised by their answer; "well you could produce our first album". I remember thinking something like, "oh yeah, how's that going to happen?" and we said goodbye and went our separate ways. Just about a year later they would come knocking on my door.

Split Enz, 1976

Split Enz – Tim Finn, 1975

The last of the five Roxy albums we recorded in that phase of the band was called *Siren*, which included what would be our only top 40 hit in America, *Love is the Drug*. Bryan later said he'd come up with the song while walking through Hyde Park kicking leaves. Yet again we adopted the same winning formula as with the previous three albums – Air Studios, with Chris producing. At the end of each day, I'd go back home and experiment with various riffs until I found one or more I was happy with. Sometimes more than one would be favoured, and so I'd play different riffs throughout the recording. Chris would then finesse the sound, and we'd move on to the next track.

The *Siren* album featured the model Jerry Hall on the sleeve and she and Bryan became an item. Jerry was (and is) strikingly tall and beautiful, with a languorous Texan drawl. She could also be a bit scatty, but then again, she can only have been about 19 at the time. They were very much a glamour couple, attracting press attention wherever they went.

Before any of us knew it, Bryan and Jerry had announced their engagement, and Jerry came to be a more or less regular additional guest on our tours. Their relationship must have been very difficult because both had busy schedules and led glamorous lives populated by glamorous people. On and off planes, in and out of hotels, photo-shoots, press interviews, and both with strong egos and separate ambitions. All taken together it didn't seem like a perfect backdrop for a romance made in heaven. I had an early inkling that things might not be exactly as they appeared when one day Bryan, Jerry, Mark Fenwick and I were being hustled into a waiting car having just got off a plane on the US tour. Suddenly Jerry was in a panic. "I've lost my engagement ring!" she shouted. Obviously this went down very badly.

Looking at what happened in those first five years of releasing two albums a year, touring all over the world, regular TV appearances and playing to packed auditoriums, it would be natural to assume that we were living the high life and accumulating a healthy bank account. But that reasonable assumption would fail to understand the structure of the industry in those days, and the extent to which young musicians who only wanted to play music and perform were taken advantage of by the business.

It's sobering, to put it midly, to consider some of the arithmetic: Roxy's share of the first album, for example, was 5%, which was to be divided between six people. Every time I asked for a statement of our earnings, I'd receive a read-out which itemised every cost of managers, secretaries, office overheads, PR people, air-travel, hotels, equipment hire, lights, costumes, make-up, hospitality, the tour bus and apparently endless hangers on – the result of which was that I joined the band in 1972 and it wasn't until twelve years later in 1984, after we stopped touring, that my bank balance was in the black for the first time.

All of us were working hard to fulfil our recording and touring obligations with Roxy, but some were also working on their own projects which could be fitted neatly within the band's schedule. I was twenty-five and having a great time with Roxy, but all the while I felt an inner voice whispering that there must be many other musical adventures out there. Maybe somewhere in my sub-conscious, the passion and excitement of those Latin-American beats which had permeated my 6-year-old head in all those exotic nightclubs were hammering to get out. I felt the need to counterbalance my Roxy music with different genres. Bryan, Andy and Brian Eno had all made solo albums, so I put my hand up and said me too please: EG and Island agreed.

When I decided to record the album, I was keen to bring together some of the people I'd enjoyed working with already, but to add some new flavours into the mix. I rented time in the famous Island Records studio at Basing Street, where Free had recorded their timeless single *Alright Now* and Bob Marley had worked so often that the aroma of weed seemed to linger in the corridors. Andy, Paul and Eddie Jobson from Roxy agreed to play, and Brian Eno was evident throughout, eventually singing on two tracks – *Big Day* and *Miss Shapiro*. The

Diamond Head album cover, 1975

album also gave me a chance to work with one of my great heroes of all time, Robert Wyatt, late of Soft Machine and Matching Mole.

Robert had suffered a terrible accident when he fell out of a fourth-floor window while at a party, and by this time was confined to a wheelchair. Ironically he said later that the accident had probably saved his life, because his drinking had been well on the way to becoming completely out of control and would have killed him. I was thrilled when he agreed to be part of the album. I'd written a track with the MacCormick brothers and had asked Robert to write some lyrics in Spanish which he would also sing.

When Robert came to perform the song in the studio, I got the impression that the lyrics consisted of a whole lot of Spanish sounding phrases joined together in a way which didn't quite make cogent sense. Nonetheless they managed to convey a tone and atmosphere with the distinctly Latin-American feel I was looking for, and I found them mesmerising. Naturally I asked him where the lyrics had come from, and he confessed that he'd consulted a Spanish dictionary and compiled a random confection of words and phrases he liked the sound of. It all added up to something you could vaguely recognise as "we've got to get to the frontier," and *Frontera* went on to be widely acclaimed as a sort of Dadaist montage which everyone who heard it fell completely in love with, including me.

The rest of the album is made up of collaborations with my chosen musician friends. The creative process was everything I'd hoped it would be. I was always looking for any chance I could find to personalise the album and so I called it *Diamond Head*, recalling my sun-drenched childhood memories of Waikiki beach.

Obviously if you're going to go to all the trouble and expense of hiring Basing Street studios, you want to get your money's worth, and so at 6pm each day we'd say goodbye to some of the musicians playing on *Diamond Head* and head downstairs to Studio 2 where there would assemble another gathering involving some overlaps and a few others from among my old friends.

Up until that point, Quiet Sun had felt somehow like unfinished business from schooldays, and I felt a need to return to it and give it the

Quiet Sun, Dave Jarrett, Charles Hayward, Bill MacCormick, me, 1975

high-quality production the music deserved. I set about reassembling the band's original musicians, plus some new collaborators. This combination included Charles Hayward, Dave Jarrett, Eno, Bill MacCormick and his brother Ian contributing back-up vocals, and we had a great time revisiting the music we'd first rehearsed just before I joined Roxy. We called the album *Mainstream*. Mostly it was instrumental in the style of the Canterbury school; exactly the recorded music I'd played at my audition for Roxy, and which Bryan and the others had so disliked. Looking back on those busy times, it's hard even for me to believe that I was working all day recording for the *Diamond Head* album, and then I'd end it by going to a different studio and recording a whole new album with my old schoolmates from Quiet Sun. The resulting work has always attracted its own cohort of fans, and even now I'm frequently urged to re-assemble the original cast and head off to Japan where the album still has a band of loyal followers.

One particular incident from that period illustrates just how insane our lives and schedule were at that time. It was early 1976 and I was on a tour with Roxy to promote the *Siren* album. I'd been full-on playing my part in all the Roxy recordings, but I was burning the candle at both ends recording *Diamond Head* and *Mainstream*. By the time we were due to board the plane which would take us to the first gig of the tour in Toronto, I was already totally exhausted.

I remember getting off the plane at the other end, checking into our hotel, and falling into the deepest imaginable slumber. A chance to make a dent in a serious sleep deficit before this leg of the tour got underway. The next thing I knew, I was awoken by the sudden and urgent sound of heavy hammering on the door. As I gradually came round and worked out who and where I was, I realized that the hammering was accompanied by shouting.

"Open up this door or we'll break it down."

What the hell …? By now I was beginning to collect my wits, so I grabbed a towel and headed towards the door. The hammering and shouting was getting louder and the voices angrier. "Police! Open up NOW!" I managed to look through the spyhole in the door, and outside were three heavy guys wearing civilian clothes and carrying large and ugly-looking handguns. "Open up or we'll break the door down."

"No," I said, "I'm not opening the door. I'm going to ring downstairs and check …". But I didn't get to the end of the sentence before the solid wooden door shattered right before my eyes, and instantly three goons piled in with the momentum of an express train but none of the subtlety. I stumbled backwards like a ninepin tumbling before a hurtling bowling ball and found myself pinned down on the bed by a body the size and shape of an orang-utan sitting astride me.

Quiet Sun album cover, 1975

While this goon held me down, the other two began searching my belongings, throwing all my stuff over everywhere until the place resembled The Young Ones' living room. They made little attempt to disguise their disappointment that they found no drugs.

"OK," said Goon One. "Do not leave this room. Do not call or warn the other members of the band," and they left.

I heard later that when they'd hammered on Bryan's door, he'd answered immediately wearing a silk dressing gown and a polka dot cravat, just as though it was 2pm rather than 2am. "Yes gentlemen? How may I help you?"

The only person whose door they didn't knock down was the tour manager who'd come from New York rather than from England and was the only one who had any drugs on him. But the Canadian Mounties were particularly hot on drugs at that time. They'd developed a habit of turning over British rock bands on tour, and if you ended up with a drug conviction, you wouldn't be able to get into Canada or the States at all. I don't remember receiving any apology, and I also didn't catch up on my sleep.

Our tours moved rapidly from one city to the next, without a moment to take in the first thing about the place you were in, other than the bland interiors of countless anonymous hotels. Places you'd heard about in movies or in the lyrics of *Route 66* came and went like squares on an endless board-game. Onto one plane, a fast change to another plane, into a bus, into a hotel, off to the venue for a sound check, do the gig, crash out as soon as possible, a few hours of sleep, and then up at the crack of dawn and off to the next one.

One time we were landing in Chicago and there had to be a very quick turnaround if we were to catch the connecting flight to the next city and the next gig. Everyone else got off the plane before me, and by the time I'd walked up the air-bridge, there was no sign of anyone I recognised, and no clue about which direction to turn. In fact the band had turned right, and then immediately turned right again to board the connecting flight. I guessed wrong and turned left, only to find myself in a vast concourse which seemed to be full of odd-looking men wearing "Jesus Saves" sandwich boards and offering to save my soul. Right at that moment though, the prospects of eternal damnation seemed to pale against the consequences of losing the band, so I started asking people, "have you seen any musicians coming this way?" "Yes", said a young kid with an excited look in his eye, "they went that way." I followed in the direction of his pointing finger, casting around in the hope of seeing a familiar face, when at last I did indeed recognise some people I knew – but unfortunately it was David Bowie's band who happened to be travelling through Chicago at the same time. By now I was in a panic.

Just at that moment I heard a voice over the Tannoy – "will Mr Manzanera go to the atrium?" I did and was met by one of our minders who informed me that everyone else had boarded the plane and left, and that he and I would have to book on the next flight out. We managed to get a later flight, which was then struck by lighting, causing my so-called minder to grab my arm in terror. We eventually arrived in the nick of time for the gig. Phew.

All this time, Bryan was undoubtedly listening to the various voices in his ear telling him that he didn't need to be making any of the compromises involved in membership of a band. "He was the main creative, he was the front man, he was the one all the TV cameras focussed on. He was Roxy Music, and the rest of us were essentially dispensable; maybe it was time to pursue his solo career." I don't know whether Jerry played a part in that persuasion, but I do know that it was led by Mark Fenwick from EG management. Once again, the musketeers were beginning to feel that "all for one, and one for all," should more accurately have ended at the comma.

Just exactly how and why it happened is probably known only to him, but these voices were obviously saying what Bryan wanted to hear, and the next thing we knew was that he'd moved to Los Angeles and was intent on pursuing a solo career. This was 1976 and it wasn't the end, but it was, (in the words of Winston Churchill) the end of the beginning.

Though we were disappointed by the way it happened, the parting of the ways didn't leave the rest of us especially angry or at a loss about what to do. Andy Mackay, Paul Thompson, and our keyboard player Eddie Jobson each had their own projects. Meanwhile I saw this as an opportunity to develop a whole lot of ambitions and collaborations I'd been pursuing with some more of the wide range of brilliant musicians whose work I admired.

Brian Eno and I had already been looking for another project to work on together, so off we went with the MacCormick brothers to a friend's country idyll in Shropshire where we planned and plotted. We had

801 live album cover, 1976

an idea to try something completely new and different, which was that we would form a band and make some music, on the understanding

801 live onstage at the Reading festival, 1976

that the whole thing would start and end within a strictly limited time. We'd perform a very small number of gigs, and then go our separate ways.

The talk was intense and earnest, and I learned later that Brian couldn't recall a single thing about any of our discussions, other than that the house we were using had been struck by a huge thunderbolt, after which we found that the telephone had melted and there was a wide crack down the chimney breast. Notwithstanding the wrath of God, at the end of our discussions, the *801 live* project was born. "801" after a lyric from an earlier Eno song, "We are The 801/We are the Central Shaft." Obviously.

Our mad idea was to combine what we described as musicians and non-musicians to see what happened. By that we meant that some members of the band, like Simon Phillips on drums and Francis Monkman (from Sky and Curved Air) on keyboards, were technically excellent musicians as well as being original talents. Meanwhile others were self-taught and may not have been technically brilliant but were instinctive players, more concerned with the texture of the music and with creating new and

Me and Eno at the Reading Festival

REVOLUCIÓN TO ROXY

Gig poster for the 801 'warm up' at West Runton pavilion, Norfolk, 1976

original sounds. Eno was the prime example of the latter – the first to say that he's a total "non-musician" but with more musical talent in one fingernail than many successful performers have in their entire bodies. We brought in the amazing Lloyd Watson on slide guitar and vocals. Lloyd was a lovely guy who'd just been named rock/folk solo artist of the year by Melody Maker.

For my part, I'd taken a considered decision much earlier in my career to actively avoid becoming too technically adept. I know that might sound strange, but I genuinely feared that the discipline involved in learning to play all those 'black dots' might constrain the free flow playing which was what really fired me up. So being self-taught but not entirely without technical competence, I saw myself as a sort of bridge between the two.

The rehearsals were long and challenging, especially for Simon, who freely admitted that he'd never worked so intensely before. Our eventual rendering of The Beatles' hit *Tomorrow Never Knows*, and the Kinks' *You Really Got Me*, both combine pop with some blues, traces of punk, prog rock, and ambient music; exactly the eclectic mix that we'd aspired to achieve from the outset. Other tracks written by Brian, Charles and Bill allowed us to try out a whole range of different sounds and textures.

Time and pressure from other commitments meant that the planned gigs were eventually whittled down to only three. One was in the unlikely resort of Cromer on the north Norfolk coast, another was at the Reading Festival, which John Peel said was the highlight of the event. But the real elusive magic of the bond between us was captured at our third and final gig at the Queen Elizabeth Hall. It was recorded on the Island Mobile and mixed by Rhett Davis who'd also worked with us on *Mainstream* and *Diamond Head* at Basing Street Studios. This was the first live album to use a closed mic approach to recording, in which all outputs from the vocal microphones, guitar amps and other instruments (except the drums) were fed directly to the mobile studio mixing desk, rather than being recorded via microphones and/or signals fed out the front-of-house PA mixer. It went on to win many plaudits for the innovation as well as for the music.

Reading Festival poster, 1976

Richard Williams of the Melody Maker, whose good opinion we had sought for so long, wrote that "during the concert these people collectively reached a point where virtually anything is possible. The music seemed to me to embody all the virtues of the very early Roxy Music, with the freedom to try and the freedom to fail. Except that they're now more confident, more able, more eloquent." I was very happy with that. The audience loved the show, and it has turned out to be one of the highlights of my fifty years in music.

SIX

Roxy – Take Two

By now I'd played on and written music for five albums with Roxy, as well as a solo album and half a dozen collaborations with other musicians, all of them recorded in different studios in various parts of the world. We'd toured all over Britain, Europe, New Zealand, Australia and the US. All this while, Sharon and I were still living in our tiny house in Acton which I'd been able to buy with some financial help from her father. We knew it was time for us to move but my lifestyle allowed me no spare time for house-hunting, so we hired the services of Perry Press from Pereds in Holland Park, who'd previously found suitable houses for members of Pink Floyd and others. He sent us to look at various places in Sunningdale and Virginia Water, but nothing seemed quite right. Then one day we were browsing the newspaper and saw an advertisement for an art deco house in Chertsey, called St Ann's Court.

Neither Sharon nor I knew that part of Surrey, but she remembered that our close friends Kevin Godley and his wife Sue lived in the area. We were close with all the members of 10cc and had recently been on holiday with all four of them. To my amazement, Sue said that St Ann's

Court was up the hill, near to their house, but that she'd never actually seen it and would be happy to take a walk over. It wasn't long before she was back on the phone.

"It's the weirdest place you've ever seen," she said. That was enough to persuade us it was worth a visit.

St Ann's Court is magnificent. The main building is known as the Round House and is a Modernist masterpiece by the renowned architect Raymond McGrath who was a disciple of Le Corbusier. He designed some of the interiors in the BBC's Broadcasting House in Portland Place as well as the penguin pool at Regent's Park Zoo. It's been described as one of the finest houses of its kind to have been built in Britain in the first half of the 20th century. The gardens were designed by the equally distinguished landscape architect Christopher Tunnard, who lived there with his male partner. It was built on the site of a Georgian mansion where the famous parliamentarian Charles James Fox lived with the infamous courtesan, Mrs Elizabeth Armitage, who was the former mistress of George IV. Charles eventually married her in secret in 1795, and she died a respectable widow in 1842 aged 92. Elizabeth is buried in a chapel in the grounds of St. Ann's Hill.

Right from the moment I saw St Ann's Court, I knew I had to have it. I didn't realise it at the time, but it was reminiscent of the style of our house in Havana. It was distinctive and brilliant, and I was excited, but at £70,000 it was way out of my price range. One way and another though, I was able to take on some kind of mortgage, and the deal was done. This was my first "rock star purchase", but I was twenty-five and feeling bullish, and for the next twenty-three years the house and grounds were a joy to own and to live in. Sure, it was an indulgence and a folly, but it also felt like a challenge, and I had a hunch that having all that land would be a good long-term investment.

St. Anns Court, Chertsey, Surrey, UK

We set about removing the flock wallpaper from some of the rooms and restoring an authentic 1930s look and feel. I bumped into an old friend from school called Paul Davis who had recently qualified as an architect, and he guided me in tracking down the history of the house and the wider Art Deco and Bauhaus movement. He also introduced me to two incredibly talented young furniture makers, Fred Baier and Chris Rose, who were students of the famous Parham House run by John Makepeace. Decorating and furnishing a round house presents all sorts of challenges, and Fred and Chris made several utterly beautiful bespoke pieces. Later I allowed the producers of the TV series Poirot to use the house to shoot interiors, and I still occasionally spot some familiar backgrounds on screen to this day.

Apart from the main house, the property included an amazing 18th century coach house which had fallen into disrepair; this gave me an idea. Having worked in dozens of different studios all around the world, I felt I had a good knowledge of the conditions musicians and producers need if they're to be at their most creative. I also knew from experience what worked and what didn't, and a plan formed in my mind. The coach house was a good size, was surrounded by a beautiful

The Coachouse, Gallery Studios, Chertsey

landscape, but was also private and far enough away from other buildings. Maybe it might be possible to create a state-of-the art recording studio – something really special.

My next-door neighbour was now Kevin Godley from 10cc. Kevin had bought his house from The Who's drummer Keith Moon, who had walked out of it after the sale, leaving absolutely every item he owned wherever it happened to be at that moment, including his clothes. Contents included a hovercraft which had been Keith's mode of transport from his front door to the pub at the end of his drive. Unfortunately, this short journey involved hovering over a pond which was situated alongside the pub car-park, so the trip had not always been completed without incident. Some years later I met Keith when we were both guests of Paul and Linda McCartney at a preview of the movie *The Buddy Holly Story* and afterwards we went to supper at Peppermint Park in Covent Garden. I've never been much of a drinker, and nor does my constitution permit me to tolerate drugs, so I had probably gone home long before Keith left with his girlfriend Annette Walter-Lax. Later the following day I turned on the news and heard that Keith had died during the night. It was a terrible shock, especially since I'd only seen him a few hours earlier very much 'alive and kicking'.

Kevin and Lol were becoming disenchanted at that time with 10cc, and the three of us were talking about forming a band together. Both were also keen to come in as partners on the studio project, which was great because they had impressive relevant experience having been a part of the 10cc Strawberry Studio in Stockport. All their famous albums were

Gallery's studio playing area

recorded there, so I was grateful for their creative, as well as for their financial input.

Building the studio was a labour of love but clearly was going to be eye-wateringly expensive. We decided to create a huge control room, so big in fact that you could bring in the instruments and actually play and record inside it. We planned to have all the latest gear and tech. It was an exciting adventure until one day out of the blue Kevin called up to tell me that he and Lol had received a huge and unexpected tax bill, and so wouldn't be partnering in the studio after all. My heart sank. What should I do? I rang my management company and had the options spelled out to me. Either I could abort the project now and cut my losses, or I could continue to build the studio and land myself even more deeply in debt for the next ten years. There was no third choice. I didn't hesitate and chose to continue, and so suddenly I was facing the prospect of yet another decade in the red.

Gallery's control room

I was working at Basing Studios one night in December 1976 when I received an unexpected call from Bryan. He was about to embark on a world tour, starting the following day in Southampton; would I like to come along to play guitar? I was taken completely by surprise, not least because I knew he'd already got Chris Spedding on board, and Chris is a great guitarist. I hesitated for a moment but then the lure of going off around the world with John Wetton on bass and the great Paul Thompson on drums was too tempting, and so I said yes. I spent the next 24 hours learning the set, and the next night I was on stage and on a Bryan Ferry solo tour. The tour went well and after Europe we went on to Australia where Roxy had always enjoyed a loyal fan-base, and Bryan's iconic song *Let's Stick Together* hit number one. I was slightly mystified about what was going on in Bryan's head and found myself wondering if he thought of me as some sort of talisman.

The whole thing turned out to be really enjoyable and so we went on to work our way across the US, eventually reaching the east coast. We were in New York when by chance I ran into Andy Mackay, and it was great to catch up. In and among the conversation he mentioned in passing that Bryan's girlfriend Jerry Hall had been seen out the night before with Mick Jagger. When later we played the gig at the Bottom Line club in the city, and it came time to perform *Let's Stick Together*, Jerry came on stage and was dancing alongside Bryan as she does in the video. The chemistry felt very strange, and when I looked at the way she and Bryan were interacting with each other, I remember thinking that this wasn't going to end well. A few weeks later, Bryan was in Switzerland when he read in the Daily Mail's Nigel Dempster column that his fiancée Jerry had been seen out and about with Mick. The gossip turned out to be true, and the next thing was that she had jilted Bryan for the Rolling Stones' front man.

I was sorry to hear the news because I knew Bryan would be hurting, but nonetheless I was surprised when I received a midnight call from him some months later. He was now back in London and sounding sad and lonely, but then astonished me by saying he'd been wondering if Roxy should re-form. Things obviously weren't going well in his world and maybe he felt the need of some musketeers back for the ride. A possible distraction from a huge heartbreak. I told him that I loved Roxy and always would, but that I'd already committed to forming a band with Kevin and Lol and we had an album deal with Phonogram Records. Bryan didn't see that as a problem, and immediately said, "don't worry, you can do both." I wasn't sure that was realistic, but I was badly in need of more funds to continue the studio project at St Ann's Court, so I told EG Management that if they wanted me to re-join Roxy, they'd have to lend me the money to do so. Slightly to my surprise, they quickly agreed, and so I undertook to do whatever was necessary to be the guitarist in both bands. In reality of course, this plan quickly proved logistically impossible, so what would have been the imaginatively named group GCM became just Godley and Creme, and my guitar parts on the duo's first album were contributed as a guest artist rather than as a permanent member of the band.

Getting a core team back together which would be recognisable as Roxy Music wasn't going to be a simple matter because everyone had also become involved in their own projects. Andy Mackay was immersed in the highly successful TV series *Rock Follies*, Paul Thompson was in a band called Concrete Blond, and Eddie Jobson had joined the legendary Frank Zappa, who was well known for hiring only sensational musicians but also for ruling his band with a rod of iron. One way and another though, over the following weeks Andy and Paul were tempted back, and we brought in the amazing Paul Carrack on keyboards and bass guitarist Alan Spenner from Joe Cocker's Grease band.

Now that Roxy Music was back in business, I had a sufficient source of funding to press on with building the studio. It took two years to complete but my vision was beyond realised. I named it Gallery Studios, and over the following years it was used by everyone from Siouxsie and the Banshees, the Moody Blues, Duran Duran, Dire Straits, and even Cliff Richard which was a thrill for me. Later a re-formed Roxy would record most of both the *Flesh and Blood* and *Avalon* albums there.

My appetite for producing had been sharpened by the various experimental journeys and collaborations I'd undertaken recording *Diamond Head*, and with Quiet Sun and 801, so I was happy to receive a call one day from the management of Split Enz, which was the band I'd first met during the *Country Life* tour of Australia. They wanted to come to London and were asking if I was still interested in producing them, which I was. Michael Gudinski from their Australian label, Mushroom, got them a deal with Chrysalis Records, and we went into Basing Street studios where I produced what would be their first UK album called *Mental Notes*. Later they released it in Australia as *Second Thoughts*. The whole thing was a great experience and the start of a lifelong friendship with Neil and Tim Finn.

Now Bryan and I started looking around for a suitable residential studio. We eventually alighted on Ridge Farm near Gatwick which had everything we needed, as well as tennis courts and a swimming pool for a bit of relaxation to break up any creative tension. All of which was fine until one day when I was jogging round St Ann's Hill with my Alsatian puppy Gibson trailing behind. I looked back to see where he'd got to, and suddenly the ground disappeared beneath my feet. I felt a stab of excruciating pain and looked down to see that I'd fallen down an open manhole. My leg was broken – yet again. So now I had to suffer the indignity and discomfort of being carted around in an armchair in the back of a Transit van with no windows, and of sitting on the side-lines watching while everyone else swam and practiced their backhand returns at Ridge Farm. If that wasn't bad enough, the studio was in a converted barn and the control room was up a ladder, so we'd record a take, everyone would climb up the ladder to listen to the track, and I'd still be struggling to get up there when someone would say "no good" and would try not to knock me over on their way down.

We eventually headed off to Atlantic Studios in New York for the recording of the next Roxy Music album which would end up being called *Manifesto*. Bryan in particular was very plugged in to the stylish and arty

Atlantic Studios, New York, 1978

set, and my main memory was that we were holed up in a slightly dodgy hotel near Central Park which reeked of faded glamour but was cheap. There were lots of parties involving scores of hip New York celebrities and the Studio 54 crowd.

The album included a track called *Dance Away* which turned into a surprise hit courtesy of an unexpected intervention by the legendary boss of Atlantic Records, Ahmet Ertegun. The year was 1978 and the two prevailing music crazes at the time were of course punk and disco, so when Ahmet heard our first recording of *Dance Away*, he immediately said, "that's great, but you should put fours on the bass-drum." We listened politely because Ahmet was Ahmet, but as soon as he'd gone, we said, "we're *not* doing disco; we're *not* putting fours on the bass drum," and continued as before. Then later, by another amazing coincidence, we were mastering the track in London when Ahmet passed by again. "Where are the fours on the bass drum?" This time we complied and remixed, and the single went to number four in the charts and gave a welcome boost to our otherwise quite shaky re-emergence. I guess that's why Ahmet was a Titan of the industry.

In the end, the disco undercurrent bled into some of the other songs on the *Manifesto* album and we ended up releasing three singles. The development didn't please everyone: "Roxy Music has not gone disco," exclaimed Rolling Stone magazine. "Roxy Music has not particularly gone anywhere else either." Ouch.

So now we were off again. The passing of a few years meant that we felt able to abandon the wacky outfits in favour of smart suits in pastel colours designed by Antony Price, who had continued to be responsible for our album sleeves, as well as for dressing David Bowie, Robert Palmer, and Duran Duran among others.

Many people were surprised when our next album *Flesh and Blood* included two covers alongside the new tracks. We decided to include *In the Midnight Hour*, because the song had gone down a storm when Kenny Everett asked us to play it on his New Year's Eve show. Having paid homage to the Motown aspect of the 60s, which we loved, we decided we'd do the same to the psychedelia side of the decade, so we chose *Eight Miles High* by the Byrds. By now we felt confidently back as Roxy Music,

Compass Point Studio, Nassau

and back in the groove with our recording and touring.

When we came to think about starting work on the album which would end up as *Avalon*, we did a lot of the early preparation at my Gallery Studios at St Ann's Court. Several of the rest of us had worked very successfully with Rhett Davies as engineer, but Bryan hadn't been keen. Eventually we managed to persuade him of Rhett's talents, and the two ended up working together on and off for the next thirty years. I always think of the *Avalon* album as the first occasion when we really began to use the studio as an instrument; using the technology to produce new and original sounds, often very different from those the kit had been designed for.

Things were progressing well in my studio, but then we were advised for tax reasons to do some of the actual recording outside of the UK. Somehow, we were directed to the Compass Point studio in Nassau which was owned by Chris Blackwell.

This arrangement worked okay for Bryan, but by now our gorgeous baby daughter Chloe had been born and at this point was only three months old. Andy had a one-year old daughter called Venice: a trip to Nassau was a daunting prospect.

Bryan and I were getting on okay for some of the time, but I was aware that tensions were rising. Looking back on it, I realise that part of the reason I was feeling unfulfilled was because I'd become used to being close to the centre of decision-making when working on my own or other collaborative projects. Here I was, once again, with Roxy, in which I had to find out what was going on more or less by accident. Different session musicians would be hired apparently at random for different tracks, without discussion or agreement. For example, the high-pitched scatting which became so much a feature of the *Avalon* single was recorded without my knowledge using a session vocalist in New York. I'm not saying I didn't often like the outcomes, but sometimes it felt as though I was not much more than a session player in my own band.

Bryan, Rhett and Engineer Compass Point

Indeed Andy and I might easily have been mistaken for session players when we were told to turn up at a country house in Buckinghamshire called Mentmore Towers, to record the video for the *Avalon* single. The video was co-directed by Ridley Scott and Howard Guard. When we arrived, we were told that we'd be appearing alongside two actual session musicians, neither of whom I'd met before and nor had they played on the recording. The storyline featured Bryan 'pursuing' the beautiful model Sophie Ward, while elegant diners were treated to the music of a more or less anonymous backing group. Andy and I appeared briefly alongside the session guys, ending up with rather less time on screen than the stunt-falcon.

All that might sound a bit petty and wouldn't have troubled me too much if I'd been enjoying the music. The bottom line is that I wasn't very excited by where we were musically. I'd absolutely loved what we'd produced for the first three Roxy albums, but the newer material seemed to be getting more middle-of-the-road, less rocky, and too smooth. There was less room for any of the improvised and strong guitar solos which I'd occasionally been able to include in the past. I shouldn't have been unhappy because Roxy's work was every bit as popular as ever, and we were doing well. It just wasn't where my heart was, and I was feeling once again that Roxy band members were getting fed up with each other.

I was back at my home in St Ann's Court on 8 December 1980 when news came in that John Lennon had been shot and killed by a crazed fan in New York. Instantly I found that tears were streaming down my face. It felt like the end of something, of a kind of innocence, of something which had been born in the sixties and which had informed and inspired a generation of us with limitless possibilities. John Lennon, evangelist for peace, had been gunned down by a madman just a few yards from his home. To the millions of people who loved The Beatles it felt like a personal loss. It certainly did for me.

I can't remember who had the idea for us to record John's famous and beautiful song *Jealous Guy*. I do remember driving to Chertsey High Street, buying a copy of *Imagine*, the album that had the song on it, and taking it back to the studio so we could all learn the chords. The song suited Bryan's voice and we had a feeling that our version would be big. We took a break from working in the studio at St Ann's Court and I went off for a family holiday, assuming that we would record *Jealous Guy* when we all returned in January. So I was shocked to learn that Bryan had gone back into my studio in the New Year without me, had hired another guitarist, Neil Hubbard, and was recording the song. When I got back from my holiday I added a guitar solo and some other guitar parts, but this was the beginning of the end of for me. I was committed to proceeding with the *Avalon* tour but was already thinking of ways to free myself from the constant tension. One way and another, once again, Roxy Music felt as though it was drifting apart.

Bryan must obviously have been feeling something rather similar and continued to treat Andy and myself more as part of his backing group rather than as full band members. Paul had already left the band

Avalon tour, 1981

in 1981, and once again "all for one and one for all," had become more like "all about one."

It all came to a head on 28th May 1982 when I was sitting in my suite at the Carlyle Hotel, New York on East 76th street near Central Park. I was feeling happy because we had only one gig left of our biggest tour of the USA in ten years, and we seemed finally to be breaking through. With the *Avalon* album and tour, it felt that America might be 'getting' Roxy Music at last. But my good feeling began to fade when I was interviewed for Rolling Stone magazine by a journalist who told me he'd just come from his interview with Bryan. He let me know that Bryan had said he'd be going solo after the end of the tour, but if it didn't work out, he'd continue with Roxy. The reporter was obviously sensing a big "Roxy Rift" headline and hoping I'd take the bait, but I managed to hide my reaction and changed the subject, giving away nothing of the turmoil building inside.

REVOLUCIÓN TO ROXY

An hour later I went down to the lobby, passing the sign advertising that Woody Allen was there every Monday playing his jazz. I got into a black Cadillac limo with Bryan and we headed off on the drive to Philadelphia. I said nothing about what had happened but was quietly fuming, and when we arrived at the Spectrum theatre I rang the tour manager and asked about the first flight out after the gig. He said it was the Concorde, and I said I wanted to be on it.

I told Andy about the conversation with the journalist and that I'd decided I was leaving the band. His instant response was that he was coming with me. I was unable to ease my fury during the gig and remember attacking my solos with a manic gusto. It all went really well, and it felt like a big moment as we took a bow. Then we went straight off-stage into a waiting limo and back to the hotel where our bags were already packed. Andy and I came out of our rooms, headed for the elevator, and pressed the button for the lobby. The elevator stopped, the door opened and there, standing waiting to get in, was Bryan. I took a step forward, shook his hand and said, "it's been a great pressure working with you. Goodbye."

It would be eighteen years before we all worked together again.

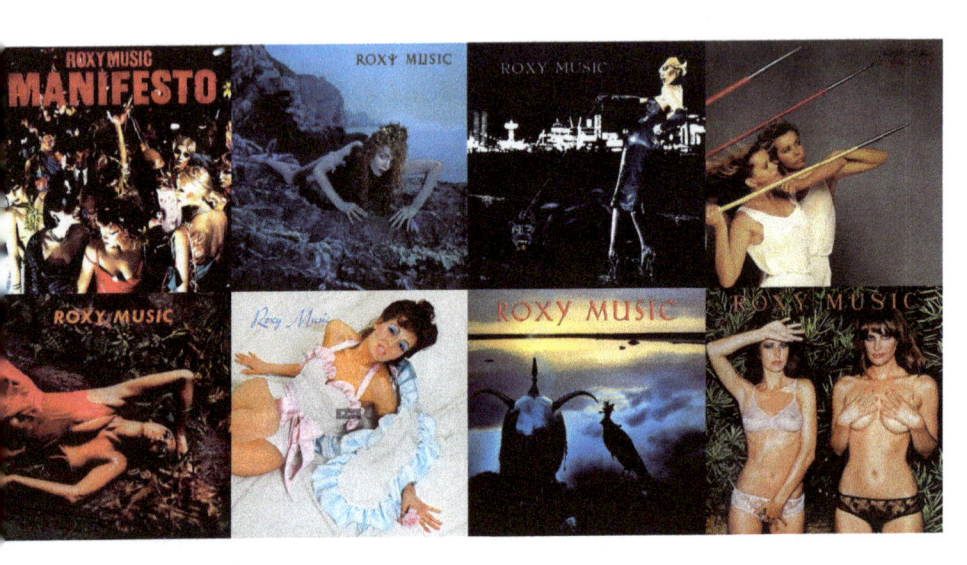

Roxy Music albums

SEVEN

The Beat Goes On...

Sitting alongside Andy on Concorde back to London, my mind turned to the future, and the world seemed to be full of possibilities. I was lucky to have made some great friends in the music business, and once again I looked forward to enjoying the prospect of working with different combinations of them and to make the kind of music that made me happy. I'd had enough of all the politics and squabbling and was glad to be free of it.

I'd been represented by EG management for all my time with Roxy, but now I regarded them as a big part of the problem, and certainly not part of the solution. I'd frequently run in to Steve O'Rourke who was Pink Floyd's manager, and his was the first name to come to mind when I realised that I needed a new manager for my post-Roxy life. Among the many of life's advantages enjoyed by Steve was that he was bloody huge, so when I sent him into EG Management to suggest that they release me from my contract, he wasn't at all phased when Mark Fenwick offered to throw him down the stairs. Steve didn't take any prisoners, and soon emerged unscathed.

"You're free," he told me, and I was.

It didn't take long for Andy Mackay and me to decide we should start a band together. Between us we made up two-thirds of the core of Roxy Music, which had just had an enormous hit with *Avalon*, so we were hot. I wanted to bring in Paul Carrack as our vocalist, but Andy said he knew a terrific singer called James Wraith. We made some demos and Steve was able to work his magic and get a substantial record deal for us from Virgin, they said they loved it. We were all set. We called ourselves The Explorers, because we were determined to explore new sounds and a new musical direction? It seemed fitting, but I honestly can't remember.

Just at that time Andy was obliged for tax reasons to live in Ireland and so we all headed off to Kenmare on the west coast with a mobile recording studio. It was out of the tourist season so we were able to get started with rehearsals in the empty dining room of the Park Hotel. Steve O'Rourke came with us, and I regret to say that we probably spent as much time in the bar as we did on the music. One day one of the locals told us about the lakes of Killarney where there was a legendary and haunting echo that floated off the water. Most sensible people would have recognised this for the blarney it undoubtedly was but, as ever in search of new and interesting sounds, this was too tempting, so bright and early the following morning we all headed off to find this lake. We hoped that the mix of morning mist and Gaelic magic would produce a uniquely sounding reverb from Andy's oboe. We should have known better.

First, access to the lake was next to a road, which wasn't especially busy, but suffice to say that cars passed by at intervals which were just frequent enough to spoil any chance of a clean recording. Next, we popped Andy into a boat and shoved him out over the water, but he very soon disappeared, shrouded in the gloom: we couldn't't hear a damned thing.

By now we were creating something of an attraction for tourists, who were no doubt enjoying watching these eejits from London making fools of themselves alongside one of their beauty spots. All in all, the whole venture was a total disaster and we soon realised that, although we were having great fun, we weren't going to achieve much on the west coast of Ireland.

By this time Sharon and I had had our son Charlie, and Andy also had a new baby boy, called Will, so a "working holiday" felt like a good idea. Steve O'Rourke and his wife Angie said they'd like to join us, and someone had the genius idea of spending yet more of the money we'd been advanced for the album by heading off to record at Eddy Grant's studio in Barbados. We rented a magnificent house on the west coast belonging to the property developer Mike Pemberton, which would have been fine except that no-one thought to inform Mike's wife Lynne, who had been planning a house-party to celebrate her birthday. She was understandably a bit put out when we turned up. Our mental picture of Eddy Grant's studio was of something overlooking the Caribbean where the biggest challenge would be keeping out the sound of waves gently breaking on a golden beach. What we found was an ancient building a little way inland from the ferocious Atlantic coast, with solid walls and absolutely no windows looking in any direction. We could have soaked up a more authentic spirit of the Caribbean if we'd stayed in Notting Hill. But the misadventures were not quite over yet. We had brought over with us an engineer I'd trained up at my studio at St Ann's Court, and who I'd managed to get a gig recording with Duran Duran. He was very talented but turned out to be a heroin addict, and we weren't all that thrilled when we learned that he'd been scouring the back streets of Bridgetown trying to score.

Andy Mackay 'Exploring' the lakes of Kilarney, 1983

We'd only just managed to sort out some rehab for him and put him on a plane back to London when we got a phone call from Eric Stewart, late of 10cc, who was holidaying on the island with his wife Gloria. "Paul and Linda have been busted," he told us, and went on to say that the

McCartneys were currently being held in a prison cell in Holetown. Apparently they'd been smoking a little bit of weed at dinner on the previous evening, and someone had (excuse the pun) grassed them up to the police. Eric wanted to know if Eddy Grant could be persuaded to intervene with his friend the Prime Minister and hopefully get them set free. He did, and they were, only to be arrested by the British police when they arrived back at Heathrow because Linda still had some weed in her suitcase.

Having now 'explored' several different ways of burning through the budget, The Explorers did eventually record their album – in my studio in Chertsey. The album was released to a deafening silence but, undeterred we did a UK tour, a concert for Radio One and some dates in Europe. Having secured an advance for the second album, we merrily went back into Gallery Studios to start work. We were all having a good time but I think Andy and I knew that something wasn't working, and we were both getting restless and interested in other projects. So by mutual agreement the Explorers stopped exploring and decided to get on with pursuing our solo careers.

* * *

Bands falling out and going their separate ways is commonplace, and probably the most spectacular and mutually destructive example at that time involved my friends in Pink Floyd. As with Bryan Ferry and Brian Eno in Roxy, David Gilmour and Roger Waters in Floyd were strong and very different personalities, each with their set ideas about how things should run. Sometimes this kind of creative tension in a band can be constructive and productive, but when it's bad, it can be very bad indeed. And in the Floyd, it was.

Roger is of athletic build, and is very keen on all kinds of sport, and is very competitive. So am I. I remember playing a game on tennis with him when we were both on holiday in the South of France. I'd assumed that the game was a bit of fun, but Roger contested every rally with the intensity of a championship point at Wimbledon. Of course he beat me, but I was able to turn the tables on him with our ping pong contest. When we raced in the swimming pool, he had no way to know that he was up against the Dulwich school swimming captain and I duly trounced him. Then, one day he asked me if I could water-ski. "Just a bit," I answered, "but the only thing is that I'm absolutely hopeless with a mono-ski." We arranged to meet at his speedboat at the Bay des Anges at 6am the following morning. It was my turn first so I jumped into the water, at which point Roger threw me a mono-ski, turned away, and before I knew it the boat was fifty yards off and about to drag me up and along. I struggled to get my feet into position, and then spent a shattering half an hour being dragged around the bay on this single ski, desperately trying to pretend to be enjoying myself.

The Floyd debacle is a case where everyone involved said and did things they probably later regretted, and the emotional and financial fallout from the rift made many headlines. The situation was somewhere near its nadir of legal actions and mutual recriminations at Christmas 1986 when Sharon and I held a party at St Ann's Court. By then we had started to host what would become a regular Christmas gathering of friends and family, and among our guests that year were David Gilmour and Steve O'Rourke.

David was working hard at the time on a new album which he hoped would re-establish Pink Floyd in the post-Roger era. The stakes were high because Roger was taking every opportunity to hurl public abuse at their efforts. Whatever came next would be make or break for David and the remaining band members. To make matters worse, not having played for some months, neither keyboard player Richard Wright or drummer Nick Mason were match-fit, so David was bringing in lots of session musicians and was also still very much on the lookout for material.

At some point during that recording, Steve told David that he thought they needed a single for the album, and later he called me to ask if I fancied spending a day writing with David in my studio. Of course, I said yes, and David came over and I played him two instrumental tracks I'd been working on and we had a jam. At the end of the day, he took the tracks away so he could try to write a top line and lyrics.

Nothing more was said, but then many months later I was invited to Astoria, his houseboat studio, to listen to work in progress. I was enjoying what I was hearing and when they came to play what they said might

David Gilmour's Astoria studio on the river Thames

become the title track, I thought I recognised it. It was the demo track that I'd given David to work on but now my guitar part had been replaced by a sequencer, and with an overlay of his guitars. It was called *One Slip*, the lyrics of which included the line, "A Momentary Lapse of Reason."

Later our shared manager Steve took me out for a very nice lunch, at which a good deal of alcohol was taken and where he very carefully and unambiguously explained that the re-formed Pink Floyd needed the publishing rights to my track, and here was the deal. It would be too tempting to say that at this point I had a momentary lapse of reason, so I won't, and will say only that of course I was delighted and proud to have a credit on a Pink Floyd album. The pluses and minuses of having Steve O'Rourke as a manager.

Back on the home front, our daughter Chloe was now five years old, our son Charlie was three and then we were lucky enough to have another beautiful daughter, Sophie, born in 1988. People say your life changes when you have children, but you never quite believe it until it happens. There I was doing the school run and enjoying being a dad. Sharon had

THE BEAT GOES ON…

opened and was running a clothes shop in Weybridge in partnership with our friend Sue Godley, and later we managed to acquire an apartment near to the shop which my mum moved into, so she could be close by. It all seemed to be going well but I felt a constant need to be industrious and to make sure I could support my growing family financially.

Whenever I found myself falling back on my own resources, searching inside myself for inspiration, I could always feel the stirrings of the deep-rooted sounds and rhythms which had swirled around the tables of those Cuban nightclubs, permeating my young and impressionable brain, and establishing themselves as part of my musical core. Also among the other important things I'd inherited from my father was an inborn and lifelong fascination with gadgets. Dad was always doing fun things with his 8mm movie camera, or his Leica stills camera. He liked to have the best quality stuff and as already mentioned, had a Telefunken tape recorder and those amazing Zenith short-wave radios. My next-generation version of that same trait was a consuming interest in all kinds of music-related "gear"; getting the hi-fi speakers to work, or the different sounds you could get from various guitar pickups. As soon as I realised you could record and play-back your own music, I became pre-occupied by the potential, and then meeting and befriending Brian Eno had helped me to understand that anything was possible.

Alongside that same growing consciousness, and in common with just about everyone else of my generation and background, we were reading Karl Marx and beginning to understand that if you wanted to avoid labouring under the yolk of "the man", it was very important to own the means of production. So I came to realise that if you could afford to buy your own kit and know enough about what you were doing with it, you didn't need anyone else's permission to make a record. You could be free to do your own thing, make the music you wanted to make, with the people you wanted to make it with. The only further hurdle would be how to get it out there to reach the people who might want to listen to it. This was of course long before social media came along and enabled artists to connect directly with their fans. So, ever the optimist and nudged on by Bill and Ian Mac, I decided to act on the idea that had been percolating around my brain for a while, and to start my own record label.

By this time the original promoter of the Greyhound in Croydon, Steve Mason had developed a thriving business helping to manage and distribute independent record labels, called Pinnacle, and so I called him and told him my plan.

"No problem," he said, and in that moment Expression Records was born. Simple as that.

An early priority was to explore potential partnerships in the States, and when I saw that Pink Floyd's first tour without Roger was due to play in Los Angeles, I decided to combine a business trip with the gig. It would be a thrill to watch the band performing my song, and I could make contacts which would be useful for the new label. It turned out to be a memorable few days for me because my friend Tim Finn was in LA recording a solo album, and Peter Gabriel and Johnny Marr were also in town.

The next thing I had to do was to get myself to the annual record industry gathering at Midem in Cannes, South of France, where indie bands look for labels and labels look for bands. I wanted Bill MacCormick to be involved, and so he and I set off together to the south of France. It wasn't long before we started meeting terrific people from the Spanish music industry who were wondering how to channel the new-found freedom they were gradually beginning to enjoy following the recent death of their country's fascist dictator General Franco. We discovered that there seemed to be no-one else in the UK music industry who spoke Spanish and had the necessary knowledge of production. Straight away I was asked to produce a band called Los Mosquitos, so we made arrangements for them to come over to my studio in Chertsey to record. We were within just a few days of starting the label, and already we were up and running in the *Rock en Español* genre.

Word soon spread to Madrid, and shortly after that I was contacted about a young but up and coming band called Héroes del Silencio. The band had originally come from Zaragoza and had been struggling for two or more years to get noticed in a market dominated by musicians based in Madrid or Barcelona. I arranged to go to see them play live at the Rocodromo in Calatayud and was picked up at the airport in a very nice Alfa Romeo convertible by their ultra-cool manager Pito Cubillas.

THE BEAT GOES ON...

Me and Héroes del Silencio cartoon in Rolling Stone magazine

Pito was managing several new bands, and had also opened a terrace bar which was very popular with the local bohemians such as the brilliant and radical film director Pedro Almodóvar.

Pito let me know that he was a huge Roxy fan, and I soon discovered that he was also a mover and shaker in an underground punk rock and synth pop movement called La Movida, which had surged up in the 80's, once Spain had got its democracy back after Franco's death.

The concert happened late at night, as is the Spanish way, and it was about 1am when Heroes del Silencio finally took to the stage. It was soon apparent that they had everything it takes to be successful. Their singer, Enrique Bunbury, looked like a young Jim Morrison, with a startling lion's roar of a voice, the fans loved it. I thought they were brilliant and it felt like watching a Spanish version of U2 in the way they connected and created excitement between the audience and band. It was clear to me that I needed to capture on record what I'd just witnessed on stage, so I met them after the gig, and we were talking about what I could do for them when my mobile rang. It was my sister Rosemary; she was calling to tell me that our mum, who had earlier been diagnosed with ovarian cancer, had taken an unexpected turn for the worse and was in the last

Héroes del Silencio, 1990

hours of her life. I was desperately needed at her bedside.

My mum was part of that generation for whom the very word cancer seemed to spell certain and painful death, and so when she'd gone to see her doctor with early symptoms, I had managed to shield her from his preliminary diagnosis. I'd suggested to Mum that we should get a second opinion, and arranged for us to see a family friend called Martin Gore who was a senior oncologist at the Royal Marsden. She agreed to do so, but I was anxious about the likely outcome, so I asked to see him ahead of the appointment. Martin sat me down and showed me a video which spelled out that the life expectancy for women suffering from ovarian cancer at that time was a maximum of five years. Of course I was mortified, but immediately I felt that the effect on Mum of hearing the news would be devastating. I made clear to Martin that I'd like him to see and treat her, but that on no account should he tell her she had cancer. We duly went to the appointment and, totally ignoring what I'd requested, he immediately told her about her condition and what he could do to help. I realise now that my instinct to shield Mum from the harsh truth probably wasn't the right thing to do.

Scroll forward three years, and by the time the news reached me in Spain that Mum was suddenly on her death bed, my brother Eugen and our sister Rosemary were at her side. I dropped all my plans and hurried to Madrid's Barajas airport, only to discover that the Gulf war had broken out that very day, and all planes in every direction were cancelled. There followed a period of 24 hours in which I explored every possible means to get home, to the point where I was demented, but by the time I arrived at the hospital, Mum had died. She was 69.

Magdalena Targett-Adams, née Manzanera, had been born in a lower middle-class family in Colombia, one of eight siblings who'd managed to remain close over the years despite the challenges of time and distance. I long ago lost count of the cousins who came and went, staying with her at the house in Clapham, and helping her to keep in touch with her roots. Latterly she had been spending two or three months of every year back in her home country, where she had methodically and systematically bored everyone she met about how proud she was of her children. Eugen had studied at Cambridge, Rosemary was working for the Foreign office, and from the moment I'd become a "rock star" nobody could escape from her lengthy and detailed updates of my TV appearances, record sales, and celebrity friends.

There's never a good time for a parent to die, and it seems to me that when that happens, you begin to confront your own mortality and to take stock of where you are in your own life.

EIGHT

In Search of Roots

The first album recorded by Héroes del Silencio two years earlier in 1988 had sold a disappointing 30,000 copies, and when I listened to it, the reason seemed obvious. While the appeal of the band was all about their electrifying live performance, the recording seemed very over-produced and pop oriented. When I told them that I'd want to try to capture the sound and vibe they created live on stage, they were delighted.

We went into Kirios Studios in Madrid which had been equipped with a huge old Neve EMI mixing desk imported from Abbey Road. It had all the space I thought we needed to replicate what made them great. Their years of gigging hadn't diminished any of their passion and commitment for the music, and there was a great energy in the studio. I felt that we were managing to record the rawness of their performance, and everyone seemed to be having a good time and enjoying the process. The only real revelation for me was more to do with their approach to time management. Every studio recording I'd been involved so far had been characterised by focused work, with everyone taking just enough

Producing Héroes del Silencio in Kírios Studios, Madrid, 1990

time to grab a sandwich or a slice of pizza for lunch, so it took me a while to get used to the idea that these guys wanted to take an extended break for lunch and dinner a la Español.

All the songs, including the singles *Entre Dos Tierras* and *Maldito Duende* were recorded in Spanish, but of course international record companies always have an eye on the English-speaking markets, and so they asked me to try recording the singles in English too. I was against the idea from the start, but I did a rough translation, and then sent the English version to Ian MacDonald, asking him to craft them into singable lyrics. We gave it our best shot, but it simply didn't work, so the English versions were never released. The album, *Senderos de Traición,* sold 100,000 copies within a few weeks, eventually going platinum. Singing only in Spanish, they achieved the rare feat of charting in Germany, France and Italy. Their album completely transformed the Héroes profile and gained them commercial success all over Europe, except for the UK, which remains apparently impermeable to any song sung in a foreign language.

IN SEARCH OF ROOTS

In the following few months Héroes del Silencio performed well over a hundred packed out concerts in Spain, and then set off to perform across Europe, playing venues ranging from tiny bars to small halls. If ever there was a case where a band's passion for their music was reflected in hard work and then success, this was it. Inevitably though, the Héroes' reputation for excess was growing along with the size of their audiences, and some of the troubles which bedevil so many successful bands were not far away.

Héroes del Silencio Senderos de Traición album

When they asked me to produce their next album, I suggested we use my Gallery Studios, where we had the space to get the same kind

Playing with Héroes del Silencio at Las Ventas Madrid, 1991

127

of feel which had been so successful for *Senderos de Traición*. A date was set for the first week of January, but of course the band turned up without warning ten days too early on the day after Christmas. It was with only the slightest trepidation that I told them they could use the studio for rehearsals and songwriting, on the strict understanding that I wouldn't't be seeing them and, more importantly, I wouldn't' be hearing them either. They readily agreed and I settled down to enjoy those quiet few days between Christmas and New Year with family and friends.

What I hadn't counted on was that the band had either brought with them, or had otherwise managed to acquire, a huge stash of drugs, and they embarked on ten days of narcotic and alcohol-fuelled madness, during which very little serious rehearsal was done. What they did manage to do was to write a lot of songs; so many in fact that they now wanted to record a double album. My heart sank; a producer's nightmare is often an over-long, self-indulgent album, rather than an infinitely preferable, tight, ten-track record.

Recording was due to start early January, and it instantly became clear that my challenge would be to distil something recognisable out of the drug-induced haze. The guitarist Juan Valdivia insisted he could only play his best stuff at 3am, to which I said, "good luck, but unfortunately I won't be here to record it." The others would wake when they woke, eat just enough food to remain alive, take whatever stimulants they needed to get them through the day, make some music and then fall back to sleep again. I found it necessary to explain to anyone smoking weed close to me that I'd be likely to fall asleep, so they were required to stand next to an open door or window, outside the control room and blowing the smoke in the opposite direction. Only then were they allowed to come back in to listen to the latest take.

Notwithstanding the mayhem, they were all great guys and we had a terrific time. I worked them hard because I knew how important this album was for their career. The music was more Led Zeppelin or Guns N' Roses than anything they'd done before, and the songs *Nuestros Nombres* and *La Herida* went on to be number one hits in several European countries. Three year later musical differences, excessive touring and the rock n roll lifestyle took its toll and the great Héroes Del Silencio burnt out. Sounds familiar?

However, for the lead singer and main lyricist, Enrique Bunbury, this was the start of his highly successful Grammy award-winning solo career. I met him when he was aged just 20 and am immensely proud of what he has achieved in the 35 years since. I was delighted when Enrique asked me to produce his first solo album. At crucial moments in his career he's consulted me when he felt he needed a change in direction, and often I was able to suggest a new way forward. I feel I was able to mentor him a little from those early days, and that he heeded my advice to listen to a wide range of music genres and styles. Also, he subscribes to my view that the supposed lines between different kinds of music are meaningless and arbitrary: rather there is only good music and bad music. He has remained a good friend and ally.

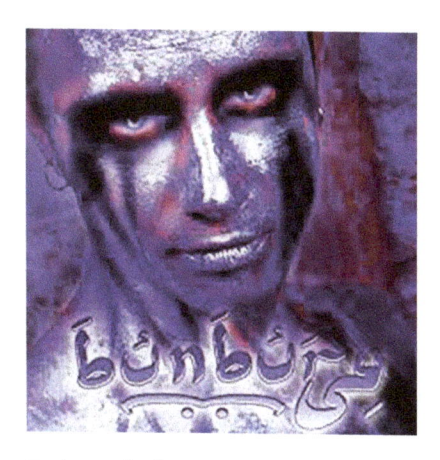

Heroes del Silencio El Espíritu del Vino album

Bunbury solo albums

Enrique is one of the hardest working and most talented musicians I have ever met, and I am in awe of his creativity and songwriting. When I watched 100,000 people in Mexico City in 2022 singing back to him the words of many of his songs, I knew that my appreciation of what I saw that night in Calatayud wasn't wrong. He has an incredible ability to connect with audiences in the Spanish speaking world and I like to think of him as the David Bowie of Spain and Rock en Español.

Enrique and Jose Girl

* * *

It's 2nd March 1992 and I am at the San Remo TV festival in Italy with a band I'd put together for the show. I've been teamed up with a Neapolitan musician who's very famous in Italy called Eduardo de Crescenzo. We're going to perform a version of his song in English together, which is what international artists tend to be asked to do. The singer is Phil Saatchi, who's one of the Saatchi brothers, but is a blues artist rather than a marketing magnate, and we'll be accompanied by a full orchestra. The whole show is going out live on RAI Uno, which is the main TV station in Italy, so it feels like a big occasion.

The TV presenters are a very good-looking man and woman, but both seem to be slightly more interested in themselves than by what's coming up next. When they announce me onto the stage, I find that no-one has remembered to plug in the power to my amp. I look bemused at the camera and say, just as calmly as I know how, "I would love to start if someone would just plug in my amplifier." There is general nervous laughter, we play our song, and before I know it, it's all gone well, and I am back in my dressing room.

I hear the welcome sound of excited Spanish voices and discover that a Cuban band called Groupo Moncada are also on the show, and are occupying the dressing room next to me. I hear them calling out to me, "Epa Manzanera venga hablar con nosotros." I pop my head in, and my brain does that strange instant switch when returning to the language I love. One thing I have found all around the world is that if I find someone who speaks Spanish, I immediately adopt my Latin persona and it's as if I'm talking to a long-lost friend or family member, with all the accompanying gesticulations. These guys from Groupo Moncada seem not only to have heard of me but have been following my career since they discovered my Cuban connection. I'm flattered but also surprised, and say something like, "I thought that what with the US blockade and no access to international media or TV, you guys must be kinda cut off?"

"We have ways and means," they say enigmatically, and proceed to display an encyclopedic and impressive knowledge of every genre of modern music since the revolution. We are getting on well, and eventually they invite me to come back to Cuba to play with them on a tour they'll be doing in December. Having fled from Havana in 1959, the idea of returning to Cuba is instantly appealing but I assume that this is just another example of Latin American courtesy.

"Isn't it difficult for Westerners to go in and out of Cuba?"

"Just leave that to us," they reply. We all shook hands and parted company, and I got on with my life and forgot about it. A return trip to a country which had such a profound impact on me as a boy would be a thrill, but it didn't seem at all likely that it would actually happen.

Several months passed by, many emails were exchanged, and eventually I received a message to tell me they'd booked the flights. I of course had not the slightest idea of what I'd be expected to play, or even what their music was like, but I just wanted to get back there. I packed my bags, grabbed my guitar, and retraced the air journey I'd last taken 25 years before with my mum, dad, sister and brother, but this time I travelled with my own young family via Madrid, Santa Domingo and on to Havana. When we eventually arrived at José Martí airport, we were greeted by the joyful and exuberant Groupo Moncada who promptly handed out the mojitos. I was back in a place where I had so many childhood memories.

What they hadn't mentioned was that because of Glasnost and the fall of the Berlin Wall two years previously, Cuba was in what was being called "the Special Period", which turned out to be special, but not quite in the way I might have hoped. For example, Russia had previously supported Cuba by trading sugar for oil, but now that deal was off and there was a chronic shortage of fuel. Consequently the entire tour would be undertaken in an old bus instead of on any oil-guzzling internal flights. Let's say that maintaining the roads had not been a high priority for the revolutionary government of Fidel Castro, and the going wasn't to be smooth or easy.

Despite the inauspicious travel arrangements, I soon discovered that Grupo Moncada were incredibly famous in Cuba, and very well connected with the government. We played to a magnificent crowd of 100,000 music fans, all of them in full-on Cuban party mode, at a free concert on La Rampa, which is next to Hotel Naciónal. Important members of the government were rumoured to be attending and the whole thing was televised. Our very handsome lead singer, Augusto Enriquez, had been a doctor earlier in his career, and so dozens of women were coming up to thank him for having delivered their babies.

Something similar happened in Santa Clara, and next we were getting ready for a New Year's Eve concert in Santiago de Cuba. This was 1992, nearly a quarter of a century since that traumatic night of the revolution, and we played to a vast crowd of happy and carefree partygoers.

Me with Grupo Moncada, Havana, 1991

I was having a great time, but in and among the busy schedule, I was hoping to take some time out to locate the house we'd lived in when I was a child, so I used a radio interview to appeal for information. "Does anyone know the address of General Tabernilla's house back in 1958? Mine was opposite his and I would love to visit." It worked, and a listener rang with the address, but on that occasion I'd run out of time for anything more than a fleeting look.

When I next visited the island a few years later, I found myself experiencing that strange and unique sensation of walking as an adult in the steps I'd last taken as a child nearly three decades earlier. So much had changed, and yet so much was the same. The heat of the sun, the clear blue skies, the smells of the trees and flowers. A few paces further on, and around some more corners, and I was walking along the road towards the house we'd lived in. I felt apprehensive as I pressed the bell, and after a few minutes the door was opened by a smart looking gentleman aged about 65. I introduced myself and told him I used to live here before and at the start of the revolution.

The man was instantly welcoming and interested to know the circumstances, and he invited me inside. Straight away the rooms and spaces before my eyes began to morph into the ones stored in my long-term memory; it all seemed the same but, in some ways, very different. Everything felt much smaller than I'd remembered, but that was probably because I was now seeing things from a height of 6 feet rather than 4.

My host told me he'd been a student leader and had been given the house in 1963. After the revolution he'd been appointed as Cuba's ambassador to Russia and was based in Moscow. He rooted out a photo album and proudly showed me pictures of himself and his wife. They looked like a golden couple, good looking, and a spitting image of Desi Arnaz and Lucille Ball from *I Love Lucy*. One photo showed them standing alongside none other than the former Soviet President Nikita Khrushchev.

After I'd enjoyed all his warmth and hospitality, he gently asked if I could do something for him. He was writing a book, he told me, on the brief British rule over Cuba in 1762. Could I go to the British Library back in London and do some research for him? Of course, I agreed,

Visiting our former home in Miramar, Havana, Cuba, 1992

and he gave me some notes about the details he wanted to learn more about.

After saying my goodbyes, I took a walk around the neighbourhood, and I began to feel a rising tide of emotion as the waves of memories from my childhood came flooding back. Random images of carefree days with my mum and dad, parties and music everywhere, and what seemed like endless sunshine. All such a long time ago, and now only surviving in the remote corners of my memory. At one point an old lady put her head out of a window, and we started chatting. 'Si, recuerdo a ese muchachito inglés, ¿eres tú?' ("Yes, I remember that little English boy. Is that you?") It was, and I felt myself losing control, the tears flooding down my face.

I returned to Cuba several times over the next twenty years, sometimes as a guest of the Cuban government, sometimes on private visits. On one occasion we made Cuban history by recording a live album with Moncada on a 16-track analogue tape recorder. There was only one machine like it on the island, but it was out of service. Fortunately I'd brought with me a very clever British sound engineer, Keith Bessey, who managed to fix it. We loaded the recorder into a van and installed it in the theatre, which I discovered was just along the road from the apartment block where we had been relocated before being obliged to leave Havana in 1959. The place had previously been known as the Teatro Blanquita but had latterly been renamed the Karl Marx theatre. It held 5,500 people and at the time was the biggest covered auditorium in South America. Previous performers included Cuban superstars such as Silvio Rodríguez and Pablo Milanés, and much earlier its stage had been graced by none other than the inimitable pianist and show-business legend, Liberace.

Moncada Manzanera Live at The Karl Marx

We called the album *Moncada Manzanera Live at the Karl Marx*, and it amused me to think that Frank Zappa and the Mothers of Invention would have approved. Years later the same Karl Marx theatre would host a gig by the Manic Street Preachers, which Fidel Castro was due to attend. Someone thought it wise to warn him that the music would be very loud, to which he replied, "you cannot be louder than war!" No doubt MSP gave it their best shot.

NINE

Serendipity

The funny thing about rock and roll is that you can have some amazingly good times, some fairly difficult times, and just now and again something happens which makes you think that someone up there is looking out for you.

Something like that happened early in 1991 when I received a call out of the blue from a man who introduced himself as Tony Hollingsworth and said something like, "I am organising a pre-event for Expo 92 in Seville. As Seville is the home of the Spanish guitar, we have in mind to run a spectacular festival of guitar music. We want to invite the best guitarists in the world, it'll last five days, the budget is $7m and it'll be broadcast live in the USA and on the BBC." I was still trying to absorb the scale of the ambition and wondering where all this was headed, when he said, "and we'd like you to be the musical director and to perform. If you agree to do it, you'll have a pretty free hand to organise it however you like."

My mind flicked rapidly through a Rolodex of my various friends who might have thought it funny to play a practical joke at my expense, but then quickly realised that nothing about this call was amusing. I did my best to sound as if it was the kind of thing that happens every day.

"So let me get this straight. I get to organise the five nights any way I want, and can invite anyone I admire so long as they're a great guitarist?" Yes, said Tony, that was the deal. I paused again to allow it all to compute. "Just let me consult my calendar," I said, and then held the receiver away from my ear for a full ten seconds. "Yes, I think I can clear the schedule enough to make that do-able. Where do I sign?"

Can you imagine? A blank canvas, a decent budget, and complete liberty to programme the five days any way I saw fit so long as we were celebrating the guitar. And all taking place in one of the spiritual homes of guitar music and celebrating the instrument I love best in the world. I grabbed my contacts book and began scanning the pages.

Guitar Legends logo

The first thing was to think of a plan for how the five concerts could be scheduled. Five nights, maybe five different genres? I quickly worked out that we could have a blues night, a rock night, a folk night and a jazz night, and I appointed a separate musical director for each of the first four evenings. For the fifth concert, having run-out of genres, I decided I would curate myself.

Who did we manage to persuade to come to the five-day Guitar Legends festival in Seville in October 1991 to herald the opening of the Expo? The short answer is – just about everybody. The eventual cast would include Brian May, Bo Diddley, Joe Walsh, Albert Collins, BB King,

Steve Cropper, Keith Richards, George Benson, Robert Cray, Roger McGuinn, Steve Vai and Joe Satriani among the guitarists. Then of course we would need vocalists, percussion, bass etc, and so for good measure we also had Roger Waters, Jack Bruce, Joe Cocker, Ray Cooper, Rick Wakeman, Roger McGuinn, Pino Palladino and Simon Phillips among many others. I even got to play alongside the legendary Les Paul himself, after which he duly signed my Les Paul guitar.

The only notable absentees were Eric Clapton, Mark Knopfler, David Gilmour, and Jeff Beck, who were all genuinely away on tours. Apart from those, the whole programme was looking like a who's who of guitar greats.

I was feeling fairly pleased with myself when I arrived in Seville ahead of the festival, to be met by a strikingly attractive woman who introduced herself as Claire and told me she was in charge of the PR. All was going well until I checked into the room I'd been allocated and found it to be rather modest and unprepossessing, and so I immediately went back downstairs to demand a suite more appropriate for the musical director. Claire looked at me wryly and pointed to the desk which said Hotel Reservations. Fortunately things got better after that because all this was thirty years ago, and Claire and I have been having musical adventures together ever since.

The recording producer of the event was Phil Ramone who has worked with a pantheon of the greatest artists of all time, including Burt Bacharach, Quincy Jones and Paul Simon. We had purpose-built stages designed and lit by Fisher Park, the Pink Floyd team, so that one performer could be setting up while another was playing. TV companies from all around the world were making enquiries, and some parts of the final shows ended up being broadcast in over 100 countries.

Since the location was Seville, I was determined that local musicians should be well represented, and I discovered a young and little-know Flamenco guitarist called Vicente Amigo. His playing was absolutely amazing, and I asked him to see what would happen if he put down his acoustic, picked up an electric and plugged in. He and I had great fun experimenting, and the resulting sound was like *Hendrix goes Flamenco:*, and was filmed for a BBC 2 documentary. Next we needed to book some flamenco dancers, and it was an amazing privilege for me to find a troupe called *El Ballet Flamenco de Mario Maya*. So frantic was the schedule that we had zero time to rehearse, and all I could do was send them my music track, which was an instrumental version of *Frontera*, and ask them to work out some choreography. Quite literally the first time I got to see the whole thing put together was at the live gig. It was astounding. Their performance looked for all the world as though it had been rehearsed for hours, and the call and response between my echo guitar triplets and their flamenco zapateo, foot stamping, was even better than I'd dared hope. Everything on the night was going like a dream, but then no sooner had the dancers left the stage than my guitar suddenly stopped working in the middle of a musical transition. Panic. I was on live TV. What was I going to do? Fortunately, the cool calm professionalism of The Miami Horns kicked in without prompting, and they just took over and improvised until miraculously the sound came back on my guitar rig. The whole debacle probably lasted only a couple of minutes but felt like an eternity.

Me at Guitar Legends soundcheck with Keith Richards, Robert Cray and Bob Dylan, Seville, 1991

The strange thing about events like this is that they take months and months to organise, and when the moment finally comes, each day seems to slip by in speeded up time, and all you're thinking is "that's another great day over." However at no point could I allow myself an instant to relax because my greatest challenge was still ahead of me. Among the performers scheduled to play on my night were Jack Bruce, Joe Cocker, Steve Cropper, Keith Richards, and Spanish artists Vicente Amigo and Miguel Bosé. Undoubtedly the highlight of my night however, was to be none other than Bob Dylan.

Like so many of my generation, I'd more or less worshipped Bob Dylan since he first appeared on the scene. In the pantheon of modern music Bob Dylan was definitely up there with The Beatles, the Stones and Hendrix. A poet, a revolutionary, an entirely original and unique talent. I remember being just a bit apprehensive when I first met Paul McCartney, keen not to make a fool of myself. Now not only was I going to meet Bob Dylan, I was also going to rehearse him, introduce him onto the stage and then perform with him, all the while making sure that the whole of the rest of the live performance went like clockwork. So no pressure then.

We were all so happy when he'd agreed to appear at the event, that none of us had quite summoned the nerve to ask what he was going to play. I'd taken the precaution of going to HMV in Oxford Street and buying every album he'd ever recorded, so I was well prepared. Meanwhile the rest of the supporting musicians were about as gifted and experienced as they come, so none of them had much worry about being able to keep up.

The Man was due to arrive a couple of days before his scheduled performance. I felt a bit nervous when he eventually turned up in the rehearsal room but I did what I always do in these situations and just jumped in. The first to speak was his young manager, Jeff Rosen.

"Hi Phil, this is Bob," he said, and then half-turned. "Bob this is Phil."

There was no response from beneath the hooded Parka.

"Hi Bob," I filled the stony silence with introductions. "This is Jack Bruce. This is Simon Phillips …". I managed to complete the formalities. "We were just wondering which songs you'd like to play?" I was thinking

Me and Bob

the answer might be *Subterranean Homesick Blues*, or maybe *Forever Young*, *A Hard Rain's Gonna Fall*, or possibly *Mr Tambourine Man*, but I shouldn't have been so naive.

"Do you happen to know a Tex-Mex song, I think it was written about 1948, I'm not sure what it's called or who wrote it?"

I was a bit taken aback and then realised he could be thinking that with a surname like Manzanera, I might be Mexican myself, but I was still trying to remain calm.

"It doesn't come to mind, but maybe if you played it, we can work it out?"

Bob grabbed a guitar and played some chords of a song none of us recognised, accompanied by a few mumbled words we couldn't decipher. Jack was scratching his head. Simon was getting edgy. I was at a loss about what to do.

"Could you just play it again, so we can try to get a handle on it?"

Well not to put too fine a point on it, Bob proceeded to play what he claimed was the same song six times in a row, and no two versions had anything in common with each other. Different words, in different keys and different tempos. After a while of trying to figure it out, Simon said, "I promised to call home about now. I'll just head off and do that and I'll be back soon," and he left. One by one the other musicians must have felt the will to live draining from their bodies, because one by one they drifted away, leaving just me and Bob.

"I know what," Bob eventually said to me, "why don't you and I just do the song as a duet on two acoustics?"

My level of anxiety was now going through the roof, and still there was something I hadn't quite gotten around to mentioning.

"The only firm request we have from the organisers is that you should play *All Along the Watchtower*." I paused for a moment to allow the idea to register, and then continued, "but if you don't mind, they'd like us to play the Hendrix version rather than your original."

I was still looking for a reaction, but none came, and so in the hope that the silence indicated assent, I dragooned some of the band back in so we could have a run through. The song has only three chords and of course everyone knew it, so all was going well until we got to the vocals, at which point Bob didn't sing. We kept on playing, I improvised a solo in the middle, it came to the next verse, and still Bob didn't sing. Eventually we finished the number and Bob hadn't sung a note.

By now our allocated time in the rehearsal room was nearly over and we were about to pack up and leave when Keith Richards appeared. There'd been a suggestion that the two would

Provisional track listing for the 17th October concert

play something together. Keith looked over at Bob and said, "Oi you, Bob, over here, sing." And he did. It was only then that I realised my mistake may have been that I was too polite. Later Bob's manager came over to me and I took the opportunity to ask the question which was on everyone's minds.

"Erm, I noticed that Bob didn't sing during the rehearsal?"

The manager didn't seem at all concerned. "Yes well, Bob might sing on the night, but then again he might not. You should probably have a contingency plan in case he doesn't feel like it. However, if he does come on, make sure you introduce him."

I needed a plan B in case Bob didn't feel like singing on the night? His appearance was a big deal, and he was being paid a fortune. His performance was scheduled to be the climax of five days of performances by some of the most exciting, brilliant, and committed musicians of our times, and we'd be going on stage not knowing whether or not Bob was going to sing one of the most famous songs in pop history.

I turned to my friend Jack Bruce, who of course had one of the finest blues voices of our generation. "If Bob decides not to sing *All Along the Watchtower* would you mind stepping in and singing it? Jack paused, smiled at me and then gave the only response any reasonable Glaswegian person in those circumstances could give. "Fuck that!" he said.

Now increasingly desperate, I remembered that our producer Phil Ramone had worked extensively with Bob in the past. How would he deal with the problem?

"You just have to go with the flow," said Phil, "after all he's Bob. If he wants one hundred takes, you do a hundred takes. If he wants just one, you do just one. If he wants to sing, he'll sing; if he doesn't, he won't. He's Bob." I found this clear but not necessarily helpful.

Have you ever had one of those nightmares in which you're on the eve of a life-changing examination, and you haven't done the revision and now it's too late? That's what it felt like, but a thousand times worse. If something else didn't happen, I could find myself alone on stage with the most iconic performer of the modern age, with half the western world watching live, and due to accompany him on a song I didn't even know the name of, let alone the opening chords.

SERENDIPITY

Then I had a brainwave. I remembered hearing somewhere that Bob was a big fan of Richard Thompson, formerly of Fairport Convention. Maybe if I could track Richard down, he might be able to get more information out of our top-of-the-bill performer, such as what he wanted to play and whether he would be likely to want to sing on the night. I discovered that Richard was in Amsterdam, so I called.

"Richard," I said, "I've heard that Bob Dylan is a big fan of yours?" Richard said he'd heard the same thing too and was flattered. "So Richard, how would you like to play with Bob tomorrow night?" Of course, the answer was yes. "Well could you get on a plane, and be here by the morning?" Once again, the answer was yes. Thank you, Richard. Thank you, God.

Richard was as good as his word, and we sent him in to see Bob to act as our representative on the planet earth. I did my own set, it went really well, and then I accompanied Jack playing *Sunshine of Your Love*, a

Bob's set with me, Bob, Richard Thompson and Jack Bruce

riff every guitarist wants to play. Then the Dylan moment was upon us. I peered into the off-stage darkness behind me, hoping to see evidence of our star, and in the distance I thought I could make out someone wearing that famous black shirt with white spots, which I know Bob favours. Yep, that's him, so I go to the microphone. "Señores y Señoras, El señor Bob Dylan!" I breathed a sigh of relief when I saw The Man walk on stage, guitar slung over his shoulder.

He of course said nothing, and just looked around appearing slightly tense and a bit confused. After a few seconds, the rest of us struck up the first notes of *All Along the Watchtower*. I looked over and was happy to see that Bob was playing the chords, but unfortunately, he was giving no indication of whether or not he was planning to sing. Everyone was looking at each other, they all looked at me, and no-one else was showing any inclination to take the initiative. Finally, just when I thought it might all be going horribly wrong, Bob seemed to remember what he'd come for, and stepped right up to the microphone.

"There must be some way out of here," he spoke the words, there was a pause, "said the joker to the thief." Phew. Bob was kind of singing, if not exactly present, on stage, and vocal. Richard played a solo, I played a solo, then we all looked at Bob for some idea of what would happen next. Nothing did, and so we all kept on playing until Bob seemed to feel as though he'd had enough, and the song ground to a halt. The crowd was ecstatic. The first hurdle was over.

Next on the running order was the song we'd discovered courtesy of Richard called *Boots of Spanish Leather*. Bob started to strum and sing, and none of the rest of us had a clue how the number went or where it was headed. We looked carefully at Bob's chord shapes on the fretboard and, through a mix of sign language and mouthing, the rest of us swapped information about the direction of the song. Even now I don't quite know how we did it, but if you watch the performance on YouTube, I think you might be prepared to believe that the number had been rehearsed. It was only twenty-five years later when Richard came to my studio to do some recording that he told me what had happened in Bob Dylan's dressing room before we all went on stage. "He asked me if I knew this Tex Mex song from 1947," to which Richard replied, "No, but you play it and I'll learn it." Bob had gone on to play the song half a dozen different ways, and Richard had eventually come out on stage just as bemused as the rest of us.

The final highlight of every evening in the festival was when all that day's performers returned to the stage for a jam session, and on this last day it fell to me to decide which song we'd all play together. Once again, I felt I was on a hiding to nothing. Do I tell Keith Richards we're playing a Beatles song? Do I tell Jack Bruce we're playing something by Fleetwood Mac? Maybe you could call it a cop-out, but I decided that the answer might lie in democracy. I found a huge blackboard, grabbed some chalk, wrote down the titles of twelve songs, and placed it in the rehearsal room. My plan worked. They talked amongst themselves and chose *Can't Turn You Loose*, written by Otis Redding.

If ever I look back at the video of me lining up to play *Can't Turn You Loose*, on stage with Keith Richards, Steve Cropper, Bob Dylan, Robert Cray, Dave Edmonds and Jack Bruce, all I can ever think of is that I look and feel a bit like Forrest Gump – you remember all those photos when he's popping up in the back of pictures of presidents and prime ministers in great moments in history? Tom Hanks in the movie managed to produce a smile of simple pleasure and disbelief, and that's exactly how it all felt to me.

And Bob Dylan? Well, the way I think about the whole thing is much the same as I used to think about my first visit to various foreign countries. I'm really keen to go, really keen to get to know their individual customs and idiosyncrasies, but having been there and done that, I don't necessarily ever feel the urge to revisit. Likewise with Bob Dylan. "Bob, I'm ready to give that Tex Mex song from 1947 a go!" "Hey, he's Bob Dylan he can do what he likes." Over the years I've read that George Harrison at The Concert for Bangladesh and Robbie Robertson at the Last Waltz concert had the same experience with "his Bobness" and I realised that this was his modus operandi, so none of it was personal.

TEN

The Things You Do

We've probably all had moments in our lives that we look back on and think, what the hell was I thinking? That's precisely how I reflect on the moment when the brilliant Colombian bass guitarist Chucho Merchan asked me if I would be willing to play a charity concert in Cali, Colombia and I said yes. He also mentioned that he'd also invited David Gilmour and Roger Daltrey, but not for a moment did I think that either would agree.

Six years earlier the Nevado del Ruíz volcano in Colombia had erupted suddenly, destroying the town of Armero and killing an estimated 23,000 people. Many more had been left injured or homeless and the need was real. Now the Eco Mundo conservation group was organising a conference in Cali, and the concert would draw attention to their aims and raise funds for local causes. None of the performers would be paid, but all our travel and hotel expenses would be covered.

At this point my mum's cautionary voice should have popped into my head, repeating the warning I'd frequently heard from her; "don't go back to Colombia, it's too dangerous!" She said it so often in normal times, but this was the absolute height of the blood-soaked rivalries between the Medellín and Cali drug cartels, in which murder and kidnapping were daily occurrences. The notorious Cali leader Pablo Escobar was on the run and something close to all-out war was raging. Some crazy naïve English/Colombian bloke, who would no doubt be perceived as a rich rock star well able to come up with a generous ransom payment, was an easy and obvious target for the professional kidnappers whose activities had been all too vividly reported. It was by no means unusual for hesitant families to be encouraged to pay when various bits of their loved-one's anatomies were received through the mail.

Poster for Cali concert, 1992

There were many reasons why a sensible person would politely but firmly decline the kind invitation. On the other hand, it had been nearly twenty-five years since I'd been back to my mother's home country – last visited shortly after my father died – and I had some sixty cousins in Colombia, many of whom would no doubt welcome me back and look out for my wellbeing. I was amazed to discover that David Gilmour and Roger Daltrey had both said yes and since neither of them had played in South America before, we were clearly in for an adventure. David's partner Polly Samson and his manager Steve O'Rourke would come along for the ride, and everyone would add on a few days of holiday after the gig. What could possibly go wrong?

When it came to making travel plans, I recalled that several of my cousins were qualified pilots working for commercial airlines in Colombia. Maybe if we took the British Airways flight to Bogotá, one of them could fly us down to the gig in Cali. I told David and Roger, and everyone thought that sounded like a great idea. None of us reflected that the airspace above Colombia was thick with small planes buzzing back and forth to Miami carrying cargoes of cocaine, and that bullets flying between them and the American DEA were a commonplace.

No sooner had we landed in Bogotá than my cousin Pacho came to the plane to greet us and directed us to a scheduled flight he was piloting down to Cali. Yes, that's right; two of the most famous and successful rock stars in the world were being led without bodyguards or protection of any kind, like lambs to the slaughter into the deepest darkest den of drugs and iniquity anywhere on the planet.

Our flight was uneventful, thank heavens, and we landed safely in Cali. Leaving aside the fact that the airport was populated by men toting machine guns, all seemed relatively calm. We were driven through the streets and installed in our hotel. So far so good. We relaxed and went to the bar.

Next morning, I was awoken by the phone ringing. Another of my cousins had arrived downstairs. Could he come up? Sure thing, of course he could. A few minutes later there was a knock on the door. He threw his arms around me, conveyed greetings from what seemed like scores of aunts and uncles I'd never met or even heard of, and then suddenly he became serious.

"Have you seen the newspapers?" Of course, I hadn't, so he produced a copy, and my eyes followed a headline written in huge bold letters across the top of the front page.

'DON'T GO TO THE CHARITY CONCERT!' it screamed, or words to that effect. Amazed and confused, my eyes began scanning the story. 'The concert is a front for money-laundering,' was the sub-heading, 'and it's taking place on a football field controlled by the Cali cartel. The police are preparing for the likelihood of violence between rival cartels.'

"Oh dear" I said, or words to that effect, and was hoping that the calmness of my voice was disguising my blind panic.

Straight away I went to find Steve O'Rourke whose instant reaction mirrored my own, except that his was mixed with an equivalent level of uncontrolled fury which I can only describe as awesome.

"Where the hell is Chucho?" he shouted, and ran out of the room, apparently determined to hunt down the hapless Colombian and murder him on the spot. I was not far behind when Steve eventually came across

Chucho in a corridor, immediately grabbing him by the lapels and lifting him bodily against a wall, so that the poor man's feet were dangling in mid-air like a cartoon character pedalling over the edge of a cliff.

"What the hell have you gotten us into?" he yelled.

"What?" Chucho was struggling for breath. "What's the problem?"

"Look at this!" he continued. "Any minute now I'm going to be reading headlines saying 'Pink Floyd's David Gilmour involved in drug money laundering scam.' Bang goes the next tour! We'll be banned in North America. Everywhere!"

Obviously Chucho swore that he knew nothing about any money-laundering. As far as he was concerned, the organisers were straight and above board, and only doing good works in the local community.

Now we were in a dilemma. Should we pull out? Leave town? Should we make a press statement? Any alternative we could think of seemed fraught with risks of a kind none of us wished to contemplate too deeply. Eventually we decided there was nothing to do but go ahead with the concert as planned.

If I'd thought that every machine gun available for miles around had been in the hands of uniformed men at the airport, I was badly mistaken. The football stadium made the arrivals hall seem like a Boy Scout's picnic. You get used to seeing these guys depicted in movies and TV series like Narcos, but the real thing is just so much more – erm – real.

At that point we had no idea if anyone or no-one would defy the danger and advice, and turn up at the gig. Pink Floyd and The Who were and are hugely popular everywhere in South America, and so ordinarily a packed stadium would have been assured. In the event, maybe a couple of thousand people came along for what turned out to be a brilliant night in which Roger swung his microphone round his head like a gaucho's lariat, and David and I enjoyed busking our way through some of Pete Townsend's most famous guitar parts. Maybe it was more in hope than optimism that we ended our set with a quick rendering of The Beatles' *All You Need Is Love*, and hurried off the stage. If any of our guitarists' hands were shaking, I don't think it did anything other than improve our vibratos. The brave fans were well rewarded, the night ended without further incident, and we all got back to the hotel safe and sound.

The plan was that David, Polly, Steve and Roger would remain in Colombia for a week or so to take in the culture and get some sun. Meanwhile I would return to Bogotá where an aunt and uncle had arranged for a few more family members who lived further afield to come to say hello to their long-lost English relative. I packed my bags and headed for the lobby, only to be met by the hotel manager who presented me with a bill for something in the region of $4,000.

"No," I said. My fluency in Spanish was coming in useful. "There has been a misunderstanding. Our travel and hotels are being paid for by the organisers of the concert."

"No señor," said the manager. "The misunderstanding is yours. They say they have no money to pay. You must pay before you leave."

I did not have $4,000, and nor did I have any inclination to hand it over even if I had.

I confess to being unable to remember the precise sequence of events; however, my friend David claims to remember it clearly. This sounds completely out of character for me, but according to him, I skipped the hotel and did a runner. What I do recall is that I managed to arrive at the airport and to check in to the flight to Bogotá, only to find that the concierge from the hotel had followed me into the VIP departure lounge and was noisily demanding that I should be prevented from getting on the plane until the bill was paid.

Remember when I said I'd felt safe coming to Colombia because I had so many cousins who would look out for me? That's what happened next. My cousin the airline pilot confronted the hotelier and a blistering row broke out in which Pacho noisily demanded to know how this bloke could dare to shame Colombia by hassling these British guests who had only come as an act of generosity and goodwill. Meanwhile the hotelier was replying that if the bill wasn't paid, he'd lose his job or maybe worse. All this was still going on when the cabin doors were closing, and I was on my way to Bogotá. Someone told me later that poor Chucho was held at gunpoint and prevented from leaving Colombia until he had paid everyone's hotel bills.

On arrival in Bogotá I was met by more cousins and taken to my aunt and uncle's house, where I was expecting to be greeted by one or two more of my distant relatives. The scene when I arrived at their home sent me into a mild panic. There were not a couple of cousins. Not even a dozen cousins. It seemed that something closer to a hundred of them had travelled from all parts of the country to see me, shake my hand, and have photographs taken to show members of the even further extended clan back home. There was Paco and Pablo and Pacho and Judith, who had long since fallen out with Marta and Leo and Daniel and Alfonsito, and the volume of the collective cacophony emanating from my relatives was easily a match for anything I'd ever produced when standing alongside my one hundred watt amplifier. Quickly I bolted up the stairs, to be followed by my cousin Carmenza who could clearly see that I was feeling overwhelmed and discombobulated.

"What's the matter?" she seemed genuinely concerned. "Are you ill?"

"I don't know, I had no idea. I'm sorry but I just can't cope with meeting all these people."

"But some have travelled hundreds of miles to see you."

Las Tías Guille and Lígia in Tío Alfonso's house in Bogotá, Colombia

I felt wracked with guilt, but after all the trauma associated with the concert and then the debacle at the hotel, I'd had as much as I could take.

"When is the first flight back to London?" I asked. "Tonight? Please book me on it."

I'm not very proud to admit that I invented some bad news just received from London which required my immediate return. My fight or flight response had kicked in big time and my well-meaning relatives merely exacerbated it. To use the clichéé, "I made an excuse and left." Two hours later I was back at the airport and checking in for the flight to London. Once again I felt a surge of relief waft over me, but my surprises for the day were not quite over. In the departure lounge I was amazed to meet none other than David, Polly, Steve, and Roger.

"What happened?" I asked incredulously. "I thought you guys were staying for another week?"

"We were," they said, "but with everything going on down there, we thought we should quit while we were ahead and scarper while we still

Tío Tito and Tía Ligia with cousins in Tío Alfonso's house, Bogotá, Colombia

had the chance." We later heard that on the day after they left, a bomb went off on the same floor of the hotel where they'd been staying.

It would be exaggerating to say that it felt like a scene from *The Last King of Scotland* when our plane took off and we ordered a nice cup of English Breakfast tea from the British Airways steward, but it wasn't very different. I've seldom felt happier in my life than when the wheels left the tarmac. Probably none of us had ever been in the slightest danger from the Cali or any other cartel, but who in their right mind would have stuck around to find out?

ELEVEN

Family Revelations

So many times in the years since my dad died, I'd found myself thinking "I wish he was here so I could ask him that or tell him this …" or "Dad would be so pleased to see that …" Now Mum had also gone, leaving another big vacuum in the space which should be occupied by someone who loves you without hesitation or conditions.

Right about now, as it happened, I was feeling badly in need of the kind of arm round my shoulder that's best provided by someone who loves you. Even leaving aside the loss of my mum, I'd had a bruising falling out with my brother, I was having less fun than usual with my music, and I was finding it difficult to get paid for a lot of the work I'd been doing for various people in South America. Worst of all, I'd reached a point where my marriage had broken down, and eventually I had to face the hardest decision I've ever made in my life. Relationship break up and divorce feels like such a commonplace in our industry, but each story contains its own sadness for all those closely involved. One way and another I felt a strong need to talk it through, but I had no mum, no dad, and so my thoughts turned towards the only surviving senior member of my English family.

After the premature death of my dad, I'd become even closer to his two older sisters, Gigi and Gertrude, known to the family as Gerts. Gigi was married to my Uncle Charles, and the sisters lived next door to each other for a while, but then Gigi and Charles moved into a bungalow high up on a hill in Gravesend, overlooking the River Thames. As a schoolboy at Dulwich, I'd often stayed with them for half-term when I wasn't able to get back to see my parents in Caracas. Uncle Charles had been a river-boat pilot during and since the second world war, and sometimes at night-time he'd take me in the ship he was piloting from Gravesend up to Tower Bridge, where we'd disembark and be met by Auntie Gigi in the car. These were wonderful memories, and it was another huge loss when Charles and Gerts both died within a short space of time.

Gigi was not in good health herself at this point, but seemed happy to hear that I planned to visit. I wanted to tell her face to face about the divorce, and to let her know about my new partner Claire. She must have sensed that it was an important moment for me because she served tea in the best blue Denby chinaware and gave firm instructions to her noisy South African green parrot to remain quiet. Gigi had seen her own share of life's ups and downs, and she listened carefully and kindly as I poured my heart out. Just when I got to the end of my tale of woe and was thinking I could breathe again, Aunt Gigi had a surprise for me. It soon became clear that she had her own weighty matter to share.

"Since you've been so frank and open in confiding in me, I've got something to share with you which I think you need to know while I'm still here to tell you." My mind went into a whirl of silent speculation. Was she going to tell me about a secret lover, or her life as an undercover agent? I was wrong, and nothing could adequately have prepared me for what was to follow.

"Your grandfather wasn't who you think he was, and you're not really a Targett-Adams." She paused and seemed to draw a deep breath for the final part of her revelation. "Your dad and I had different fathers, and your real grandfather was a travelling musician with an opera company from Naples!"

In the course of the next couple of hours she unfolded a story which caused me to re-assess just about everything I thought I knew about

Newspaper ad for Italian Opera Company visiting Hastings, UK, 1911

my family history, and would inspire Claire and I into an investigation which took us from the dusty records of the High Court in London to the National Archive in Kew and in Naples, in what felt like my own special episode of the popular BBC series, *Who Do You Think You Are?*

It went something like this.

In 1899 a 36-year-old qualified doctor called Percy Targett-Adams went to live in South Africa. This was during the second Anglo-Boer war, and he'd been appointed Surgeon Major in the South African Medical Corps. He'd been living and working in Bloemfontein for four years when, on 5 November 1903 he married a young woman called Lizzie Buckley. Lizzie was 25 and came from Malden in Essex; by now he was 40. They went on to have four children together, all born in quick succession: Algernon in 1904, Richard in 1905, Mary (Gigi) in 1907 and Gertrude in 1908.

They sound like a couple very much in love but unfortunately, very soon after the birth of her fourth child, Lizzie returned to England, and her account of her reasons for doing so were detailed in her vivid response to a divorce petition later brought against her by her husband Percy. Colourful as it is, her story is worth quoting at length.

"The petitioner is guilty," says Lizzie, "of willful neglect, cruelty, and misconduct." She goes on to give an account of her husband's scandalous affair with their servant Annie McCabe, and continues : "That on or about Christmas Day 1907 he struck me violently in the face, gripped my arms and shook me and then otherwise assaulted me. He committed adultery with said person just ten days after my daughter Gertrude was born and continued to do so right down to the time I left South Africa, he has since co-habited with her." In an addendum Lizzie adds still more detail: "On 19 September 1908 I discovered the petitioners together in (McCabe's bedroom) in night attire. A few days later in that room I found under the mattress a syringe and a box or packet of powder which had been purchased by the petitioner for McCabe and given by him to her." Lizzie was asking the court to reject Percy's petition for divorce, but for the marriage to be dissolved and for her to have custody of the children and "relief as is meet." So apparently Percy and his mistress are having sex and abusing drugs, and when Lizzie complains about it, he beats her up. Despite these apparently ghastly circumstances, and for some reason known only to themselves, both parties decided not to proceed with the divorce.

That was all very shocking and all very tabloid, but what did it have to do with me? The answer lies in what happened next, which was that a short while after discovering her husband's affair, Lizzie returned to England. Her two sons, Algernon, and Richard, were put into the care of her parents-in-law, leaving her to look after her two daughters, Gigi and Gertrude.

With the two girls to take care of and little obvious means of support, these must have been very difficult times for Lizzie. Men were widely seen as the breadwinners, and women were still some years away from success in their long struggle for the vote. A woman living with young children but without a man was likely to be the subject of turned heads and gossip.

Lizzie moved to the coastal town of Hastings, where somehow, she managed to set herself up in a decent sized house at 3 Mount Pleasant Crescent, which she proceeded to run as a guest house. The idea of family holidays by the sea was gaining popularity in Edwardian England, and the town hosted all sorts of attractions designed to bring visitors from London for the day or the week. Among them was a music hall which provided a venue for touring entertainments of one kind or another.

Obviously visiting performers needed somewhere to stay, and on one occasion Lizzie found herself renting rooms at the boarding house to one or more singers and musicians from an Italian opera company. The language barrier did not prove an insurmountable problem because nine months after the Italian guests had returned to their homes in Naples, Lizzie gave birth to a baby son. She named him Duncan, and registered the father as her estranged husband, Percy Targett-Adams. This was Duncan Targett-Adams. My dad.

Roll forward some eighty years, and my aunt Gigi is telling me this story with some degree of apprehension, because part of her is expecting me to go ballistic. All my life I'd been brought up believing one set of facts about my family and background, and now it turns out that it's all been a lie. I wasn't descended from the Targett-Adams family after all, but from an unknown Italian opera musician. Was I angry? Was I feeling betrayed? On the contrary, I was absolutely delighted. Far from being the son of a doctor, albeit the deputy Chief Medical Officer for Bloemfontein, as I had believed, my dad was the product of a love-match between a gutsy woman trying to make her own way in the world, and a professional musician from the romantic Italian city of Naples called Mr. Sparano! And even better, was discovering that I was a quarter Italian. Molto bene.

Instantly I began to see my Grandma Lizzie in a whole new light. I'd been only ten when she died, and have few memories of her from that time, but it turned out that she was after all a heroic woman who'd had the courage to leave an abusive husband. Undaunted by a sea voyage lasting nine weeks with four young children, she returned to England to an unknown future. How I wished I could go back in time and tell her how much I admired her.

So, what happened next? As far as I could ascertain it from Gigi, some years passed and eventually Percy fell on hard times in South Africa, and she had to go out to help him return to England. Time must have proven to be a great healer because eventually, some eighteen years since their acrimonious separation, Lizzie allowed Percy to move in with her, along with Duncan and the girls who were by now living in a house in Wandsworth. Her only condition seems to have been that Percy must treat Duncan exactly the same as he treated the older four children. Percy died eleven years later, leaving the surprisingly large sum of £250,000 (in today's money) to Gigi and nothing to anyone else.

When I recovered my breath and my composure, I thanked Gigi profusely for finally allowing me into the family secret, and I left Gravesend feeling much better than I had when I'd arrived.

So now Claire and I were burning to know whatever could be discovered about my grandfather whose surname, we had gleaned, was Sparano. Such was our curiosity that we took a trip to Naples to see what could be uncovered. If we were lucky, we might even be able to track down some long-lost uncles or cousins. When we eventually located and arrived at the appropriate archive however, we were disappointed to find that they retained no records at all from the relevant period. We made further enquiries and were told that when the Nazis were retreating from the onslaught by British and American troops in 1944, they had destroyed every record they could lay their hands on. Nothing remained, and there was no other way to track down any details about anyone of that name living in Naples in the relevant period.

That seemed a shame, but now I had latched on to something which might provide a partial explanation for my dad's lifelong penchant for show business. After he left Hastings Grammar school, he appears to have found his way to London where he went in search of work as an actor in what was then the burgeoning British film industry. He seems to have become gainfully employed, and managed to get a part as an extra in a 1933 film called, *I'll Stick To You*, starring Jay Laurier and Betty Astell. Then he repeated the trick in *Love, Life and Laughter*, shot at the Ealing studios in 1935 and featuring the legendary and much-loved film star Gracie Fields. I have a copy of the movie, and if you look closely you can see a fleeting shot of my dad looking suave in full dinner jacket, twirling around the floor.

No doubt these were only occasional jobs as an extra for Dad, whose full-time employment was as the stage manager at the Coliseum theatre.

That's where he met and made friends with some of the great actors of the day, including Ralph Richardson and Vivien Leigh.

Much later Ms. Leigh visited Caracas with the Old Vic touring company. I was taken along to see her performance in Macbeth and in her dressing room, after the play, she kindly signed my programme. I have some rather wonderful grainy super eight colour film, taken by my dad, of her and the legendary Robert Helpmann at a swimming pool party hosted by him.

I've often wondered whether his knowledge of his own illegitimacy, in those much more censorious times, dissuaded my dad from seeking employment in some more formal profession where too many questions might be asked. In common with so many others who crave a career in the entertainment industry, my dad was probably having to decide between his passion for the movies, and a steady career and income. However I now wonder, was Dad always acting a part in his own personal drama, that of the quintessential Englishman abroad? Did my

Vivien Leigh, performing in Caracas with The Old Vic Company, 1964

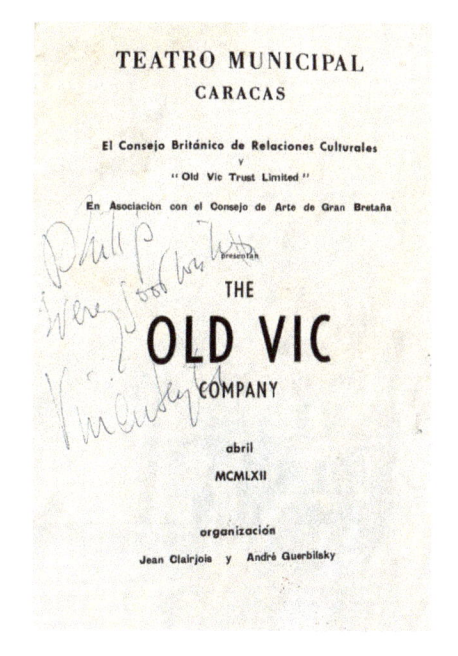

Signed Programme for Phil

mum know her husband's colourful family history? It remains a mystery to us all.

Dad's application to join the Armed Forces was turned down because of his colour blindness, and so I think he must have looked around for another way to serve King and Country. The onset of World War Two was just around the corner, and the rise of Fascism in Germany, Italy and Spain, as well as communism in Russia, had persuaded our government that it should do something to maintain and bolster what remained of British hegemony around the world. The result was the creation of the British Council, whose role was defined as, "to create in a country overseas a basis of friendly knowledge and understanding of the people of this country, of their philosophy and way of life, which will lead to a sympathetic appreciation of British foreign policy, whatever for the moment that policy may be and from whatever political conviction it may spring." Not exactly the most pithy mission statement, but you get the idea.

Dad with students at the British Council with 'special' student Mum, both dressed in white, Baranquilla, 1941

Dad applied and was accepted into the British Council in 1941 and, despite not being able to speak a word of Spanish, was immediately sent to head up the office in Barranquilla, Colombia. It must have felt like a far-flung outpost of British influence, and a letter from him to Gigi dated January 1942 refers to the Council's habit of trying "a spot of matchmaking" by sending "suitable" women out from England to provide spouses for their male staff. That plan obviously didn't work, because another letter home dated seven months later in August refers to himself as "a respectable married man." Evidently my dad had done his own matchmaking and had fallen in love with Magdalena Manzanera, who'd been born and brought up in Barranquilla. Their marriage resulted in three dramatic and consequential events, which were that: i) he was sacked for breaking a rule about consorting with local females; ii) the female in question was pregnant, and iii) he was instantly rehired by the British Council in Argentina.

For this rapid rehabilitation we have to thank the big *queso* in Buenos Aires, Sir Eugen Millington Drake. Dad was sent to head up its office in Tucumán where my brother was born rather less than nine months later and christened Eugen in tribute to his boss.

What did my dad actually do? No doubt his day job for the British Council was to promote what we now refer to as "soft power", and our various houses were consequently full of actors and writers, politicians, and diplomats. And spies too? The question was something of a mystery when I was a small child, and sadly remains so to this day. Anyone who ever operated

Mum and Dad's wedding day, Baranquilla, 1942

in the ex-pat community in any capacity knows that it was hardly possible to get by without a close working relationship with the embassy, in which the old boy network was always alive and well. Certainly, it would be impossible for anyone to navigate the bureaucracy involved in setting up inter-continental flights for BOAC, which at that time was the British government-owned airline, without a healthy dose of assistance from the diplomatic service, and no doubt the favours were suitably reciprocated. One thing we do know is that Dad had a habit of turning up in a series of countries just ahead of their revolutions, including Argentina, Paraguay, and Cuba, and making a fairly speedy getaway after they'd occurred. A series of gnomically phrased letters between him and various bosses tantalisingly refer to things like "this special task", and a request to "get me that particular book from a book shop in Charing Cross road". He was due to receive an OBE from the Queen just a month before he died, so I like to think that he was on "Her Majesty's Secret Service".

To me as a young boy, my dad was always a heroic figure. Certainly, when I read *Our Man in Havana*, and realised that its author and MI6 man Graham Greene had written it while staying in a hotel just a few hundred yards along the road from my dad's office, I allowed my imagination full flight. The book's hero Wormold works as a vacuum-cleaner salesman while moonlighting for MI6. When his boss returns to London on a Pan Am aircraft, the Chief tells him, "You should travel BOAC", and then that "our man in Havana has been turning out some pretty disquieting stuff lately." Possibly coincidence, but I choose not to think so. And meanwhile I'm still curious to know more about my opera-musician Italian 'Nonno'.

TWELVE

Producer

It takes a lot of time, as well as a lot of accumulated experience and wisdom, before any of us can get much of a handle on who we are and how we've become the person we turn out to be. There's no doubt that we're all products of our childhood, but it's only in later life that we're able to identify and differentiate some of the ingredients that came together to form our individual selves. As with so many of my contemporaries, it took some counselling support before I was finally able to come to terms with so much that has happened to me, and I thoroughly recommend it. In my case there was an exciting but sometimes scary childhood, combined with the whole business of living thousands of miles away from my parents while at boarding school, and then the shockingly premature death of my father. Each of these factors no doubt has its own chapter in the psychologists' most basic textbook, and I'm probably a very typical example of so many kids who grew up with comparable backgrounds and circumstances.

Making the whole recipe just a bit more complex for me, however, has been the effect of living large parts of my early life in the quintessentially

English and Anglo-Saxon culture of boarding school, and at the same time absorbing the Latin influences of South America and the Spanish speaking world. It's a duality which informs my character and personality, sometimes very British, measured and toned-down, sometimes the Latin: especially if I'm on stage with percussionists, singers and dancers from Italy or Spain, Colombia or Argentina, Cuba or Brazil. All I can say is that when I find myself in any part of Latin America, or even hearing the language being spoken, a vivid and distinctly different feeling comes over me, and I have a strong conviction that this is an essential part of me. It's difficult to describe but everything goes into technicolour and the temperature rises. It's obvious that these rhythms go to my very core. All rooted, no doubt, in those hypnotic beats that I absorbed as am impressionable 6 year old growing up in Cuba.

All of which may help to explain why, whenever I find myself searching the roots of my own creativity, my thoughts inevitably turn to Latin rhythms and I am drawn towards some of the many fabulous musicians and artists who live in Latin America.

I've already talked about how, from the first moment I started my own record label, my fluency in the language along with my natural aptitude for this special music made me the "go to" producer for *Rock en Español* bands. Added to which, since my earliest days with Roxy, I'd become ever more interested in the idea of exploring and producing new kinds of music, and the development of sophisticated technology offered a range of possibilities which were quite literally endless. Now though, while having a state-of-the-art studio in an 18th century coach house in the grounds of St Ann's Court was a huge asset, I was without the income from touring and recording new music with Roxy, and the studio and record label began to feel like a bath with the water running down the drain faster than I could easily fill it from the taps. My long-term bankers had been very patient but were beginning to get fed up with me.

So I embarked on a series of collaborations working as producer with some of the most exciting and talented musicians in the world. Most of these projects were good fun, several helped me to reduce the overdraft, and a handful from various countries in South America come to the forefront of my memory.

Notwithstanding the long-term dispute about the Falkland Islands (Islas Malvinas), Britain has many close and long-term ties with Argentina, which is probably the most European of the South American countries. A recurring theme in its music is the background of the perpetually volatile politics, and no-one exemplifies this more than the singer-songwriter and brilliant pianist Fito Páez. Like me, Fito had begun making music as a schoolboy playing in bars and clubs, but unlike me, his early recordings explored the difficult lives of the poor and downtrodden. His aunt and grandmother had both been assassinated at their home in Rosario in 1987, and the dark lyrics of his highly successful hit song *Ciudad de Pobres Corazones* are a tribute to them.

Fito had recently enjoyed a huge success with his 1992 recording entitled *El Amor Después del Amor* and was playing to audiences of 40,000 people. His great success meant that he had plenty of budget for the next one, so he made up his mind to enjoy the process. He would record the album's backing tracks in his hometown, spend some time in Europe, take a load of his friends along for the ride and film the entire adventure. Hang the expense; he was going to treat himself. Fito sounded just like my kind of guy, and so when I was asked to produce the album, I readily agreed. I duly flew to Buenos Aires and then to his hometown of Rosario, where I was able to find a huge empty theatre for rehearsals and where I thought we'd probably go on to make the eventual recordings. We'd need to take out the seats and make the stage an improvised control room.

Fito was an engaging and talented musician and all was going well, until he decided he had a hankering to go to Europe and record his vocals outdoors while facing towards the Mediterranean Sea. As you do. Being very fond of the Mediterranean myself, I said. "Yes, great, I know just the place." I arranged to head off to Capri Digital studios on the island of Capri, which are suitably spacious and well-equipped but also have a terrace with stunningly beautiful views across the Bay of Naples. Fito had said he wanted to sing facing the Mediterranean, and there could be no more perfect location. We thought.

What we didn't yet know, because he hadn't told us, was that Fito's wish to perform these vocals facing the Mediterranean was specifically

Capri Digital Studio with Ash Howes, sound engineer, 1993

confined to a brief period starting at 6pm each day. He didn't want to do anything much else for the rest of the time, and so we all settled in to enjoy ourselves in the sunshine, taking in the beaches and blissful boat trips to the Blue Grotto, before setting up to record in the early evening. All that would have been okay, except that when everything was prepared and we were ready to press the red record button, we discovered that 6pm was also the cue for the local church bells to start ringing, and these bells didn't merely chime six times and then fall silent. 6pm was the start of extended peeling from all around the district, which more or less prevented us from any possibility of an uninterrupted recording of Fito's vocals.

We were diligently persevering over several days in our attempts to record Fito singing without distraction, when the startling news came through from Rosario that the police had arrested some people thought to be responsible for the murder of Fito's grandmother and aunt. Suddenly his concentration and his routine were shattered, as he was frequently whisked off by various TV and radio stations from all over South America for interviews about his reaction to the arrests.

Eventually even that calmed down, but not content with recording in a theatre in Rosario or a beautifully located studio in Italy, Fito next decided that he'd like to record with a full live orchestra in London. This didn't seem to be a great idea because (between you and I) Fito's singing wasn't exactly pitch-perfect, and being accompanied by a live orchestra would leave us with limited options for helping him out. My attempts to talk him out of this course of action failed, and so we next found ourselves in George Martin's new Air Lyndhurst Studios, located in a converted church in Hampstead. It was a bright Sunday morning when a full orchestra gathered and were ready to go, but it was only at that point that one of the musicians spotted our film crew. Fito had insisted that there should be a documentary record of the entire "making of", but only now was it pointed out that the Musicians' Union demands a higher rate for filmed recording, and that no such deal had been agreed. How much more money would this cost? No-one seemed to know. It was the weekend and no-one from the M.U. was answering the telephone. What was to be done?

Fito Paez at mixing desk Capri Digital, 1993

Eventually some kind of compromise was cobbled together, the recording went ahead, and the resulting album *Circo Beat*, was well-reviewed and produced several hit songs, including *Mariposa Tecknicolor* and *Tema de Piluso*. Fito is a unique talent whose career has continued to prosper from that day to this, and he remains one of the most famous rock stars in the Latin world.

Around that time, I was also introduced to a Brazilian band called Os Paralamas do Sucesso, but always referred to simply as Paralamas. The core of the band consisted of Herbert Vianna on guitar and lead vocals, Bi Ribeiro on bass and drummer Joao Barone. They'd been around since 1982 and their music was yet another interesting fusion; in this case of ska and reggae, to which they'd later mix in some horn arrangements and Latin rhythms.

It was mid 1993 when Paralamas came to Chertsey to record what would be their seventh studio album, and what I remember most about it was that they were obsessed with the idea of asking Brian May from Queen to guest on one of their tracks. Brian is a lovely guy, and so he readily agreed to come down and play some guitar on the song *El Vampiro Bajo El Sol*.

Me and Fito recording with the orchestra at AIR Studios Lyndhurst, London, 1993

I also played on some tracks and had the wonderful experience of playing the iconic guitar that Brian's dad made with him, using an old sixpence as a plectrum as Brian famously does. The album was released under the title *Severino* in Brazil in Portuguese and initially didn't do especially

PRODUCER

well, but then it was later sung in Spanish, renamed *Dos Margaritas*, and became a huge success in the whole Hispanic market.

Herbert Vianna was later struck by tragedy when a small plane he was piloting crashed, killing his British wife Lucy, and leaving him in a coma for some three months. His recovery was slow and has led to him being confined to a wheelchair, but I was happy to see that he was well enough to sing at the ceremonial handover of the Paralympics from London to Rio in 2012.

By now my growing reputation for producing and recording Latin bands and artists led to me being asked by the guys from Sony Latino to look after the next album from a Puerto Rican artist called Robi Draco Rosa. Robi had made his name in a band with Ricky Martin called Menudo and after a series of collaborations, was striking out on his own. He was married to the actress Angela Alvarado who had a successful movie and TV career, and went on to direct promo videos for her husband's music.

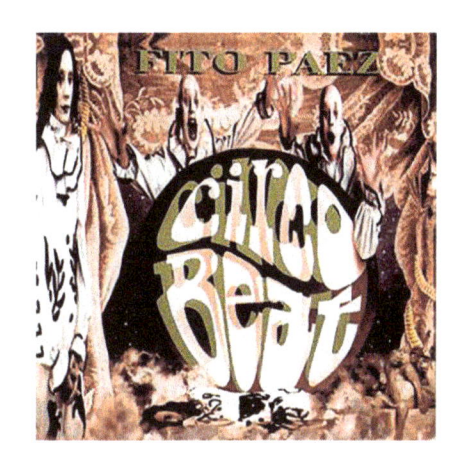

Circo Beat

The agreement with the record company was that he would come to London to record in my Gallery Studios at Chertsey. It wasn't a big budget, but Robi favoured the gnarly, strong guitar sounds of bands like Metallica and Jane's Addiction, so I knew I'd enjoy myself.

Robi brought along with him a selection of amazing musicians, including Rusty Anderson

Paralamas Dos Margaritas

173

who went on to play with Paul McCartney. I played on a few of the tracks myself, and the whole thing was special because it's a heavier and darker side of rock sung in Spanish. The eventual album, called *Vagabundo* was released to amazing reviews, and was included in Spin Magazine's list of the top ten greatest *Rock en Español* records of all time. Despite the high praise however, sales were disappointing,

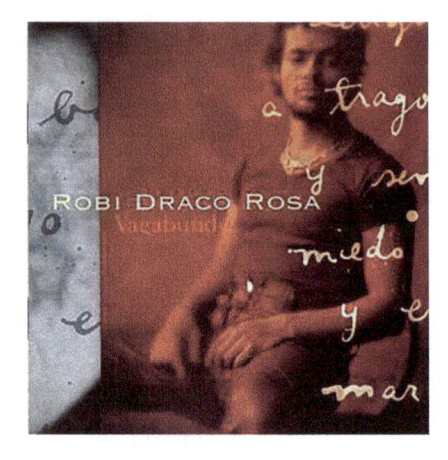

Draco Rosa Vagabundo

and when the time eventually came for Robi to return to America, he didn't even have the money for the air fare and had to plead with the label to get him home.

I didn't hear anything very much from Robi for a few years, and so it was a pleasant surprise when I received a phone call from him one evening to say he was in London and suggesting that we might meet up.

"That would be lovely," I said, "where are you staying?" He told me he'd been in town for a little while and was living at the Dorchester. "Get the hell out of there," I said. "How can you afford to stay at an expensive place like that?" He laughed. "You don't understand Phil, I'm rich now, I'm a millionaire." It turned out that a year earlier in 1998 he had written and recorded Ricky Martin's first ever album in English, which included the global smash hit single *Livin' la Vida Loca*. The album went on to sell some twenty-two million copies. I was absolutely thrilled for him.

Later Robi was diagnosed with non-Hodgkin lymphoma and embarked on a lengthy and heroic battle against the condition, first involving alternative treatments and eventually more conventional chemotherapy and bone-marrow transplants. He was declared cancer-free for a period, but then suffered a relapse in 2013. He fought back once again, and at the last check he was celebrating his seventh-year cancer-free and still winning Grammys and Latin Grammys in America.

One of the many good things which arose from my relationship with Robi was that he introduced me to another amazing South American band called Aterciopelados, which translates as "The Velvets". I was especially happy to make their acquaintance because, having worked with musicians from Cuba, Argentina, and Brazil this would be my first collaboration with a band from my mother's home country of Colombia.

In some ways Aterciopelaos are like a Latin version of the Eurythmics. Fronted by Andrea Echeverri and Hector Buitrago, they were the Annie Lennox and Dave Stewart of Colombia. While their music was an appealing mixture of punk, Latin and rock and roll, their words and deeds were all about social consciousness and activism. Andrea is a sculptor and artist as well as a musician, and wherever there was a demonstration or campaign for a good cause, they were there on the front line.

This would be their third album; the first two – *Con El Corazón en la Mano* (With my heart in my hand), and *El Dorado* (The Golden One) featured all the things I love best, including heavily distorted guitars, a rock-bolero sound, and a loud punk drumbeat. Once again we had a limited budget and it was agreed that we'd record in my studios. As luck would have it,

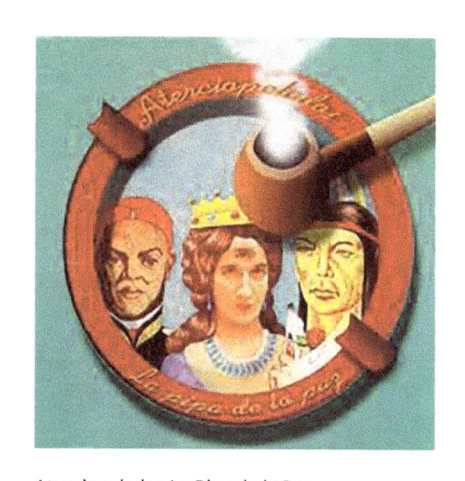

Aterciopelados La Pipa de la Paz

we discovered that a number of brilliant Colombian musicians were visiting and performing in London at the time, and so we were able to bring them down to play. I played some guitar parts myself, and even persuaded Chucho Merchan to play bass on some tracks while Enrique Bunbury from Heroes del Silencio sang some backing vocals.

The resulting album, *La Pipa de la Paz* (The Pipe of Peace) produced some of the band's best known singles and enabled them to embark on their first tour of the US. The album led to Aterciopelados becoming the first Colombian band to be nominated for a Grammy in the Best Latin Rock/Alternative category, and since then they've gone on to win two Grammys.

With these four collaborations, alongside many others with similarly inspiring artists, I've managed to keep the Latin-American part of my persona fed and watered, and marching harmoniously in step with the British man you see as the guitarist in Roxy Music. I've found over the years that if I pay attention to both characters, indulging their individual passions and aptitudes whenever I can, the two Phils – Targett-Adams and Manzanera – can manage to get along together quite nicely.

THIRTEEN

Have Guitar Will Travel ...

If you're lucky enough to discover the guitar at an early age, as I was, you know you've made a friend for life. Ever since I got my hands on my mum's guitar as a small boy, I've always tried to keep one close by. It's been my constant and faithful companion, my consolation through some tough moments, and a source of joy and celebration in the great ones. Most of all, it's been my personal passport to meeting people and going to places which no other asset could ever have made possible.

In and amongst the many opportunities I had to produce brilliant musicians like Robi Draco Rosa, Enrique Bunbury and Aterciopelados, the simple joy of

Womad Benoni, South Africa, 1994

playing music with people from all kinds of places and backgrounds has been a constant blessing. I remember a TV series as a kid called "Have Gun Will Travel" in which Richard Boone played a gunslinger/investigator who toured the Wild West righting wrongs. My version has been "Have Guitar Will Travel," in which I've slung a guitar over my shoulder and headed off in many directions pursuing new musical adventures.

One day early in 1999 I took a call from a man whose name was familiar when he introduced himself as Dan Chiorboli. Dan is well known as an accomplished percussionist who's collaborated with greats such as Brazilian guitarist Sergio Dias and Ladysmith Black Mambazo. He was phoning to ask if I'd like to to play in a forthcoming Womad (World of Music, Arts and Dance) tour of South Africa, the Canary Islands, Australia, and New Zealand.

I've always admired the whole concept behind Womad, ever since it was invented by Peter Gabriel forty-odd years ago. Using music as a shared language to cross cultural and ethnic barriers has been a constant theme underpinning so much of what I've tried to do, and so this opportunity felt tailor-made. Of course, I said yes.

Me with Ray Phiri of Graceland/Paul Simon fame, playing with The African Gypsies, 1994

The band Dan had put together was called The African Gypsies and included some of the most talented and respected musicians from the African continent. Among them was the wonderful South African guitar-player Ray Phiri, famous for his role alongside Paul Simon on the Grammy Award-winning *Graceland*. Also on the tour was the human rights campaigner Oliver "Tuku" Mtukudzi. Oliver originated from what was then Salisbury in Rhodesia, now Harare in Zimbabwe, and his songs are all about the struggle against white rule and inequality. I was sad to hear that Oliver died in 2019 from complications following diabetes. Bass for the Gypsies would be played by the equally legendary Gito Baloi from Mozambique. Gito had also worked with Paul Simon, as well as with Peter Gabriel, Sting, Tracy Chapman and Youssou N'Dour. Unfortunately Gito had a problem with drugs and later he was prevented from entering New Zealand with us because of a drugs bust; four years after that he was tragically shot and killed while trying to score some dope in Jo'burg.

There were far too many brilliant artists to name-check all of them, but the other extraordinary musician whose name can't be overlooked is the inspirational singer and guitarist Baaba Mal from Senegal. Baaba worked tirelessly for good causes, including notably for the fight against AIDS. He's also an inspirational advocate for traditional African music. In an interview in 2020, he talked about the ritual quality of traditional instruments, and how he chooses different ones to convey his songs' messages: "The spirit of the kora and the ngoni are different from the talking drum and the balafon, or the sabra and the djembe. The kora and ngoni are closer to human beings because they are made from things that had life. The talking drum, the balafon, and the sabar are made from wood, and when you listen to them your mind goes out into the forest. When you make music and write songs, you have to know about the messages. From the messages, you know what the instruments are and how to put them together underneath the lyrics." Like I said, inspirational.

I wondered how I'd fit in with all these fabulous African artists, and then I thought that maybe my immersion in Latin-American culture might help me to bridge the gap between our musical backgrounds. Still, I was looking forward to a decent spell of rehearsals with other band members so I'd be able to find my feet before going live. It was not to be.

The first gig on our journey to Africa was in Las Palmas on the Canary Islands, and the very first time I played with the band was at the live concert. It was a baptism by fire and a steep learning curve, but somehow I got through it and had a great time.

Our concert in Benoni, just outside Jo'burg, was the first ever Womad performance in South Africa and was an amazing and uplifting experience for me and for everyone involved. The audience was unlike most rock concert crowds and seemed to be made up mostly of families out for a lovely day of peaceful camaraderie, relaxed and full of the joy that only their unique style of music and dance can bring. The Womad tour continued to Australia and New Zealand.

The whole thing was an exhilarating experience, and I was thrilled when I was invited back to South Africa in 2018 to take part in the celebrations for Nelson Mandela Day. I found myself joining 142 singers and musicians playing traditional instruments from all parts of the continent. Incongruous in the mix, but demonstrating the apparently boundless inclusivity of the project, we were happy to be joined by one of the Neville Brothers from New Orleans. We recorded the live performance and later released an album with some of the same musicians on my own label, calling it *The Liberation Project*.

Boring things like funding and practicality were never going to stop the spirit motivating this music and its advocates. Just a few months later I was invited to rejoin The Liberation Project on a tour of Italy. There was no money other than a nominal grant from the South Africa Arts Council, so now we found ourselves driving all over the country, cooped up in the back of two tiny transit vans. There were eleven musicians and managers on the trip, and we travelled with our gear and did all the heavy lifting between us. All a far cry from the cosseted VIP treatment and trips on Concorde I'd been used to with Roxy, but on the plus side I got to play guitar with some of the most impressive and affable musicians I've ever met. I also got to see more of the beautiful Italian countryside than I'd bargained for and was amazed by the quality of the food in the service stations … only in Italy would that happen.

Conspicuous among us was the magnificently named N'Faly Kouyate – conspicuous because he's about 6.7 and one of the coolest dressers I've come across; but neither of those is his claim to fame. N'Faly is the latest in a line of storytellers from his homeland of Guinea. He was brought up as a traditional Djeli (Griot), which means that he's a sort of ambassador of the Mandingo culture. The Griot, which literally translates from the original Mandinka as "blood of the society", is so called because, much like the blood in the body, they circulate everywhere. Griots serve as a conduit for the collective memory, as life libraries, history tellers, and counsellors for the king and the people. Not unlike the traditional Celtic bards, N'Faly stands in a line of storytellers and musicians who've been an indispensable part of West African culture for centuries.

In fact, the Celtic link goes deeper, because N'Faly is also a member of the incomparable Afro-Celt Sound System, which mixes traditional music and instruments from both cultures into a mesmerising confection which would make a marble statue stand up, clap hands and stamp its feet. Give yourself a treat and look them up on Youtube if you haven't heard them.

The Liberation Project, Johannesburg, South Africa, 2007

Joyous though the experience was, the novelty of enduring the sort of discomfort we were used to when we were aged 17 eventually wore off just a bit. Claire and I found ourselves asking why we were struggling up a pot-holed mountain road for three hours only to play for fifty people when we got there. Eventually we recorded and released another album – the aptly named *Solidarity Express* – which sealed some great memories in a time-capsule.

Dan Chiorboli's endless and endearing supply of optimism for musical adventures led him to become, for a short time, manager of the former Cream drummer, Ginger Baker. Ginger's obsession with polo had led him to relocate to South Africa and one day, when we were in the country for Dan's *Awesome Africa Festival*, he asked Claire and I if we would like to go up country to visit Ginger on his farm. Since we had a great connection with Jack Bruce, we thought that might be fun, so we agreed to go. Anyone who has seen the boggling documentary, *Beware of Mr Baker* in which Ginger is seen assaulting the filmmaker, might not be surprised at what happened next.

We arrived after a three-hour car journey at what looked like a fortified compound, where Dan led us into a very shabby room full of dogs which occupied every sofa and seat. Ginger seemed reluctant either to acknowledge our presence or to clear away any of the dogs so we could sit. Our attempts at small talk were completely ignored, and the whole thing felt like we were talking to Albert Steptoe from Steptoe and Son. We gave up after twenty minutes and left, feeling mildly relieved that at least no violence had taken place.

The next time we met Ginger Baker was at Jack Bruce's funeral at Golders Green crematorium, and if anything the experience was even less pleasant. Claire and I shared a pew with him and Eric Clapton, but to our disgust Ginger either beat time on the wooden seat or exclaimed loudly, during the valedictories, 'oh god, when is this going to be over?' I imagined Jack looking down and wanting to strangle him, and I would gladly have done so on his behalf. But even that wasn't to be our last meeting with the curmudgeon. One year after Jack had died, his wife and manager Margrit and his three children organised a tribute concert at London's Roundhouse. Many of Jack's music friends performed, including Ian Anderson, Mark

King, Bernie Marsden, Ginger Baker, and myself. On this occasion Ginger refused to talk to anyone at rehearsal, was vile to Jack's pregnant daughter Natasha, and when Ian Anderson made the mistake of trying to say hello to him, his reply was "fuck off". We were less than a minute and a half into the iconic, *Sunshine of your love* when Ginger abandoned his drum-kit altogether. Fortunately the long-suffering musical director Nitin Sawhney had taken the precaution of having another drum-kit set up and a deputy, Frank Tontoh, ready to go. Frank made the transition so seamless that the rest of us played on, completely unaware of the drama going on behind us.

The audience certainly saw it however, and we can only imagine what they thought. Knowing what I know now, it surprises me that Cream lasted as long as it did.

One project that had its roots in a chance meeting occurred one day in 2006 when I was queuing in the passport hall at Gatwick airport, and I glanced over and noticed a face I thought I recognised. The last time I'd seen my old school-chum Charles Hayward had been around 1975 when we'd recorded the Quiet Sun album at Basing Street studios. It was terrific to see him and to hear great stories about his long and successful career as a member of a John Peel favourite band called This Heat, and as a session-man playing drums for Hot Chip. Later we went to see his one-man show which was fabulously entertaining.

Lezeck, Charles, Yaron and Me at Gallery Studio, London, 2007

Charles' name came straight into mind when I had an idea for a musical experiment to go into a studio with some of my favourite people to record an as-live album. The plan was a very simple one; we would each choose a track we wanted to record or improvise on, and then all get together and just play and see what turned up.

Ever since I'd met him whilst recording David Gilmour's album *On An Island*, I'd been looking for another excuse to collaborate with the extraordinary Polish pianist Leszek Mozdzer, and this seemed like the moment. Leszek, Charles, and I got together with Yaron Stavi on bass to record an album which we named Firebird VII in honour of my trademark guitar.

Bill MacCormick contributed a track entitled *Fortunately I Had One With Me*, which was left over from the Quiet Sun album. Charles offered *After Magritte*, Yaron suggested *A Few Minutes*, and all of us contributed to *Mexican Hat*. The whole thing was exhilarating, challenging and a new experience. It gave me the chance to fulfil an ambition which I'd secretly nurtured since 1968 when I'd taken my first trip to Ronnie Scott's with Robert Wyatt and Bill Mac to see the American jazz pianist and double-bass player Charlie Mingus. There's also a quiet satisfaction for a rock guitarist to have sneaked into the citadel of British Jazz: we're not often let in.

Ronnie Scott's is widely acknowledged as the home of British jazz, but is also a kind of mecca for those of us who would never quite make

Me, Charles, David at Ronnie Scotts Club, Soho, London 2007

it into the jazz inner circle. It was the venue for Jimi Hendrix's last ever performance before his death in 1970 and is hallowed ground on which just about every musician I know aspires to play. It was the *Firebird VII* project which enabled me to fulfil the ambition, playing for three nights in February 2009. David Gilmour and Andy Mackay turned up as guests on a few numbers, and among our repertoire was *East of Asteroid* which we'd first played with 801. Exactly how it all went down with the purist jazz afficionados is unknown, but I do know that a review by one of the UK's most respected jazz-critics Jack Massarik awarded us one star. I found this a bit depressing until I learned that the same critic had also reviewed a performance by Jeff Beck, whom I regard as probably the best guitarist I've ever seen, and gave him no stars at all.

We were all having so much fun that we decided to take the band on a quick six-date tour of Leszek's home country of Poland. I piled into the back of a very dodgy van, all of us humping our own gear, and drove on a lot of roads with more potholes than the lunar surface. Every time we drove over a bump, our heads would hit the roof of the bus and Charles would shout "oh for fuck's sake!" In any spare moments during soundchecks, Leszek would mesmerise the rest of us playing his favourite Gershwin's *Rhapsody in Blue*.

All of which might easily sound and read like a lot of self-indulgent musicians just having a good time, roaming around the world playing all the stuff we loved to play and hoping there was enough of an audience here and there to pay some of the bills. And to be fair, that's exactly what it was.

Ronnie Scott's Firebird V11 gig, London, 2008

FOURTEEN

Roxy – Take Three

Every young person who has ever hankered to play music no doubt has his or her vision of what it would be like to be in a band. For me, when I met the Roxy guys at the audition in late 1971, my hopes and dreams were probably derived mostly from The Beatles, who had blazed a trail for an entire generation. "Beatlemania" was a new and unique phenomenon which gave me a vivid picture of what could be possible if my hopes became reality. Looking in from the outside, the "Fab Four" seemed to be an indivisible band of brothers, tied together with a shared objective to make great music and to have a good time.

Certainly I felt we were living something close to that in those early days of Roxy. The band was inventing its own unique sound, developing its own look and style, and creating something which people hadn't seen or heard before. It seemed as though anything might be possible, and frequently it was. We were our own band of brothers, together making music which quickly became part of the fabric of popular culture.

That moment in a performance when you realise the audience knows every lyric and every note of the song almost as well as you know them

Roxy Music tour poster, 2001

yourselves; that those licks and nuances you'd laboured over and perfected in the studio are now out there as common currency in the wide world. It felt good. We were creating something essentially for ourselves, but which also had its own individual resonance for thousands of people we would never meet or know.

But then, gradually, and perhaps inevitably, life began to move on. No matter how grateful you are for your good fortune, you can't "live the dream" every day, and eventually what might seem to outsiders like all your Christmases coming at once, begins to become your idea of normality. I don't think I ever took for granted the thrill of a rapturous crowd or the dedication of our fans, but as we began to grow and mature, our personal radars expanded and each of us developed new and wider interests. Gradually we began to discover that there was life outside the Roxy bubble.

The undeniable novelty of being young and part of a rock band and on the road, with all that entails, eventually began to fade. One by one we got married and our families and children became more important to us. Each of us wished to pursue our own projects, life took over, and we all discovered the fulfilment which comes from expanding our horizons. The desire to make music was as strong as ever for all of us, but we didn't necessarily feel it had to be within the confines or context of Roxy Music.

We'd had that first great five years together before circumstances led us to go our separate ways, then there was the second five years together which had ended with some bad feeling in Philadelphia in May 1982. So as we approached the turn of the century, it had been the best part of eighteen years since Roxy Music had last played together, and in that time I must have been asked ten thousand times if and when the band might reunite. I know the same was true for Andy and Paul, and it was probably the same for Bryan too.

Though our paths had crossed occasionally, and I had played on a few of Bryan's solo songs, we hadn't worked together as Roxy since the au revoir in Philadelphia. Then one day in the middle of 1999, shortly after I'd finished the WOMAD tour, the phone rang, and I was surprised to find it was Bryan calling. We did the usual, "how are you?" "Fine thanks, how are you?" and then he told me he was due to play with his band at Hammersmith, and would Claire and I like to come along as his guests? That seemed like a nice idea, so we went along as invited, enjoyed the gig, and at the end of the evening we went home and thought little more about it.

Then, in common with just about everyone else at that time, we were wondering what might be a fun and interesting way to celebrate the passing of the millennium and the beginning of a new one. We were still undecided when I received a call from Bryan. "I'm doing this thing at Greenwich on New Years' Eve, and I just wondered if you'd like to come along and play?" Since Greenwich Mean Time was going to be the center of the universe at the turn of the century, the idea seemed fun so I said, "yes, as long as I can bring guests and we can all have a great party," and that's what we did. While events at the Millennium Dome were organisational chaos, everything at Greenwich went like clockwork. It was a very special night and all of us had a memorable time. The warmth of the occasion melted away the last traces of any frost which might have formed between myself and Bryan, and we got along well and parted with mutual good wishes for the new century.

It was just a few weeks later that Bryan called me at home. We chatted for a while about how much fun it had been to play together on New Year's Eve and then he suggested that it might be a good idea for us to meet and talk. The only problem was that if we did so in public it would bound to set off a tidal wave of speculation which we didn't want or need. Eventually we agreed that we'd meet in a little-used country pub, which was more or less equidistant from his Sussex home and mine. I agreed, and when I turned up a few nights later, I walked into a dingy and run-down bar, only to find the whole place completely empty except for a solitary rock star sitting hunched over his drink with his collar turned up. Bryan and I chatted for an hour about family and friends, we caught up on what we'd each been up to, and then we edged into a tentative discussion of what it might be like if we got Roxy back together. Who might we involve? What material might we want to play? Neither of us made any kind of commitment, but it all seemed very promising and fortunately our secret liaison remained secret. That was step one.

Seeing us together on stage at Greenwich had set some other people thinking too, and among those who wondered about the possibility of a more formal reunion was a concert promoter called John Giddings. John had just sold his own company, Solo, to Live Nation and was in a position to orchestrate a financial offer which might be sufficiently attractive to tempt us back on the road. When John asked me if I thought the time was right to get Roxy back together, I encouraged him to do his sums and see what numbers he could come up with. When he produced the number seven followed by six noughts for a seventy-gig tour, I felt it was the proverbial 'offer you can't refuse'. I arranged a meeting with Bryan and his accountant Ronnie Harris.

"We've got a number," I said, "it's £7 million. Here it is."

"That's all very impressive," said Ronnie, "but naturally we don't feel comfortable taking the first offer we hear. We'd like to ask around to see if we can do better."

Needless to say, no other promoter in Europe could improve on the £7 million, and so the offer from John Giddings and Live Nation was approved in principle by the three of us; Bryan, Andy Mackay, and myself. That was step two.

Since it would be eighteen years since we'd played together as Roxy, we decided to make a big splash by holding a press conference to announce the tour. Our PR company, LD Communications suggested The Savoy Hotel as the venue, echoing one of our most popular songs, *Do The Strand*. Word of the likely content of the announcement was inevitably filtering out through the industry and so scores of

Me with feathered friends

journalists gathered at the appointed time, set up their microphones and cameras and waited, and waited, and then waited some more.

Why were they waiting? Because in a luxury suite several floors above their heads, Ronnie, Bryan, Andy, and I still hadn't agreed the financial split between us, and Bryan wasn't prepared to announce until we had. We went back and forth but couldn't agree, and meanwhile downstairs the vol-au-vents were getting sweaty, the copy deadlines were coming and going, and everyone was wondering what on earth was going on.

It's worth saying here that we were all aware, though no-one was saying it, that the elephant in the room was Paul Thompson. Though Paul hadn't played with us since the *Manifesto* album, he had been a key member of the original Roxy line-up and I was hoping we'd find some way to bring him back in. I thought that if Bryan, Andy, and I could only agree the deal between ourselves, we'd go ahead and make the announcement and sort out Paul later.

After what seemed hours of arguing and pacing, we eventually went downstairs and announced what by then was the worst kept secret in pop history. But if we'd imagined that no-one would refer to the elephant in the room, our hopes were quickly dashed. Prompted by Ian Macdonald, the NME journalist Charles Shaar Murray asked, "does anyone have Paul Thompson's phone number?" We all looked at each other and sheepishly replied, 'yes'.

Of course, we all loved and respected Paul, but it had been more than twenty-five years since we'd played with him in Roxy Music, and so before anyone committed, it seemed a good idea for all of us to get together to see if the old magic was still there. We convened at Rak Studios in London and when someone asked how we should begin, I said, "let's play *Virginia Plain* – it's only got four chords". We did, and instantly we sounded like the authentic Roxy Music. Step three – we were back.

Rehearsals started, the set was sorted, and a huge tour was about to begin which would eventually include the UK, most of Europe, the States, Canada, Australia, and New Zealand. We were all prepared, but then just two days before we were about to embark on the tour, Bryan sprang one of his surprises.

"I went to Quaglino's last night and there were these terrific dancers wearing feathered Samba outfits. I think we ought to hire them and bring them on tour with us."

"That sounds fun Bryan," we said, "how many of them?"

"Sixteen."

"Sorry, I must have misheard you. For a second there I thought you said 'sixteen'."

He had said sixteen, who all duly turned up to perform with us on a Top of the Pops Special at Riverside Studios Hammersmith: let's just say the stage was a bit crowded.

When the tour started in Glasgow, sixteen dancers had become a more manageable eight, and I had to admit that they brought an extra layer of glamour and pizzazz to the show. Thinking back, they reminded me of the dancers I'd so admired at the Tropicana Club in Havana. Somewhere along the line I seem to recall that the eight became four, and by the time we got to the final gig of the UK tour at the Hammersmith Odeon we were down to two, which was a great relief for Christian Wainwright who was head of wardrobe and used to refer to the dancers as the 'feathered ones'.

Lying on my red sofa at home in London, the day after the final gig of the 2001 tour, I was surprised and pleased to get a call from Bryan. "That was good fun," he said, "maybe we should do some more."

It was around about now that my divorce was being finalised, as a result of which it became inevitable that I would no longer be able to hang on to St Ann's Court and the attached studios I'd built in the Coach House. I'd had some amazing times making music there, and undoubtedly it felt like a wrench. However it was also very much like a chapter closing and another one opening up, and Claire and I found a superficially unprepossessing top floor of a Victorian warehouse tucked away in a secluded courtyard next to the railway line in Queen's Park. Nothing could have been more different from St Ann's Court, but this was where we proceeded to make our home and inevitably to build another studio. It took two years for my Gallery Studios mark two to be completed and ready to roll once again.

From the moment of the reunion in 2001, the reformed Roxy Music toured together all over the world on and off for another five years.

Me and Bryan at Roxy's Top of the Pops Special, Riverside Studio London, 2001

It all felt pretty good and was going well, and the question naturally arose about whether we might go back into the studio to record some new material. The four of us talked about it, and then we thought we might contact our old friend Chris Thomas to ask if he'd like to produce something. Next, I was deputed to approach our original band-member Brian Eno to see if he could be tempted to come along for the ride. Eno had more than fulfilled all the expectations promised by his immense creativity all those years before and had recently worked with Coldplay. At first, he was sceptical, but when I added the thought that perhaps we might record some of his own material, he was eventually persuaded to give it a whirl.

We booked some time in Rak recording studios, but as the day approached I felt increasingly anxious about how Bryan and Brian might get along with each other. They'd certainly met several times since the split and had remained on good terms, but this was potentially the resumption of a creative relationship which had previously ended badly. I was keen to make sure that their first meeting in rehearsals should go well, not least because it was likely to set the tone for whatever was to follow.

Ever the diplomat, I reckoned that the best way to avoid any awkwardness might be to organise some distractions. Our bass player for the session, Guy Pratt is not only an outstanding musician but is also an accomplished stand-up comedian, so I thought he'd be well able to ease any tension. I made sure that Paul Thompson was already in the car when I picked up Brian Eno, and when I dropped them both at the studio door, I took my time to park. By the time I made it inside, the four of them were chatting and the atmosphere was relaxed. I felt relieved. So far so good.

Andy, Paul, Bryan, Brian and I, five of the original members of Roxy, along with Guy on bass and with Chris Thomas producing, got on with the process of recording. It all seemed to be going well, and after a while we took a break and sat down together, at which point Eno wryly observed that we all seemed to have reverted to the same roles we'd adopted thirty-five years previously. In that moment I knew that our venture was doomed to failure, and that whatever music we made together was never going to see the light of day. Like the good old troopers we undoubtedly were, we soldiered on in the face of certain defeat, and no-one died in the process. Eno went back to being Eno and the rest of us continued with other projects. We all felt that we'd given it a good go but also, since we were so proud of the original music we'd made together, it seemed wrong to add to it with material which we wouldn't be completely proud of.

I've been asked many times over the years to explain how and why Roxy Music came and went and came back again several times and turned into a sort of episodic part of our lives. I've always struggled to find a clear and simple answer, but the best explanation I've come up with so far goes something like the following, (and you'll need to bear with me because it comes in the form of a slightly extended metaphor).

One of my relatively few "rock star purchases" back in the early days was a rather splendid burgundy-coloured Rolls Royce, Mulliner Park Ward, drop-head coupé. The car was undoubtedly a thing of elegant style and eye-catching beauty, and whenever we took it out for a spin in the sunshine, passers-by would attempt to peer inside, probably expecting to see a liveried chauffeur transporting a Hollywood star or a cigar-smoking movie-mogul. Car-afficionados would watch and wait patiently as I negotiated the twelve-point turn which was usually necessary to install the Roller safely in a space in a car-park and would then feel free to engage me in conversation about aspects of its performance which were well beyond my competence or expertise to discuss.

Rolls Royce Mulliner Park Ward 'Chinese Eye' Coupé

With all its quality, appeal and attraction, the Rolls-Royce literally weighed a ton and had a very light steering wheel which caused it to roll around like a lilo in a swimming pool, which was not good for small children who became instantly car sick. In short, it was completely unsuitable as an everyday family vehicle. As a result, it spent most of its life hidden under a tarpaulin in the garage, only to be allowed out on special occasions. The car carried a famous brand name, it was sleek, stylish, and smooth, and undoubtedly in its own way it was iconic. It was a treat to take out, and whenever I did, it was admired and enjoyed by everyone who experienced it. Eventually though, the time would come when it needed to go back into the garage and once again be covered by the tarpaulin to keep it well-preserved and in good order, ready for the next outing.

I guess you can see where this is going. There was something about that Roller which felt to me to be a bit like Roxy Music. Eye-catching, stylish, and high quality, extremely enjoyable and I was proud to be associated with it. From time to time, it would be an absolute joy to take out for a ride so that it could be admired and appreciated; but the 'steering' difficulties and the resultant discomfort meant that its outings were strictly limited. After a while it had to go back under the tarpaulin so I could live my everyday life in my run-around.

FIFTEEN

The Gilmour Years

Claire and I were married on 7 May 2005 at Leatherhead Registry office and the reception was at the RAC Club in Epsom. It was a very happy day, attended by family and friends, including Robert Wyatt and Alfie Benge, David Gilmour and Polly Samson, Andy and Lucinda Mackay and Paul Thompson from Roxy. Bryan sent us a very generous wedding gift.

Since the sale of St Ann's Court, Claire and I had been living in what was by now our very cool New York loft-style apartment in Queen's Park and in a rented cottage on a farm in West Sussex, but we were on the lookout for somewhere of our own in the area. Claire saw an ad in the local paper for a house in a West Sussex village which sounded ideal for us, so we

Phil and David in the Barn

went ahead and bought it. It wasn't until later that we discovered we were a ten-minute drive away from Bryan's place in the country, just a stone's throw from Mike and Angie Rutherford, and that our nearest neighbours were none other than David Gilmour and Polly Samson. By sheer chance we had landed in what a friend drolly described as 'The Malibu of Sussex'.

Three years earlier Claire had been asked to handle the public relations for David Gilmour's concerts at the Royal Festival Hall. The event reunited David with the Pink Floyd keyboard player Richard Wright, and included contributions from Bob Geldof and from our mutual friend Robert Wyatt. The set-list consisted of a number of Pink Floyd tracks, along with some of David's solo numbers and some of Syd Barrett's. Even with all his years of playing to packed stadiums all around the world, the event was a big deal for David. It had been his first live gig for many years, and later he was quoted as saying, "I can show you places where the nerves are there. At the beginning of 'Shine On You Crazy Diamond', there's a closeup of me doing a vibrato on the acoustic guitar which is more than I'd ever intended. That was due to trembling." Despite all his misgivings, the event was a remarkable success and the press coverage had exceeded anyone's expectations.

David, Polly, Claire and I started hanging out together as friends and neighbours, and he and I undoubtedly spent a lot of time talking about music. He had accumulated quite literally hundreds of snippets of ideas for new sounds and melodies, maybe consisting of a particular effect or a short but interesting guitar riff. He always carried a tiny tape recorder, something like a dictation machine, and had myriads of bits and pieces stored away in no particular order. We were talking about these one day when I found myself offering to listen to his tapes to see if anything could be made out of them. He agreed, and before long I was listening to acres of David's guitar noodling that he'd recorded over a period of about ten years.

If I'm allowed to say it myself, this is something I'm good at. Methodically I organised and catalogued them into what turned out to be a total of 170 identifiable and potentially useable pieces. I found that I could listen to, say, piece 73, and know by instinct that it might readily fit together with piece 130. Then there could be a change of pace and tempo, maybe a key change, and we could bring in piece 52.

Taking all these individual snippets, I then went into my studio and began assembling the jigsaw. Some pieces would be sped up, others might be slowed down or reversed, and after working away at this on and off for several weeks, I eventually went back to see David and played him my work in progress. He listened for a while and then asked, "what is this we're listening to?"

"It's your stuff," I told him. "Built up from the bits and pieces of music you gave me."

He liked what he'd heard and immediately could see the potential, and so over another few weeks I further refined the sequences, and then added and mixed in accompanying bass, drums, and keyboards, all produced from my studio, so that together we could get a better idea of what an eventual album might sound like.

All this time I was only too aware, as was David, that the stakes were very high. One thing we know for sure about Pink Floyd fans is that many are close to fanatical, and after twelve years since *Division Bell* without a new album from their favourite guitar hero, expectations would be in the stratosphere. I knew we would need a theme or approach which felt rooted in the music they all loved, but also provided some significant development appropriate to the interval since the last albums.

I had of course been in the audience at the earlier Festival Hall concerts and felt that they'd been quite acoustic; putting me in mind in some ways of a performance by an English chamber orchestra. The audience had clearly loved the approach, and so I was keeping all this in my thoughts as we headed towards a recording. We managed to get some of that feeling in as the production progressed, but it's fair to say that it's scarcely identifiable in the final album.

Our next step was to head down to David's magnificent floating recording studio on the 1911 houseboat Astoria, which is moored near to Hampton Court. The vessel itself is a thing of absolute beauty, having once been owned by Charlie Chaplin's manager Fred Karno, who designed an open roof to accommodate a ninety piece orchestra. It's a fabulous environment for recording and is where David has produced some of his very best work.

I hadn't fully realised at that time that David usually doesn't write his own lyrics. Just as used to happen when we were composing with Bryan in Roxy Music, David delivers the music track to Polly, and she takes it away and eventually comes back with fantastic words for him to sing. Polly, a published and respected author, wrote the lyrics to seven of the eleven tracks on *Division Bell*, and was given grudging respect by many Pink Floyd fans. They are a brilliant writing team, in which she manages to put into words exactly what he wants to say with the music.

The excitement increased as the project developed and David, Polly, Claire, and I sat around their kitchen table on countless evenings plotting and strategizing the approach to the eventual release of the album. One of the constant subjects for debate at the time was the relative merit of analogue versus digital recording, and so important did we all think it was to make this as good as we could, that we decided to record on both. As it happened, we had old analogue machines at both Astoria and at Gallery Studios, but the only problem was there was no analogue tape to be found, and no-one was producing it anymore. Eventually someone discovered what we believed to be the last stash of it anywhere in the world in Holland, and so David bought up the entire supply and shipped it over.

Having been so immersed in all the ingredients for so long, I felt perfectly capable of mixing the recording, but after twenty-two years since his last solo album, David was keen to leave nothing to chance. So he decided to bring in Chris Thomas, whose many credits included *Dark Side of the Moon* as well as four Roxy Music albums. I was fine with this as Chris is a great mate of mine and we have a long shared history.

When we came to the point of choosing whether to proceed with analogue or digital, we decided to set ourselves a blind test. We would listen to both versions, declare which we thought was which, and then indicate a preference. We carried out the experiment in strictly controlled conditions, and I was the first to admit that I couldn't be sure which was analogue and which was digital; however I chose the second one as my preferred option, which turned out to be the digital. Chris and David claimed to be able to tell the difference; they were both correct and also preferred the digital – so that's the way we went, never to use analogue again.

We brought in the celebrated but rather volatile Polish film composer Zbigniew Preisner to write and arrange the orchestral parts, and we went into Abbey Road studios where the flamboyant and impressive Robert Ziegler was the conductor. After that we went to Mark Knopfler's British Grove studio to take advantage of the ex-Abbey Road mixing desks they'd acquired. See what I mean by leaving nothing to chance?

Finally, one of the great things about working with David is that of course he can invite anyone he wants to work on his albums, and they're very happy to oblige. So, we enjoyed the talent and the company of Jools Holland, David Crosby, Graham Nash, and Georgie Fame. Guy Pratt played bass and John Carin shared keyboard parts with Richard Wright.

It had never been envisaged that I'd play on the final recordings; I considered David a great friend and more than anything else I just wanted to help him to succeed with the album. In the event I did record some second guitar just to help out, but mostly I simply felt proud of having played a key role in the production.

The *On an Island* album was eventually released on 6 March 2006, which was David's 60th birthday, and it turned out to be the best possible birthday present because it went straight into the UK charts at number one and was his first chart-topping solo album. It was released in the US the following day where it eventually peaked at number six, and it went to number one in the European chart and number two in Canada. In short, it was a critical and commercial success.

The only downside of having such a star-studded cast recording the album comes when you plan to tour, because not everyone involved can or wants to go along for a massive odyssey across the UK, Europe, and America. David was quite diffident when he asked me if I fancied playing second guitar because, he said, "I know you are your own satellite." I wasn't immediately sure, but the first leg of the tour was scheduled round the Gilmour children's school holidays so I reckoned the commitment would be relatively short and sweet. I also knew that Richard Wright had agreed to play and so the whole thing would be likely to be good fun. The clincher was that Claire would be on the tour as travelling publicist, so it would be very much a family affair.

Though I didn't at all mind being the supporting 'fiddle' to David's brilliant guitar on stage, session playing doesn't come naturally to me; to have to play exactly the same parts, on exactly the guitars that David

REVOLUCIÓN TO ROXY

The Gilmour years

had originally used, with total precision night after night. It's just not my style. Obviously, for example, the audience wanted to hear old favourites such as *Wish You Were Here*, and just about everybody who has ever picked up a guitar can play a version of the memorable and iconic opening riff on a twelve-string, but I was damned if I could play it exactly as David had played it originally. I remember sitting in his kitchen while he tried to show me. David has wide and muscular fingers developed through a lifetime of huge and precise string bending, while mine are longer and thinner. Can you imagine the pressure to get that opening sequence perfect, especially as there was no lighting on me during that opening riff and those twelve strings are very close together. Of course I loved playing it, but at the same time it was pretty stressful.

It was a privilege to be able to spend time with Richard Wright, and of course we weren't to know just how precious that time would be. He was now free from the complications arising from all the bullshit with Roger and seemed to thrive in his on-stage relationship with David. Their interplay while performing *Echoes* was a rare opportunity on stage to let things flow a bit more naturally and led to some truly wonderful live recordings. Richard was a lovely, modest, original, and slightly eccentric guy. Very much his own man, and Claire made it her special mission to ensure that his role received appropriate recognition.

Notwithstanding any reservations about being essentially a sideman, I enjoyed much of the tour, which had more than its share of memorable moments and a lot of laughter and banter. Invariably we would all congregate in the band dressing room, and there was strong sense of camaraderie as everyone tucked into my egg sandwiches. One extra special night will always stick in my mind when we were due to play the Royal Albert Hall and there was to be a surprise appearance by one of my all-time heroes, David Bowie.

Ever since I'd first met him at the Greyhound pub all those years before, it had always felt just a bit special to be in his company, always with a big and infectious smile and a twinkle in his distinctive heterochromatic eyes. There was great excitement when he turned up in the afternoon to rehearse and sound-check, in the course of which he asked, "can I get a bit more of Phil in my monitors?" and added, "you can never get enough of Phil." A small thing in the great scheme of things, but I will always treasure that, and the sentiment behind it.

Rick made great efforts to show David how to sing *Comfortably Numb* in the way he was singing it on the tour. David listened respectfully, but when he came on stage that night and the surprised crowd went wild, he gave a rendering of their favourite song which took the collective breath away. He took an iconic number and made it entirely his own, as only a genuine artist can ever do. Looking back at the recording of the concert, you can see by the looks exchanged between Guy Pratt and me, and by the expression on David Gilmour's face, that we all knew we were witnessing something magical. We were also joined on stage that night by David Crosby and Graham Nash, and there was a very rare live appearance by Robert Wyatt. It was the first and last time I got to appear on stage with

David Gilmour's Royal Albert Hall Concert with my 'Heroes', London June 2016

David Bowie, and none of us could have known that tragically that would be his very last performance in the UK.

Then of course there was our attempt to play in Venice. Our concerts in August 2006 were set to be the first live performances by a rock band ever to take place in the unique and magnificent setting of St Mark's Square. The stage was set up at the far end of the piazza, facing the cathedral, but all the time we were doing our sound check in the afternoon we were aware of riggers still running around, scratching their heads, and looking concerned. As soon as we came off stage, someone told us that the roof had been declared unsafe and the concerts would have to be postponed for a week. So we all headed back to London for seven days, during which it must have rained torrentially, because by the time we got back the square was flooded. We performed the concerts over two nights in the pouring rain, and I found myself wondering whether the patron saints of Venice, Theodore and Mark, were trying to tell us something.

The climax of the European tour was our appearance at the shipyard at Gdansk in Poland where 50,000 people, including the legendary trade union leader and former president Lech Walesa, turned out to celebrate the founding of the Solidarity movement. This was my second encounter with the extraordinary pianist Leszek Mozdzer who joined us at the event, and with whom I formed an instant friendship which would endure for many years. On that night only we played *A Great Day for Freedom* from the *Division Bell* album, which David hadn't performed since his semi-acoustic shows in 2002. Our rendering of *Echoes* lasted half an hour, with the interplay particularly between David and Rick reaching sensational heights and lasting twenty-three minutes.

One day shortly after the tour was over, David called me up and asked if I would be interested in mixing the recording from the Gdansk show and versions of tracks from the other concerts as extras for a live album.

"That sounds like good fun," I said, "when do we start?"

"No you don't understand, *we* aren't starting," he said, "I won't be turning up."

I was confused. "You mean you'd like me to do this on my own?"

"Yes please," he said, "and I'm looking forward to hearing it."

Because I had been so invested in the tour and had thoroughly enjoyed it, I agreed to listen to no less than thirty-two hours of our recordings, and to compile the best takes for the album *David Gilmour, Live in Gdansk*, which was eventually released as a standard edition, a three-disc edition, a four-disc edition, a deluxe edition, a vinyl edition and an iTunes edition. I think that's what's known as "waste not want not".

SIXTEEN

Going Solo

I don't consider what I do as 'work' in the traditional meaning of that word. Certainly there are times when there's a lot of graft and attention to detail, but the joy of working with talented musicians and vocalists makes what I have done and do a real pleasure. To have made a living out of music for over fifty years is a privilege, a miracle and I count myself very lucky indeed. I love the great sense of camaraderie when you're all focused on making the best of a piece of music and trying to create something exceptional for the listener.

I think this desire for camaraderie goes back to my early childhood, before I went to school in the UK, when I felt almost like an only child. I wanted to go to boarding school to make more friends and I did. I enjoyed being in sports teams, and being in a band was an extension of this collective endeavour, but with the focus on making music with friends.

Leaving school, it was important for me to maintain these friendships, which I did with Bill Mac and Charles Hayward. I've said elsewhere that Roxy Music felt from the outset like more than the sum of its parts, and there's no doubt that when everybody is on their best game and the muse is with you, it can be possible for a group of like-minded musicians to conjure up magic.

That said, it's also true that being in a band of supposed equals inevitably involves some element of compromise with fellow band members and after a while this can feel restricting: sometimes you just simply want your own way. The refrain, 'great idea Phil, but save it for your solo album', could often be heard echoing round the control room. So I did; in ten solo albums and counting. An example was the time, when I was living at St Ann's Court but hadn't yet built Gallery Studios, and was working on my album K Scope. My friend John Wetton knew a fellow bass player from Yes called Chris Squire, who lived ten minutes away and had his own studio beneath the living room of a large, thatched house he owned on the Wentworth estate. It was called Sun Park and was a lovely facility, except that the noise leaking into the house above must have been alarming. Chris was a slightly larger than life person, generous and lovely and very "rock'n roll" and when I asked him if I could use the place he said, "sure, man".

Getting the musicians together was an opportunity for a reunion with some of my favourite people, and I asked old school-mates Bill and Ian MacCormick to get involved. Simon Phillips and Paul Thompson played drums, John Wetton was on bass, and Kevin Godley and Lol Creme provided some backing vocals. My friends Tim and Neil Finn, and Eddie Rayner from Split Enz had been trying to break through in London for a couple of years, and by now were struggling financially and unable to get the money together for the fare home. As it turned out, their fees for session work on the album were enough to get them back to Australia, and the rest is very highly successful pop history. This album, which I called *K Scope*, was never going to be a great hit, but it gave me the means to continue making my own music alongside my work with Roxy, which was important to me. A long way down the line, *K Scope* would crop up once again in very happy circumstances, of which more later.

My commitments to Roxy Music then took over my life again and for the next three years I had no opportunity for more solo work, but by the time I was ready to record my next album, Gallery Studios had been built. I decided I wanted to make an entirely instrumental album and would 'do a Mike Oldfield', playing all the instruments myself. We were recording the *Avalon* album with Roxy at the same time, which was of course terrific in so many ways, but which gave me no real opportunity to let rip with my guitar as I'd loved doing in the early days. It was about serving the song. I wanted my album to be entirely instrumental, focusing on my style of guitar playing, which I thought was best described as "primitive", so I called the album *Primitive Guitars*.

As things worked out, the solo album was released at the same time as *Avalon* and so I was keen to discover whether any of the music press would notice the coincidence. Roxy Music was touring Australia at the time and I was in the airport in Sydney when I spotted a copy of Rolling Stone magazine on a news-stand. The famous RS writer Kurt Loder gave *Avalon* a four-star rating, and I was delighted that his article included a review of *Primitive Guitars*, in which he perceptively noted that 'guitarist Phil Manzanera is poorly utilized on *Avalon*, at times he sounds like he is walking through his parts, perhaps he saved his inspiration for his own album *Primitive Guitars*'. Thank you, Kurt, I remember thinking, you're spot on. I kept the magazine to myself and didn't share a word of it with Bryan or Andy.

By the time Roxy had stopped working together in 1983 I felt it was time to embark on some more solo work, and once again I decided to look to my South American roots for inspiration. I was still collaborating on writing lyrics with the MacCormick brothers, and I was lucky that, ten years after we had last worked together, Tim Finn was also passing through the UK. I managed to get the four of us together so I could explain something about my own musical roots, and to share my thoughts about what I wanted the album to be about. In the end the music was a cross between Latin and rock, and it was Ian who had the idea to call the album *Southern Cross*, which was a clever wordplay based on the astronomical connection between the two musical genres.

The words of *A Million Reasons Why* reveal more than a glimpse of my state of mind at that particular time.

Can't feed the world on greed and power.
Dictators changing by the hour

A voice of freedom goes to jail
The politicians feed corruption
As people disappear by the gun
It's up to us to tell the tale.

The themes of each of the songs reflect a different aspect of my life up to that point; for example there's a track called *Fidel* which tells the story of one of my most vivid and traumatic experiences as a 6 year old in Cuba.

A child is awake, he watches in silence
A truckload of soldiers pulls up in the night
A man makes a run – he's shot in the back
A child takes a snapshot and shivers inside.

Tim's special contribution to the album was the bossa nova *Astrud* and the brilliant *Venceremos*. I even did a version of *Guantanamera*, which is perhaps the most quintessentially Cuban song of all time, and we especially pleased my mum by sticking to the original lyrics by the 19th century poet and liberator of Cuba, José Martí.

By the time we got to the end of the 90s, all that had been a while ago, and now I was feeling at a strange and slightly unstable period of my life. Both of my parents had long since passed away, my marriage had split, there had been lengthy and sometimes acrimonious divisions with Roxy, and one way and another I was feeling in need of some help. The best thing about my life was (and is) Claire, and when she suggested that I should get some therapy to try to sort out a few things in my head, it felt like good advice and proved to be invaluable. Now it was time for me to write and sing about how I felt.

I started writing what turned into a series of what I **call my** "white albums", so named because the covers were all white other than the title logos. The first was *Vozero* which is a word I made up on the basis that it sounded a bit Latin and had something to do with the voice and speaking out. Later again I got some of my greatest friends together to record an album which we called *6PM*, for the very good reason that (if we include Diamond Head) it was my sixth solo adventure. Once again Brian Eno,

Robert Wyatt, Andy Mackay, and Paul Thompson played on some tracks, and Enrique Bunbury of Héroes del Silencio contributed vocals. David Gilmour also helped out on guitar, which in turn planted more of the seeds which would grow into our long-standing and productive collaborations. And then two years after that I recorded *50 Minutes Later* for the blindingly obvious reason it was just about fifty minutes long: I don't tend to overthink the titles of my albums.

Each of the tracks was in some way a reflection of what was going around in my head about my life and situation. One example was called *Tuesday* because my mum had always believed that every important thing that ever happened to her happened on that day of the week. *Rayo De Bala* is more about the gun battle I'd witnessed as a small boy growing up in Havana. I managed to persuade Claire to sing the lead vocals on a song called *Hymn* which is about my dad, and *Desaparecido* is a song about anger and despair. Equally autobiographical are the words I wrote for the song *Technicolor UFO*.

6pm phil manzanera

6PM album

vozero phil manzanera

Vozero album

50 minutes later phil manzanera

50 minutes Later album

There's Kevin Ayers
Sitting in a corner
Singing from the bottom of a well
Robert Ellidge pouring the drinks
And I must say that he's looking swell
Captain Beefheart's sweeping the floor
Pickin' up the bottles and the butts
Bill and Ian toking in the corner
Two Brians standing at the jukebox

Meanwhile anyone trying to track the progress of my mental state through the album, might be relieved by the much more sanguine place I'd arrived at by the time I wrote the words for *That's All I Know*.

Let's put another log
On the Meadow fire
And feel the warmth
Of love surrounding us
And in the morning
When we see the robin fly
We'll look up to the
Ever changing sky

Whatever anyone may think are the merits or otherwise of my home-grown lyrics, what can be said for sure is that they accurately summed up how and what I was feeling at the time and, as "the little sparrow" Edith Piaf memorably put it, "je ne regrette rien". I also realised that the words were so personal that I couldn't have asked anyone else to sing them. I don't doubt that getting them out there was cathartic, and part of what turned out to be a successful process of reconciliation with myself. Having written them, and having expressed them with my own voice, I feel absolutely no need to write or sing any of my own words in the future: I've said what I've got to say in that way, sung it, and it was time to move on. To quote Joséé Martí: 'Hechar mis versos al aire,' (to release my verses into the air.)

SEVENTEEN

Endless River

When Richard Wright died in September 2008, all of us who knew him were devastated, feeling the loss of a rare talent and valued friend. David correctly declared that it would be wrong to try to continue with Pink Floyd without him, but nonetheless was looking for an appropriate way to pay tribute to his work, and finally to tie up the loose ends of the band. Once again we were standing in his kitchen when he said something like, "When Rick, Nick and I were working on *The Division Bell*, we did a lot of jamming together which we've recorded … maybe you'd like to have a listen and see if anything could be made of it?" David told me that Andy Jackson, who'd worked as an engineer for Floyd since 1980, had done something similar with the same material some while before, and suggested that I should speak to him. I did, but I wanted to avoid listening to anything he'd produced for fear that I might subconsciously borrow his ideas.

Over the following six weeks I found myself listening to hours upon hours of recordings, finding some of it unremarkable, but occasionally coming across moments of genius which stood out from everything

Trophies

else. I resurrected my process of separating, numbering, and cataloguing individual fragments, hoping to get some inspiration about how they might work as a cogent album. I made copious notes itemising the issues: what was the real essence of a Pink Floyd album? What did I like about Richard's playing? What did I like about David's playing? How could this all come together with Nick's drums in a way which would satisfy David's ambitions as well as the expectations of the loyal audience?

Wishing to immerse myself still further in the task, I sat down and listened carefully once again to the entire Pink Floyd oeuvre; this was going to be the last ever Pink Floyd album, and so we would need to be certain that we had the right material within these largely ad hoc recordings to be able to build something which would live up to the legacy.

Eventually my thoughts developed into a structure with four movements along the lines of a classical composition, with returning themes and echoes featuring riffs and sequences which the three men had produced while jamming. I even drew a storyboard to represent a sort of narrative, which I didn't eventually have the nerve to show to anyone other than Claire.

When I had eventually put together something I was ready to play to David, he said, "I think there's something there. You should play it to Nick to see what he thinks."

"I'm not playing it to Nick," I said, "you should do it."

"I'm not playing it to Nick," he said, "but he needs to hear it."

The truth was that I wasn't keen to play the recordings to Nick for the simple reason that there was hardly anything recognisable as his original

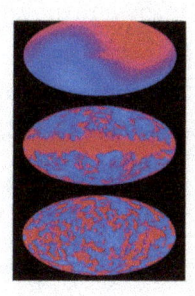

ENDLESS RIVER

ASTORIA PARTS 1,2,3,4

SUSPEND ALL DISBELIEF

Brief was to create the ultimate' Pink Floyd ambient album out of the 20 hours of jamming at Astoria,Olympic and Britannia Row that occurred in 1991prior to recording Division Bell.

In order to make sense of this, and select what I wanted to use from the above, I decided to create 4 x 12 minute approx parts with a visual narrative that in my mind would help me to create the different soundscapes.

ASTORIA Parts 1,2,3,4

Intro 45seconds
Imagine the night sky with a multitude of stars or dots and one of these dots is heading towards Earth, this one dot represents cosmic background radiation, which is electromagnetic radiation with no discernible source. Its discovery is considered one of the major confirmations of the big bang theory and this radiation is present in everything. Dee then calculated that this radiation wave expressed as a tone would be b7.

Part 3   12 minutes
They arrive on an Acoustic, Blakeian planet, a bit like Danny Boyle's set for the opening ceremony, which is very British Pastoral, full of streams, birds, and Granchester Meadows and High Hopes church bells. Full of 12string acoustic guitars and English folk romps.

Part 4   12 minutes
Leaving the previous Planet they head off through the PF world of the 90's back in time to Dark side period ending on a wistful blues-like jam ,off into space ,with a reverse of the intro ending in the cosmic background radiation having examined a moment in time.

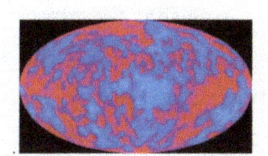

Part 1   12 minutes

An ebow and keyboard, almost a classical piece, where DG and Rick channel Vaughan Williams, in the context of the cosmic sounds which occur randomly.

Part 2   12 minutes
At this point the cosmos sounds reappear and Astoria seems to take off into space (stick with me} Must be listened to watching the star screen saver above the Neve desk) .With the DG, Nick and Rick crew off to explore the interstellar world, channelling Live at Pompeii, the middle section of Echoes and Saucerful of Secrets. It finally resolves with an almost hymn- like piece, which leads to part 3.

Endless River Idea

217

drumming in the mix, and I thought he might well be unhappy. I'd taken a few of his phrases and fragments, but once again they'd been sped up or slowed down or looped, supplemented, or replaced. It was with some considerable trepidation that I eventually invited Nick to my studio. Unable to countenance the idea of watching him while he listened, I decided to turn down the lights and I put a Floyd-style screensaver on the monitor so we could listen together in darkness.

I did. We did. And eventually he said, "I think we might have something there", and went to ask his manager Tony Smith to speak to David's manager Paul Loasby to discuss how the album might come to fruition. We were one step closer. Nick's other suggestion at the time was that we should meet the Wachowski brothers – who latterly became the Wachowski sisters – to see if they would be interested in using some of the music for their next film. The pair had made a name for themselves with their work on futuristic movies such as The Matrix, so we all trooped off to Pinewood where they were currently working, but for one reason or another the idea came to nothing, which might be just as well because their next venture after that was a flop.

After that, everything went quiet for something like nine months, during which time I was getting on with my various collaborations in Europe and South America. Later I heard that David had played the work in progress to Youth (stage name of bass guitarist from Killing Joke, Martin Glover) who loved it.

"Why don't we get you, me, Nick and Youth down to the studio in Brighton to see if we can finish it off like a band?" said David, and so we brought Andy Jackson back as engineer and got to work. Nick came in and played drums, which were great, and he'd lost none of what Robert Wyatt describes as his unique Pink Floyd timing. All the while we had in our minds that the album could be a fitting tribute to Rick, a sort of goodbye and 'that's it' from Pink Floyd. In the event only one song on the album would not be an instrumental. Polly wrote poignant lyrics to the track *Louder Than Words*, and as usual she captured the essence of the band.

We bitch and we fight
Diss each other on sight
But this thing that we do
These times together
Rain or shine or stormy weather
This thing we do
With word-weary grace
We've taken our places
We could curse it or nurse it or give it a name
Or stay at home by the fire, felled by desire
Stoking the flame
But we're here for the ride.

Writing in Rolling Stone, David Fricke said that: "Wright was the steady, binding majesty in the Floyd's explorations. This album is an unexpected, welcome epitaph," while The Observer called the album, "an understated affair but unmistakably the Floyd .. a pretty good way to call it a day," which felt about right. I'd loved working with David, Polly, and the team, and was proud to have co-producer credits on albums by David Gilmour and Pink Floyd.

EIGHTEEN

A Rainbow With a Pot of Gold

One of the many great things about being in the music industry is that you never know what's going to happen next. One minute the sun is shining bright and all is well with the world, and then suddenly a huge black cloud looms and drenches you. In an amongst it all, occasionally a rainbow might appear.

One such rainbow came out for me on a wet afternoon in March 2012 when I was driving up the Harrow Road with my son Charlie. We'd just passed Sainsbury's when the phone rang from an unknown number and the voice that followed had a strong New York accent.

"Hello is that Phil Manzanera?" I hesitated, but then confirmed that it was. "It's Roc-A-Fella Records, New York here," he said. "I'm calling

Watch the Throne Jay Z and Kanye West

to let you know that Jay Z and Kanye West have sampled one of your guitar riffs on an album they've been working on together, and it's due to be released next week."

"It's nice of you to call," I said, "but I'm afraid I think you've made a mistake. I'm sometimes confused with Ray Manzarek who's from The Doors. I think you probably mean him."

There was a pause and a Transatlantic shuffling of paper.

"There's no mistake Mr. Manzanera," drawled the voice on the line. "Obviously I can't send you the track before it's released, but if you like I can play it down the phone and you can see if you recognise it."

By this time, I had sufficiently taken control of my wits to indicate to Charlie that he should start recording it on his phone. The track played for a few seconds and then stopped.

"Well that certainly sounds as though it could be me," I said. "Maybe someone has slowed it down a bit?" He wasn't sure if it had been slowed down, or of very much else for that matter. "That's very nice,' I said, and ended the call.

When Charlie and I got back to my studio, we played the track again from his recording and certainly there was something about it that sounded familiar. It was a brief sequence of maybe twenty notes, and eventually I recognised the riff as one I'd included on the solo album I'd released in 1976 called K-Scope. Delving as deep as I knew how into the furthest recesses of my memory, I vaguely recalled being near the end of recording and at a loss for something new to play. One evening I'd been sitting on the sofa and noodling with my guitar when I came across this riff which I quite liked. I played it only a few times, recorded it in the studio the next day, and then forgot all about it.

Now I was confused. The man had said that the track was due to be released the following week. Didn't someone need to ask my permission? You could say that my knowledge of the music and work of Jay Z and Kanye West is not encyclopedic, and this was way before what at the time of writing I take to be Kanye's very public mental breakdown, but suppose they had used my riff alongside words of the "smack my bitch up" variety, which I certainly wouldn't agree to?

I called the Business Affairs people at Virgin and spoke to an executive. I told her about the phone call from Roc-A-Fella Records and asked if she knew anything about it.

"Oh yes we know about it," she said cheerfully, "we've been discussing it with them for weeks."

"Are you allowed to do this?" I asked. "Don't you need my permission?"

"Well no actually we don't because we own the copyright," came the response, "but I think you'll be happy with the outcome." She went on to explain that they had negotiated a division of the royalties resulting from sales of the track, and that my share would be one-third. "Actually," she continued, "I think you'll probably earn more from it than either Jay Z or Kanye West."

While I wasn't too thrilled to discover that I had no say in the matter of who used my music, or how they reproduced it, I did feel that receiving a healthy share of the resulting revenue was some sort of consolation. I said goodbye, but then a moment later I realised that not only had I played the riff, but I'd also written it – so wasn't I also entitled to a share of the publishing revenues? I then called Universal, who handled my publishing, and told them all about the phone call.

"Oh yes we know all about that," came the matter of fact response, "we've been speaking to them about it for weeks."

"Without bothering to mention it to me?"

Ignoring my apparent naivety, he once again confirmed that they didn't need my permission. "But I think you'll be happy with the outcome," he said, and went on to tell me that they had negotiated a one-third share of the publishing revenue. "And as a matter of fact, you'll probably earn more from this than either Jay Z or Kanye West."

One week later, the album *Watch the Throne* was released. It was the first joint album between Jay Z and Kanye West so was hugely hyped. *No Church in the Wild* was the first track, with my guitar riff playing throughout the whole song and included vocals by Frank Ocean and The-Dream. The album went gold in the UK and Italy, and platinum in the United States and Denmark. It was used in the trailer and in a scene in the film *The Great Gatsby*, was in an advertisement for Audi cars, and in another TV ad for Dodge Dart which ran in the half-time break of the Superbowl.

Who knew that I would earn more money from a short guitar riff that I wrote one evening on a sofa in front of the telly in 1978 than I ever earned in the entire fifty years as a member of Roxy Music? Thank you, Kanye West, thank you Jay Z, thank you Virgin and Universal, and thank you to the capricious mistress that is rock and roll.

But the irony was that I couldn't work out how to play it! I played the track to David Gilmour, but neither he nor I could figure it out. Then finally Claire's nephew Toby worked out the fingering and talked me through it. The original sequence is in E flat which is damn-near impossible to play. It's just a bit easier in the key of A, but even then, it's a stretch.

While still basking in the warm glow of my potential good fortune, I was curious to discover how it had come about, and so I embarked on my education about a whole industry in which people listen to different types of music, from every different genre, from every different era, and on every kind of medium. They're looking for sequences which can be recorded, mixed and manipulated for use as "beats" or samples which provide the background sounds for the words written by rappers.

Delving still further into the origins of this particular piece of luck, I discovered that there was a man who went to school with Kanye West, and who specialised in listening out for sequences to sample from music recorded on vinyl in 1975-1979. Niche or what? His moniker is 88-Keys – so-named, of course, after the number of keys on a piano. One day in 2011, 88-Keys had been running around town, busy with a lot of errands, when he took a call from his friend Kanye. He was holed up with Jay Z in a huge suite in The Mercer Hotel in New York, and they were at a loss for new beats; did he have anything?

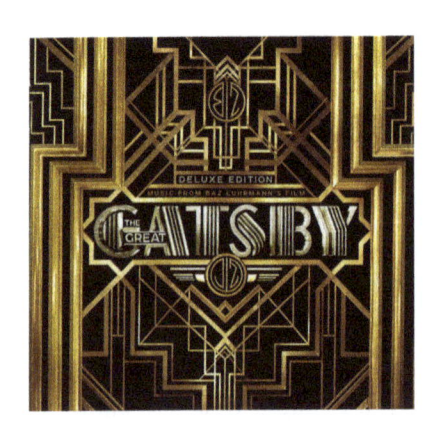

The Great Gatsby film

"No man, and I'm running late to get back to my wife, rushing around town with loads of stuff I have to get done."

"Come on man," said Kanye. "We're desperate. We've nearly finished the album and we just need one more beat."

"But I just don't have anything, and even if I did I don't have time to come over."

I'll spare you more of the imaginary details of the conversations they may have had. Suffice to say that 88-Keys was persuaded to abandon his chores and hightail it over to the hotel where Kanye and Jay Z were waiting. One version of the story has it that 88-Keys had just five brief samples; another says it was twenty. In any event, he played what he had, the two rappers loved mine, and with that the dark clouds in the sky parted and the rainbow appeared, leading to a 'pot full of gold discs.'

Some while later I was in New York and due to play at Radio City with David Gilmour, when it occurred to me how nice it would be to meet 88-Keys and thank him personally. When word reached Mr Keys, it transpired that he had never heard of Pink Floyd or David Gilmour, so he tweeted all his friends and Kanye that he was off to meet Phil Manzanera who was playing at Radio City. I had to quickly disabuse him of the idea that I was the main attraction, but nevertheless this friendly guy with dreads came along to the concert that evening. He was a real force of nature who didn't seem to mind being surrounded by thousands of hard core Gilmour fans. 88-Keys came backstage after the show, we all shook his hand and had a drink together, and I signed his vinyl copy of my album *K-Scope*. We congratulated each other on a very successful and lucrative collaboration.

NINETEEN

Pizzica in Puglia

"Two minutes to on-air Phil ... 90 seconds ... 60 seconds ... oh, oh – just a minute Phil – we have a problem."

It's 8th August 2015 and I'm standing on a stage with my black Fender Strat' slung over my shoulder. I'm looking out over a sea of heads stretching as far as the eye can see and beyond. An estimated 200,000 people have been waiting in the ferocious heat for several hours, and the "on-air" that is about to begin is a programme lasting four hours and transmitting live on Italy's primary TV channel, RAI Uno. The show will consist of performances from dozens of fabulous musicians and dancers, including some of the most famous stars in the whole of Italy,

Notte della Taranta soundcheck
Melpignano Italy

but the opening flourish consists of some solo notes played by myself. Except that we have one of those "Houston we have a problem" moments which stops the heart. The next words I hear through my earpiece make my blood run cold.

"We've lost sound from Phil's guitar."

I tentatively pluck the bottom E string and sure enough, I can't hear a thing. So now it feels as though every TV camera in the Northern Hemisphere is pointing directly at me, and when the red light goes on in just a few seconds from now, what am I going to do? My fluency in Spanish enables me to get by in some areas of Italy, but we are in Puglia where the local dialect, Grikos, is unique, and I've been compelled to use the services of an interpreter to organise and rehearse the show. If my guitar doesn't start working soon, I won't even be able to welcome the audience in words they'll comprehend.

"Twenty seconds ... fifteen ... ten, nine, eight, seven ... it's OK Phil. We're back on."

The first notes ring out over the crowd, other musicians join in, the singers begin to sing their beautiful song, and I can breathe again.

200,000 punters at Notte

It's seven months since my phone rang, just before Christmas, and it was Brian Eno's brother-in-law Dominic. He proceeded to talk to me about a massive project coming up in Italy. I'm afraid I was immediately slightly suspicious.

"This isn't something Brian has been offered and turned down is it?"

He assured me that it wasn't and went on to tell me about an annual festival which takes place in Puglia and is all about celebrating pizzica, which is a particular style of folk music unique to the region. The occasion has the dramatic name *La Notte della Taranta* and is a free open-air concert which is also televised live. Each year they have a different highly distinguished musical director, and next year they'd like it to be me.

"I love the idea," I said, "but I don't know the first thing about pizzica music."

"That's all to the good," said Dominic, "because they would like you to completely re-imagine pizzica, and produce and present a whole new version of it taking into account the original field recordings of Alan Lomax done in the 1950s."

Over the following days I discovered that Alan Lomax was born in Texas in 1915 and had made an extraordinary career as an ethnomusicologist. He made it his business to track down folk and blues musicians from the widest possible range of different communities, and to record their work for posterity. He had an amazing life and is well worth looking up, but in a nutshell, he managed to get around much of America, England, Spain and Italy, recording, preserving and publishing singers and musicians whose work would otherwise never have been made popular. Among those he's credited for bringing to a wider audience are Robert Johnson, Woody Guthrie, Pete Seeger, and Lead Belly. He made no money himself and was forced out of the United States by the McCarthyite witch-hunts of suspected communists when he came to England and began working for the BBC. From here he was sent to Spain and Italy, where he made a series of field recordings of the pizzica music of Puglia.

The proposal was that I would produce the event taking place the following August, somehow bringing together the original spirit of the folk music, taking into account Alan Lomax's recordings, but also bringing in other influences and styles as I thought appropriate. All in all, it sounded like good fun. My only reservation was that after my close collaborations with David Gilmour on the *On an Island* and *Endless River* albums, a new project was in the offing. I'd been doing whatever I could to push the thing along, but nothing had been said to me officially, and I was waiting to learn more about his intentions. In the absence of any kind of commitment from David's management, I thought maybe I'd be able to squeeze this in and still do whatever they needed me to do whenever they told me what that was, so I agreed to do it.

My first task was to understand as much as I could about Puglia and pizzica music. The region is of course in the heel of Italy, more or less opposite Albania. Over many centuries its location has put it in the way of influences and invasions from just about everyone, including Neapolitans, Albanians, Greeks, Spanish and Phoenicians. As a result, many local people speak Grikos, which is a sort of hybrid of Greek and Italian.

Pizzica music is said to be based on the cult of Dionysius and tends to have a very repetitive and hypnotic beat. People working in the fields cultivating tobacco or whatever it was, were at risk of being bitten by tarantulas, and the music and associated folk dance was part of a sort of cult of exorcism. That might not be the full picture but it's as close as I could understand it. Original and authentic pizzica dancing usually involves two women together, but occasionally it will include a man and a woman, and very rarely two men. However more modern takes are like a kind of Irish clogdancing laced with voodoo – if you can imagine it – incredibly powerful and mesmerising to watch. Try as you might, you just can't listen to it and remain still.

What I hadn't realised, but became clear quite quickly, was that the organisers expected me to spend most if not all of my time in Puglia for the entire six months before the event. I was assured that all my distinguished predecessors as Maestro Concertatore had done so, though I knew for sure that at least one of them, Stuart Copeland, certainly had not. Of course, this was impossible, but I undertook to come for a few days at least once a month, and would move in full time for the last month before the concert.

I set off to Puglia before Christmas to meet the local concert organisers. The area is stunningly beautiful, and the precise location of the concert in Melpignano was to be a huge open space just next to a ruined monastery. All very promising. Local musicians included a thirty-piece orchestra featuring a bagpipe made out of a pig's bladder, a mandolin, guitars, percussion, fiddle-players and and ten one-man drum kits called a tamborello. There were also six singers singing in Grikos, the local dialect, and twelve dancers. The rhythms were incredible and exhilarating, and I was really looking forward to finding ways to adapt it.

I was also introduced to the mayor of the local village, who was a serious-looking fellow who left us in no doubt that he was the man in charge of everything. If there was anything amiss, I didn't sense it at the time, and I promised to return to the region early in the New Year.

Christmas came and went and I returned to Puglia as planned, but was immediately disconcerted to discover that one of the key music advisers and director of the orchestra had died unexpectedly, and ranks seemed to have closed around the cause of his sudden demise. Nevertheless we stayed for a few days, did what we had to do, and went home promising to return again the following month. I also decided to wait until after the project had finished before I started reading the book I'd recently purchased about the Apulia Mafia.

On returning in February, I found that once again one of the key musicians we had met before was no longer anywhere in evidence. What had previously been merely disturbing was quickly becoming alarming, and I was determined to find out what had happened to him. All I knew was that his name was Claudio, and with some difficulty I tracked him down. He was reluctant to speak openly, but eventually he revealed that he'd been sacked from the project and told by the mayor that he would never work again.

"What no-one has told you," he confided, "is that just before you arrived, the musicians went to the Mayor asking for a pay-rise. His reaction was to threaten to fire all of us, so that when you came in December, we were all feeling under pressure but could say nothing. I've been considered to be one of the ringleaders, so I've been sacked, but the others are still unhappy and I suspect that I won't be the last."

Now incensed and feeling I'd been the victim of a deception, I immediately went to see the mayor to have it out with him. I found him in his impressive boardroom in the mayor's office.

"What the hell has happened to Claudio?" I asked him.

"He will never work again," said the Mayor.

"Look," I said, casting caution to the wind, "this has got to stop. You can't go on running things like this. One day you will be dead, and the Foundation will need young people like Claudio to carry on this music and tradition."

I can't say for certain that it was a frank exchange of views because of course I could scarcely be sure of what he was saying. The gist was that it was all political in ways I probably wouldn't understand, but one way and another I left with sufficient confidence that I'd be able to do my job without undue further interference.

So how to re-interpret pizzica taking into account the recordings of Alan Lomax and some of my own sensibilities? I began to imagine a mix of the original sounds with some South American and African, and maybe a bit of rock n' roll and even some punk. I booked Andrea Echeverri from the Colombian Aterciopelados, Paul Simonon, the bass player from The Clash as well as the brilliant Afrobeat drummer Tony Allen. These were very exciting guests, and the organisers were suitably impressed. However, when I told them that I'd also been able to persuade Luciano Ligabue, who was and is probably the biggest rock star in Italy, they were absolutely ecstatic. Luciano is commonly known by just his surname, and is a talented writer, singer, and director. He is handsome and charismatic, and his performances are characterised by women screaming and fainting with adulation.

I wanted to do as much as I could from home, and I was lucky that a really good pizzica band happened to be working in London so I could bring them down to my home studio. Their cumbia rhythms were in the 6/8-time signature I've always loved. With their help I began to get a handle on what the four hours could consist of, and I went back and forth to Puglia each month, taking care to stay as far away from the mayor as possible. In the intervals in between visits, I went to all possible lengths to ensure that I was on hand for anything David Gilmour might need for his next album and tour.

With the event only a month away, I was obliged to make good on my promise to live full time in the area, but I was keen to put as much distance as I could between ourselves and what were euphemistically being called "the politics". We therefore located and rented a vast compound with villa, traditional trullis and a huge pool which was a two hour drive away, but which overlooked the sea so that on a clear day you could just make out the coast of Albania.

Final preparations were going well, but time was of the essence, and so when I received a call from the mayor telling me I had to turn up to do some promotion for Mercedes because they were supplying the cars, I swiftly declined. Undeterred, he waited until the next time I was at the venue, at which point I was more or less bundled into a car and driven away to participate in the promotion. Clearly, he wasn't a 'don' who was used to having his orders disobeyed.

We scheduled a final press conference in Salento on the day before the concert. It was all a huge deal and dozens of TV, radio and press journalists turned out. Since we were being broadcast live on Italian TV, and not being one to miss an opportunity, I gave a quick outline of the story of my grandfather being an Italian opera musician and inviting anyone with further information to contact me. They didn't seem very interested, but what they were very interested in was the appearance of rock singer Ligabue. In fact, "interested" doesn't come close to describing it; they went absolutely crazy. Demented. Dozens of flashbulbs were exploding as

Press conference chaos: the mayor, Ligabue, me and Paul Simonon

La Notte della Taranta night

photographers clamoured to get close, and journalists jostled with cameramen and radio reporters thrusting microphones under our noses.

It was at this point that the mayor intervened, grabbed hold of Ligabue, ignoring me and the rest of the star-spangled cast I'd assembled, and before I knew it the Italian singer had been hi-jacked and taken into an adjoining room. What happened next? I went berserk – that's what happened next. Live on Italian TV I can be seen going absolutely bonkers and haranguing the mayor, assorted police officers, and an embarrassed Ligabue. Eventually Ligabue was restored to us, and order was restored too.

After the initial debacle with the malfunctioning guitar, the four hours of music and dancing was a triumph. There's something about pizzica music that reverberates, creating a physical reaction, making your heart and feet beat in time to the rhythm. The crowd went crazy as only Italian audiences know how, and everyone had the time of their lives. The people of the

The beautiful location of the Festival

Puglia region are warm and friendly and delightful, the food and wine are fabulous, and the scenery is breathtaking. When I look back on it all and think about the way dissent is sometimes dealt with in those parts, I'm only surprised that I came out alive.

* * *

For most of 2015 I'd been working non-stop with David Gilmour and Polly Samson, in his Brighton studio, co-producing his next solo album which would become *Rattle That Lock*. It was a busy but enjoyable time organising the recording process and helping both manage their time productively. Setting deadlines was crucial if we were to hit the agreed release date. In the course of the recording our intended saxophonist dropped out and I found a brilliant young replacement called Joao Mello for the tour, whom I recommended to David, and he loved straight away. My only other obligation at the time was the two or three days a month Claire and I were spending in Puglia preparing for the festival, but otherwise my time was devoted to the album project. Claire was David's long-term publicist and her PR company, LD Communications, had publicized all his projects since 2002.

I had no choice but to be in Puglia for the weeks leading up to the pizzica festival, but on the morning after the concert, Claire and I flew directly to London, dumped our luggage in the hallway and then dashed to the rehearsal rooms in Brighton. We immediately felt a 'chill' in the air, which was not just from the nearby sea. No-one had set up any of my equipment and I discovered that rehearsals had gone ahead with a session man playing second guitar.

Rattle That Lock was released in September 2015, and I was delighted that once again it went to number 1 in thirteen different countries, including the US and UK. I'd been booked to do the European, South American, and North American tours, but once on the road the atmosphere wasn't good. The petty jealousies and playground politics which sometimes accompany these tours were rife, and no-one seemed to be having a great time. I think we all hoped to re-create the good fun we'd had on the 2006 *On An Island* tour, but Rick was no longer with us, we were playing bigger venues and suddenly it all seemed too serious.

A few days after we all arrived home in January and were preparing for the next leg of the tour in North America, I received a call from David.

"I feel I need to change the band," he said.

"OK," I said, even then not suspecting what might be coming. "What sort of thing do you have in mind?"

"I need to make some changes in the band," he repeated, "and that includes you."

It still took me a moment to compute what he was saying, not least because the American tour was about to begin, and he went on to say that he had in mind that I'd stay for those gigs but not do the remaining ones in Europe. The same applied to several others he was firing at the same time. Probably he meant well by putting me on notice rather than pulling the rug out straight away, but it did mean that Guy Pratt, John Carin, and I trailed through the following itinerary knowing we were facing the firing squad, and so between us we dubbed it "The Walking Dead Tour". The last gig I played with David was in aid of the Teenage Cancer Trust at The Royal Albert Hall, after which we all went our separate ways: except for Guy, who had a last-minute reprieve.

My friend Brian Eno used to say that when you find yourself on stage thinking about your laundry, you should move on. To be honest, I remember that I did have exactly that thought at the Madison Square Garden show and so probably should have heeded Brian's advice. Maybe by that point, some of the joy of playing second guitar in Pink Floyd and David's songs had started to wane for me, and his decision was the right one for the tour.

Goodbye

TWENTY

Pirates of the Caribbean

I've always considered myself a European. I've had a lifetime of working and holiday in many European countries, particularly Spain, France, Germany and Italy so you can probably guess my feelings when Britain voted to leave the European Union. I was very upset, angry and totally bewildered. Freedom of movement and labour between EU countries has been crucial to so much of my work and, more than that, throughout my life I've taken every possible opportunity to break down cross-cultural barriers. So, in a strange way the Brexit vote felt almost like a personal affront.

Then one day I was leafing through the newspaper, still wondering how I came to be living in a time when Theresa May was the British prime minister and Jeremy Corbyn was the leader of the Opposition, when I came across an article which caught my eye. The Spanish and Portuguese governments had announced that if you could prove you had a Sephardic Jewish background, they would welcome you as a citizen. ¡Dios mio! I cast my mind back to the dim distant past and recalled hearing a rumour that my mother's long-since buried family might have some

Jewish heritage. Could this literally be my passport back into citizenship of the EU?

'Yo me explico' or let me give you a brief and potted history lesson taking us back more than five hundred years to 1492, when Queen Isabella and Ferdinand II issued the Alhambra Decree, which stated that Jews living in Spain were obliged to convert to Catholicism or face exile. 200,000 converted but somewhere between 40,000 and 100,000 decided to leave, many of them ending up in Holland. Even here they faced discrimination, including restrictions on the trades they were allowed to follow, which is one reason that many resorted to moneylending. Much later, in 1656, Oliver Cromwell let it be known that Sephardic Jews would be welcome and allowed to practice their faith freely in England: his motives weren't entirely philanthropic. Cromwell saw the Jews as an important part of Amsterdam's financial success and hoped they would do the same for London. Many came to London from Spain, Portugal and Holland. The influx led to the establishment of Bevis Marks which was the first synagogue in London.

At the same time there was a further diaspora of Jews from Holland to the Dutch colony of Curacao, and from there, after Simón Bolívar liberated many South American countries from the Spanish, a further leap took some to Gran Colombia which included Venezuela, Panama,

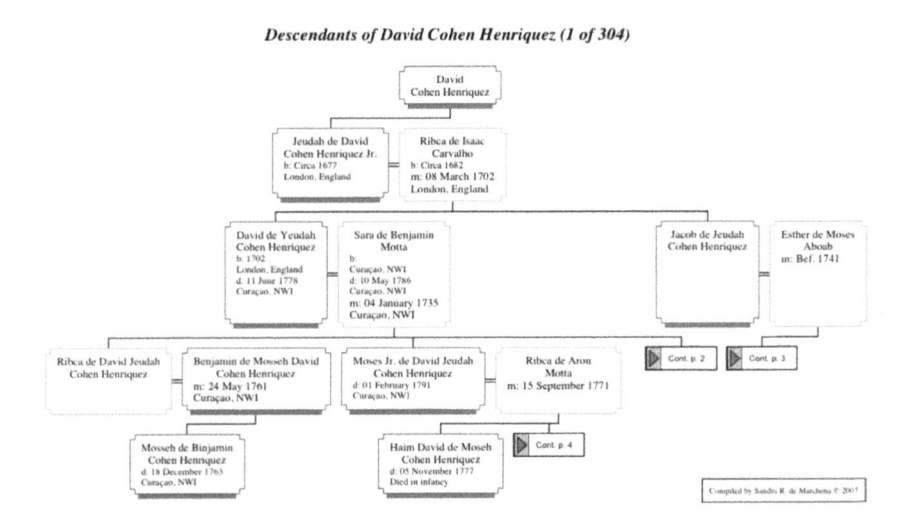

Descendants of David Cohen Henriquez (1 of 304)

and Colombia. Among those ending up in Barranquilla was my great grandmother whose maiden name, I discovered, was Henriquez Cohen. We were getting warmer.

Looking further back at the family tree, I spotted the name Benjamin Cohen and Googled him, only to discover that he was one of the most notorious pirates of the Caribbean – second only in notoriety to Captain Morgan and Johnny Depp. My great great great (I've lost track of how many greats) Uncle Benjamin Cohen turned out to be the right-hand man of Captain Morgan, and was running around between the islands with a huge bounty on his head. It seems that he had attacked and ransacked a ship carrying a cargo of gold back to Spain, valued at what would be literally billions in today's money. Running for his life, he first headed off to Brazil where he bought an island. All seemed fine for a while, but then when the Portuguese captured the country he scarpered once again and remained on the run and was never captured.

I was in the middle of discovering all this when I happened to bump into my lawyer friend John Cohen, and I said, "you're not going to believe this John, but I think we may be related." I told him the story of the Jewish pirate and suggested it had the makings of a West End musical,

Paddle Steamer on the río Magadalena, Girardot.

but that a hurdle in the way of my plan to achieve Spanish or Portuguese citizenship was that you had to document your Jewish ancestry and have it verified by a rabbi. As far as I recall I'd never even met one, so John suggested I should go to his North London synagogue and meet his rabbi, who turned out to be a young very cool guy who loved my story and said he'd do everything he could to help. This is to be continued.

Meanwhile in Barranquilla, my grandma Zilah Cohen met and was being courted by a very glamorous captain who skippered a passenger and cargo paddle-steamer. His name was Capitán Manzanera, and his regular route up the river Magdalena was the same one taken by the Conquistadors to the foothills of the Andes. The Nobel-prize winning author Gabriel García Márquez tells in his autobiography how he travelled on that same vessel, and I like to think my grandad was the captain. Capitán Manzanera and his new wife named their daughter after the river Magdalena, and thirty years later she was my very own Mamá.

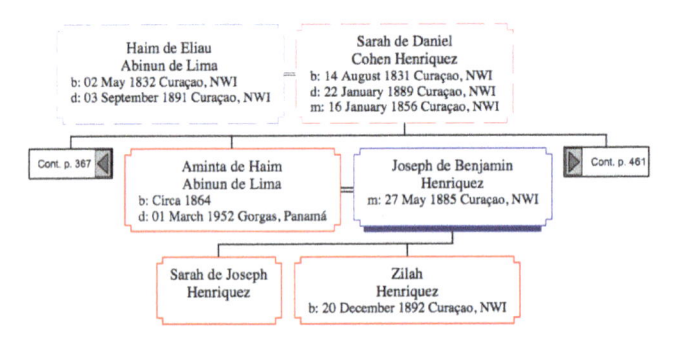

```
Haim de Eliau                    Sarah de Daniel
Abinun de Lima          =        Cohen Henriquez
b: 02 May 1832 Curaçao, NWI      b: 14 August 1831 Curaçao, NWI
d: 03 September 1891 Curaçao, NWI d: 22 January 1889 Curaçao, NWI
                                 m: 16 January 1856 Curaçao, NWI

                ┌────────────────┴────────────────┐
[Cont. p. 367]  Aminta de Haim        Joseph de Benjamin   [Cont. p. 461]
                Abinun de Lima    =   Henriquez
                b: Circa 1864         m: 27 May 1885 Curaçao, NWI
                d: 01 March 1952 Gorgas, Panamá

                    ┌────────────────┴────────────────┐
                    Sarah de Joseph       Zilah
                    Henriquez             Henriquez
                                          b: 20 December 1892 Curaçao, NWI
```

Zilah Henriquez Manzanera

Now feeling very optimistic that I could prove my ancestry to a level of certainty which would permit me to gain citizenship of Spain or Portugal, I visited the Bevis Marks synagogue in the City of London to search their records and this is work in progress. Such has been the popularity of the scheme however, that Spain eventually rescinded it, but at the time of writing, the opportunity remains open in Portugal and I'm still working on it.

Note to self – must acquire a Portuguese phrase book.

TWENTY-ONE

Return to Cuba and Other Adventures

I've always been very aware of my good fortune in having a life which has taken me to many of the most interesting, exotic, and exciting places in the world. In the early days of touring my visits had been limited to seeing the airport, the road into town, the biggest arena for some distance around, and the inside of a hotel room. Nonetheless my passion for travel and for aircraft which was born when I boarded that Stratocruiser in 1957 has never left me.

Any time I've ever had the chance to do so, I've grabbed the opportunity to return to one of my favourite places in the world, which is of course Cuba. The last time I played there was in 2012 when I was invited to a festival being staged by the island's well-known cigar industry. The organisers encouraged me to bring along some other musicians, and I knew that my old friend Jack Bruce was a fan of Cuban music, so I called him up. "Would you like to come to Havana and play with some top Cuban musicians?" I asked. It took Jack about a second to give me his answer. "Si por favor," in 'Glaswegian Spanish'. I didn't want to dampen his instant enthusiasm, but I felt the need to check that he wasn't a rabid

Me and Jack Bruce at the Hotel Naciónal, Havana

anti-smoker, so I mentioned that the event was sponsored by the cigar people. Jack's response was that the great jazz drummer Tony Williams had taught him all there was to know about cigars and rum back in the 70s, and he wasn't worried at all. Jack's wife Margrit, also his manager, came with us for the adventure and we did the whole Cuban thing: staying at the Naciónal Hotel, wearing the obligatory white suits, and drinking lots of mojitos.

Since the concert was sponsored by the cigar festival, we found ourselves obliged to sample the product simply out of courtesy to our hosts. Having had a traumatic experience when trying my dad's cigars as a child, being a non-smoker and not having the slightest idea how to smoke a cigar, this was going to be a challenge. I amused everyone by trying to cut the wrong end of a very expensive Cohiba, at which point Jack took it from me and expertly snipped it and handed it back. I pretended to smoke it, turned ashen and took a long swig of the vintage rum.

Naturally enough our hosts didn't have much actual money to pay us, but they did seem to have a lot of lobsters, of which we consumed copious amounts. It turned out that the other thing they were short of was any suitable stage equipment, and it soon emerged that the only bass amplifier on the island belonged to a bass-player who was due to use it the same day as our scheduled performance. Eventually it was agreed that we would use the amp for our soundcheck, then he would take it away for his gig in the afternoon and would return it to the famous Karl Marx theatre in time for the concert in the evening. When we arrived back at the venue however, Jack discovered that all his settings on the amp had been changed and

Onstage with Jack Bruce in the Karl Marx theatre Havana

there was no time for another soundcheck. He was incandescent and declared that he wasn't going to perform. Over the years I've learned to stay calm in the face of an artist meltdown, and so I continued to attempt to change my strings, while saying "okay, your decision" but praying that the Glaswegian storm would blow over. It did.

We went on to play a version of *Sunshine Of Your Love* Cuban style. I say 'Cuban style' because of course these fabulously talented Latin musicians have very little aptitude for playing rock and roll beats, and so it was all a bit too loose, but Jack got into the Latin version. I enjoyed the night, it was great to have the opportunity to play with him again, and the crowd went wild. Rest in peace Jack, a great friend and musician who is sorely missed.

The last time I visited Cuba was a year later, in 2016, on our way back from Chile after the Gilmour tour. I awoke in the cabin of a sailing boat in the Bahia de Cienfuegos to find a text on my phone saying that David Bowie had died. David had been a part of my musical landscape just as he had for so many of my generation, and he meant a lot to me. Cuba had been harbouring many emotional memories for me, and maybe the terrible news triggered something inside that had been there for so many years, just waiting to come out. I found that I couldn't stop crying.

* * *

In all my trips to various parts of South America I'd still never managed to visit Barranquilla, where my mother was born and brought up and where she met my dad. When I was invited to speak at the Hay Festival in Cartagena in 2017, I jumped at the opportunity to visit the Caribbean coast of Colombia and to go on to Barranquilla. The festival originated at Hay-on-Wye on the Welsh borders, but when the organisers invited the Nobel-prize winning author Gabriel García Márquez to come and he declined, they decided to take the festival to him. There's been a Hay Festival in Cartagena ever since.

Me and David Bowie backstage at the Radio City Music Hall, New York.

My other motive was that I was just about to bring out a new Spanish language album which I had reason to think would cause a stir in Colombia, and the festival seemed a good place to launch it.

The Corroncho project had begun with a conversation I'd been having with my friend, the Colombian artist and sculptor Lucho Brieva, who was married at that time to Chrissie Hynde of the Pretenders. Lucho and Chrissie had bought the flat on the first floor of our building, and we were good friends. One day we were kidding around, and we suggested to Chrissie that she should re-record some of her songs in Spanish. We argued that she'd be opening a whole new market for her music, which would then spread all over the Latin world. Chrissie was understandably sceptical, so Lucho and I offered to translate some of her songs and then to sing them back to her in Spanish. We did exactly that, and instead of being impressed and motivated to learn the language and go back into the recording studio, Chrissie's reaction was to collapse on the floor laughing her head off. She said it sounded like the Canadian/American comedy duo Cheech and Chong, and suggested that Lucho and I should record a whole album together. We decided that we'd do exactly that, and in the end Chrissie agreed to join us on the musical escapade, and the final recording included contributions from Annie Lennox, Enrique Bunbury, Robert Wyatt, and even Paul Thompson.

We had to think of a name for the project and it was Lucho who suggested *Corroncho*, which is a fairly offensive term of abuse used by Colombians from Bogotá about the people living on the Caribbean coast. It's also the name of the ugliest fish on earth, so ugly that when fishermen catch one, they usually throw it back. The resultant album is themed around the adventures of two fictitious "corroncho" characters from the Caribbean coast and consists of music played in Latin rhythms from Colombia, including salsa, cumbia and boleros. We included a cover version of the Dylan song *Forever Young*, which we translated into Spanish, 'Tu Juventud', which turned out sounding like a hymn to the young nations of South America. Chrissie told me later that she'd played our track to Dylan himself and that he'd expressed his approval, so that was good enough for me.

Hay Festival Cartagena, Colombia, 2017

Our concern about how the controversial name might be greeted was vindicated when we eventually launched the album and the story made the front page of the national newspaper El Tiempo. Some approved of the audacity of using such a word, while others were appalled. One way or the other the album received all the attention I'd hoped for, shining a light on prejudice and absurdity.

My talk at the Cartagena festival, which I gave in Spanish, was all about my own Latin roots and history. It seemed to go down well, and next we were off on a sentimental journey to my maternal family home in Barranquilla. It was a very emotional trip for me as we stayed in the Hotel Prado, which was the very same one that my dad first stayed in when he arrived there in 1941. We also visited the church where Mum and Dad were married and were shown their entry in the wedding register. Our tour guide was my Uncle Tito, who was the youngest of my mum's eight siblings, and who sadly died in 2022. Later we returned to Cartagena and visited a local island called La Isla Grande where the notorious drug-lord Pablo Escobar had a huge compound, more like a palace, where he used to party. We then discovered that two of my Manzanera cousins, submariner admirals based in Cartagena, spent most of the 90s chasing the drug lords' submersibles on their routes to Florida. Never a dull moment.

* * *

Corroncho gig Bazurto Social Club Cartagena

RETURN TO CUBA AND OTHER ADVENTURES

By now it must be obvious that the idea of bringing together what may seem to be a random collection of brilliant and passionate musicians, and then seeing what comes out of the mix, has been a source of continuous joy for me for fifty years and counting. Another of these adventures would take me back to Japan, where I'd last visited with Roxy in 2010, playing the Fuji rock festival.

I'd always been glad to know that there was a dedicated audience for my music in Japan, most notably because of the recording I'd made as Quiet Sun back in 1975. I thought I'd be unlikely to return there anytime soon, but then I got involved with yet another group of talented friends in a project we called *The Sound of Blue*. The band featured the fabulous young Portuguese vocalist Sonia Bernardo, as well as ex-Stereophonics drummer Javier Weyler from Argentina, Yaron Stavi from Israel on bass, Joao Mello from Brazil playing sax and keys and Lucas Polo, from Spain, on guitar and vocals. We were honoured that Hotei, a guitar hero in Japan, joined us for one of the concerts.

Tokyo Sound of Blue Band with Hotei

The whole visit was scheduled to last for just about a week, but what I hadn't realised when I glanced at the schedule was that we were booked to play two sets per night, which meant six in Tokyo and two in Osaka. This was a career first, never to be repeated, but I was buoyed along by the sheer talent, exuberance, and youthful enthusiasm of the band, with an average age (not including me) of about thirty.

I'd intended Japan to be the end of the tour, but once again the lure of South America proved too strong to be resisted, and in November 2017 I found myself agreeing to go with Sonia and Lucas to Argentina. There we performed with a whole host of Argentina's most famous musicians at the Centro Cultural Kirchner in Buenos Aires. The CCK arena is this amazing whale-shaped capsule seemingly suspended within a huge auditorium, and the place was packed to the rafters with nosily enthusiastic fans. It was recorded and shown on national TV, and turned out to be one of the best and most enjoyable gigs I've ever played.

Buenos Aires CCK concert

TWENTY-TWO

It's Only Rock n' Roll But We Like It ...

In common with the TV and the film industries, the music business is awash with award ceremonies, and although of course it's very lovely to be recognised, the truth is that only a very select few of them carry great prestige: the American Rock and Roll Hall of Fame is definitely one of them. The project was founded in 1983 by the legendary head of Atlantic Records Ahmet Ertegun, and the first set of inductees included Elvis Presley, James Brown, Little Richard, Fats Domino, Ray Charles, Chuck Berry, Sam Cooke, the Everly brothers, Buddy Holly, Jerry Lee Lewis, and Robert Johnson. Since then, it's gone on to include all the music heavyweights from The Beatles to Joni Mitchell, from Prince to Jay Z. Membership of this exclusive club would indeed be an honour worth having.

The way it works is that artists or bands become eligible for induction into the Hall of Fame twenty-five years after the release of their first recording. The Foundation's nominating committee selects candidates who are then voted on by an international body of some five hundred rock experts who decide whether you're going to be among the chosen few. Quite often people are nominated initially but then fall at subsequent hurdles, so that when we heard early in 2019 that Roxy had been nominated for the first time, we tried not to get too excited. But then it wasn't long before news came through that we'd cleared all the hurdles on this first outing, and would be inducted at the next ceremony. We were quietly thrilled – or at least I know I was.

The Hall of Fame machine continues to work in mysterious ways, and it seems that a group of people there get into a huddle, and then issue a list of the individuals they deem to be members of the band. In our case their published list named Bryan, Andy, and I, obviously. Phil Thompson, also fair enough and of course Eno. But then it went on to include Eddie Jobson whom none of us could remember having seen since about 1976 and, more importantly, was never a full band member; and finally, Graham Simpson who, the organisers possibly hadn't realised, had sadly died in 2012.

This was the line-up which the august body wanted to honour, and who were we to argue? The only questions for us to decide were who would attend on the night, who would say what, and what songs we would play at the ceremony, if any. When I called Bryan to ask how he wanted to handle things, his first reply was along the lines of "I'm not sure I want to do it". I said that was no problem and that Andy and I would be very happy to go along to say a few words, at which point he began to warm to the idea that he might at least turn up.

That was progress, but were we also going to play?

Bearing in mind that we hadn't done anything together as Roxy Music since we'd gone our separate ways in New Zealand eight years earlier, and that the Rock and Roll Hall of Fame is a huge extravaganza which is broadcast all around the world, this was going to take some serious thinking about. Apart from a potential TV audience of many millions, we'd be surrounded on the night by lots of other bands and inductees whom we respected. Among them would be Radiohead, Stevie Nicks and other Fleetwood Mac band members, Def Leppard, and The Zombies all of whom were being inducted on the same night. I was very keen that if we were going to do it, we'd give a good account of ourselves.

We heard very quickly from Brian Eno that while he was pleased that we were being inducted, he wasn't travelling by air for environmental reasons. This felt like an authentic Eno response and one that would brook no argument. Paul Thompson also wasn't keen, and we were unable to talk him round. Having decided that we would play, we called on Bryan's touring band, which included Chris Spedding, Neil Jason, Tawatha Agee and Fonzi Thornton, all of whom had played with Roxy over the years.

We booked a rehearsal space in Brooklyn for five days leading up to the event. It all felt a bit strange at first, but before long we got back into the general mild bickering and mutual irritation which is part of what makes us our unique selves, and before you knew it, it felt like we were Roxy Music once again.

Our task was to choose three or possibly four songs, and I assumed that Bryan would want us to perform our biggest hits, which he did. We rehearsed *Out of the Blue*, *Love Is The Drug*, *More Than This* and *Avalon* so that we could choose what to do on the night. I thought that would be that, but then I was surprised when Bryan said he also wanted us to play *In Every Dream Home a Heartache*. I say surprised, because of course the song is in part about an inflatable sex doll, and includes the lyrics:

I bought you mail order
My plain wrapper baby
Your skin is like vinyl
The perfect companion
You float in my new pool
De luxe and delightful
Inflatable doll

I thought it unlikely that American TV would be willing to broadcast the song, and indeed they didn't. However, since it involves a long guitar solo at the end, which I'd get to play at this prestigious event, I was happy.

We learned that we were being inducted for the honour by our old friends Simon le Bon and John Taylor from Duran Duran. We thought that was lovely, not least because we knew they were genuine Roxy fans. Simon talked about his memories of our first ever appearance on Top of the Pops which he recalled as "a psychedelic Sinatra crooning pop-art poetry over driving drums, over saxophones and oboes, heavily treated electric guitar and the most out-there synthesizer parts you ever heard." Nice.

The usual routine with these things is that every individual being inducted steps up to the microphone in turn and thanks their primary school teacher, their mum and dad, their grandparents, siblings, agent, manager, record company and finally their partner, and it all seems to go on until you're so bored you lose the will to live. Since part of Roxy's brand has always been to do things slightly differently, none of us was keen to do all that. We also thought that if we agreed to keep any speeches short, we might have time for an extra song.

When it came time for the soundcheck, each inductee was allocated a fixed amount of time to rehearse both the music and their acceptance speeches. In true Roxy style we hadn't agreed what was going to be said and by whom, so I assumed we were going to divvy up the speeches between Bryan, Andy, and me. However when I approached the microphone and spotted the autocue way off in the far distance, I realised that I'd never be able to read it in a million years. Andy felt the same, so we suggested to Bryan that he should read it. Bryan started reading, but quickly stopped and said, "who the hell wrote this?" Everyone looked at each other and then Bryan's son Isaac, who occasionally acts as his assistant, said, "Well I had to put something up there." At this point the floor manager said, "time's up," and so we never got a proper chance to look at the speech, which ended up with a roll call of no fewer than thirteen different Roxy bass players.

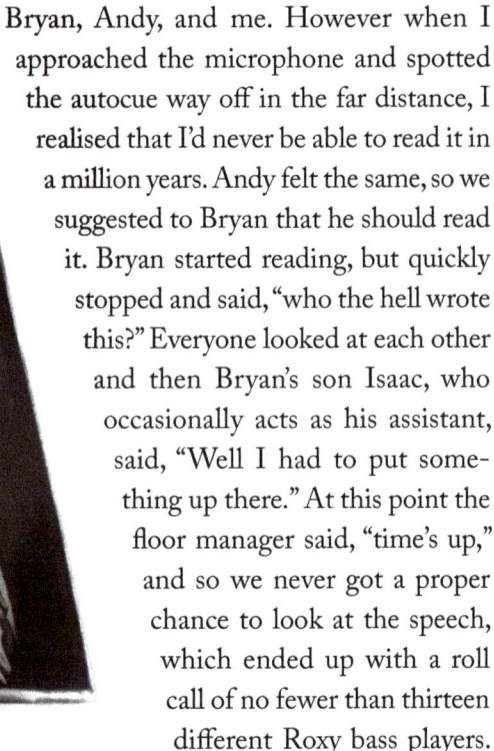

The trophy

Somehow it seemed like a classic Roxy moment, in which we managed to take something that should have been easy and turned it into something difficult. I thought the whole thing was hilarious, but little did I know that there was even more jeopardy to come.

After the speech we were due to go straight on stage to play our set, but first we'd have to disappear briefly behind a curtain so we could be fitted with our ear monitors. At the sound-check, the floor manager had clearly instructed us that once the ear monitors were in, we should start the set. He added that there was no rush because the TV show was being recorded and any gap could easily be edited. The only important thing, he said, was that we didn't go on before we were all properly ready. So as soon as the speeches had finished, we headed back behind the curtain. Bryan's monitors were put in by the tour manager and off he went to the stage, where the rest of the band was ready and waiting. The same thing then happened for Andy, and off he went too. But then when my roadie Lucas came to fit my ear-monitors, there was a tangle of wires which couldn't be sorted quickly, especially when hands were shaking. When I next looked around, everyone else had gone, leaving me alone with a still struggling Lucas. Spotting us in trouble, our tour manager Cath came to the rescue, but then to my horror, just a few seconds later, I could hear the opening notes of *In Every Dream* striking up. It seemed that neither Bryan nor Andy had noticed that one musketeer was missing. I can only think that nerves got the better of them and they'd forgotten what the floor manager had said.

So, it's the Barclay Centre. There are twenty thousand people in the hall. Among them are Brian May, Stevie Nicks, Janet Jackson, and many of the glitterati of the rock and roll world. Claire was sitting at the table with my daughter Sophie, and both momentarily worried that maybe I'd had one of my not infrequent mishaps backstage and the whole thing was headed for humiliating disaster. Luckily for me, *In Every Dream…* begins with an extended section in which Bryan sings accompanied only by the keyboards, and he'd been doing so for at least a minute when, aided by low lighting, I strolled onto the stage behind him, strapped on my guitar, and was ready to play just in the nick of time. I think that if anything I may have looked rather cool and casual. Several friends who watched on TV told me later that they'd assumed my late entry had been rehearsed. If only.

It was all great fun being Roxy Music again and I was very proud of our performance. After playing our set, I returned to our table and watched the rest of the ceremony. An enjoyable event was rounded off nicely when all the inductees were invited back on the stage to sing *All the Young Dudes*. I always feel a bit naked on stage without a guitar, especially since I'm not the world's greatest singer, but there I was alongside Ian Hunter, Brian May, Rod Argent, Susanna Hoffs, Steven Van Zandt, and the guys from Def Leppard, singing my heart out to one of my favourite Bowie songs. Carpe Diem.

After show party with Rany Hoffman and Neil Finn, Rock and Roll Hall of Fame, Brooklyn

IT'S ONLY ROCK N' ROLL BUT WE LIKE IT...

All the old Dudes!

Among the many old friends, I ran into that evening at Stevie Nick's after-show party was Neil Finn from Split Enz and Crowded House. Stevie was touring with Fleetwood Mac at the time and Neil was in the band for their tour. He and I had a photo taken together and later I sent a copy of the picture to his brother Tim, who was at home in New Zealand, with a note saying, "guess who I ran into in New York?" When Tim replied, he asked if I would put guitar on some tracks that he and Split Enz keyboard supremo Eddie Rayner were working on called *Forenzics*. Of course, I said yes, and the tracks were sent to me and I became a member of the Forenzics.

A year later, in March 2020, the whole world was in the grip of the Covid lockdown, and I was sitting in my writing room in the garden, which doubles as my home studio. I was idly staring at my screensaver of an island in the Pacific, when an email popped into my in-box which turned out to be from an island in the Pacific. It was Tim, also locked down but in Auckland, asking if I had any slow Latin American-style grooves that he could write to. I'd been storing away a few ideas with a thought of releasing a new *Corroncho* album, so I raided my 'musical cupboard' to see what I could find. Over the following days I polished up a series of backing tracks and sent a few of them to Tim. Since the end of my working day coincided with the beginning of his, we got started on a kind of shift pattern in which I'd send him some music overnight, and by the time I woke up the following morning, he'd have sent back a version with his recorded lyrics.

I'm not sure how best to describe the pleasure of waking up in the morning, clicking the mouse on an icon, opening up a file, only to hear Tim's melodic

Caught by the Heart album

Tim and Phil, 2021

The Ghost of Santiago

voice echoing around my home studio, singing lyrics which sounded as though they had been crafted in the course of several weeks rather than a few hours. The whole project felt like a beautiful and fitting outcome of a friendship which has lasted for half a century and counting, somehow magically encapsulating anything and everything that he and I have learned in all that time. After listening to each track for the first time I would then go for a walk in the beautiful West Sussex countryside and continue listening.

And the great thing about a fifty-year friendship between people who've both achieved a bit, is that you don't mind if the other one says, "hey Phil, that was great, but I think you could do this part a bit better," and that did happen a few times. Tim would tell me if he wasn't completely happy with something, and every time he did, I thought, "yeah I know, he's right," and I'd do some more work on it. Rather than heading back into a fully equipped and state of the art studio, I'd sit in my garden room with my Shure SM57 microphone, which is linked to a Universal Audio Ox, pick up my trusted Firebird, and just play the track and record what came into my head. Other times I'd try things out on a 1951 Telecaster I keep here, or my Epiphone Flying V. It was all so "home-studio" that I even used the side of a fountain pen as my slide. Then I'd send what I'd put together to my friend Mike Boddy who is a brilliant sound engineer and has all the proper up to date plug-ins, just so the completed package sounded totally right, which in the end it did.

It's hard to put into words what it feels like . There's something almost primordial about it, like the glow of a wood-burning stove on a winter's day, or the feeling of the sun on your back. The album of ten songs was released in 2021 and we called it *Caught By The Heart*. We knew that we'd managed to produce something special, but it's always very gratifying to get great reviews, which we did.

News of the release of the follow-up album of ten tracks, *The Ghost of Santiago*, coincided with the announcement of The Roxy Music 50th Anniversary tour, which proved to be yet another moment when solo and band careers were able to happily co-exist.

Tim and Phil at the Borderline Club, London 16th June, 1993

50th Celebration Tour, North America, 2022

IT'S ONLY ROCK N' ROLL BUT WE LIKE IT…

Roxy Music, UK Tour, 2022

TWENTY-THREE

The Seventies

It's 15th Oct 2022 and I find myself arriving back at our 17th century cottage in West Sussex. Last night we played a sold-out concert at the O2 Arena in London to 16,000 enthusiastic fans, followed by a big after-show party. Claire and I were chauffeured home in a huge and shiny Mercedes saloon, only to discover that we needed to buy milk and food for an empty fridge, collect the dry cleaning, and fix the heating which, sometime in the six weeks we've been away, has developed an unexplained fault. It's bloody freezing.

As if by magic the Roxy world where every need and every desire is catered for, has vanished. Down to earth with a bump. It's as if you've woken up from a fairytale, the Roxy Cinderella coach has turned into a pumpkin which, as if to taunt us, has miraculously appeared outside the front door because it's coming up to Halloween.

There'll be no more relying on the dressing-room rider for sandwiches and fruit, no more crew-catering, no more hotel room-service, no more wardrobe-assistant to fetch freshly laundered clothes, and no more tour-manager to cater for every whim. And so off I go next morning to the local supermarket to deal, on my own, with trying to find a shopping trolley that doesn't have a wobbly wheel, and the dodgy scanning machine at check-out.

It's an abrupt reminder of how the trappings and illusions of rock stardom come and go, and you suddenly find yourself sitting alone in your home-studio trying to process what you did for the past two months. Of course, this or something similar has happened to me so many times that I've lost count. However, this last tour was special because it marked fifty years since the band's beginning, which for me also marked half a century as a professional musician. And as if that wasn't enough, on 31st January 2021 I reached the ripe old age of 70.

Scroll back to Christmas 2020 when I went round to see Bryan at his home, which is near mine in the country, with a view to catching up on how we'd all fared through Covid and to listen to some of his latest music. We chatted about what he'd been doing, then about what I'd been doing, and how the lockdowns had given all of us a chance to reflect on so much we'd done together and what we'd done apart. Inevitably we got round to remarking that it was coming up to a very big milestone since we first got together as Roxy Music, and we did a bit of reminiscing about all the good times we've had and some of the mistakes we've made. I guess the question was inevitable, and it was Bryan who asked it first.

"Do you fancy doing some gigs?" he said. "My agent in the US says we should get Roxy back together and do ten."

My default answer to anything to do with playing live music is usually yes, and sometimes it's only later that I regret it. In this case I didn't hesitate and heard myself saying, "I guess we should do something to celebrate the fiftieth. If you really are up for it, I am too."

Like the man from Del Monte, he say, "Sí!"

It was as simple as that. Well, nearly. Obviously we needed to find out if Andy and Paul were also able and willing and, after just a bit of persuading, both agreed.

The idea was for a North American tour which would include The Forum in Los Angeles and Madison Square Gardens in New York, both of which are very big venues that we hadn't played before. Meanwhile, if we were going to get back together for an American tour, we obviously

THE SEVENTIES

wanted to include the UK in the celebration, so we selected Glasgow, Manchester, and a final evening in London.

At first Andy had some doubts about whether we'd be able to fill the biggest of the American venues, but I reckoned that selling the tickets was someone else's problem. Our only job was to make sure that after ten years since we'd last played a concert together, the band was as good as we'd need it to be. We've all spent our entire professional lives making sure we look and sound our best, and the last thing we'd ever want to do is to let anyone down.

We first got together in the 70s, and now we're all in our 70s. Paul is the same age as me, but Bryan and Andy are a bit older. We've all had our little health scares of one kind or another, but we're not doing badly for old guys. Fortunately we're not the Rolling Stones, so our act doesn't involve running around the stage and gyrating like twenty year olds; nonetheless, a thirteen-city tour playing some of the biggest arenas all over America and the UK was not to be undertaken lightly.

First off, we'd need a manager, and I suggested Wendy Laister who looks after Duran Duran and I knew well as an old friend and colleague of Claire's. Wendy met Bryan, they got along well, and so I knew we'd be in good hands along with Bryan's personal manager Millie. Bryan also had recent experience of a lot of excellent sound and production people through his solo touring, so we were off to a good start.

With the aftermath of the lockdowns and everyone's commitments to plan around, we wouldn't be able to start proper rehearsals until a month before the first gig, so I knew I'd have to get my fingers working again on some numbers I hadn't played for ten years. The challenge was made even greater because the passage of time has brought about small but significant changes in Bryan's voice, and so there'd be some changes of key. This was an arithmetical problem for me as I attempted to transpose complicated riffs on the fretboard, at times finding myself sitting with paper and pencil and working it out like something between sudoku and a crossword puzzle. Everything got a bit simpler when I re-tuned the strings from E to F, which made some of the fingering more straightforward. The whole thing would prove to be a bigger challenge for Andy because some of the notes he needed to find just don't exist on the oboe or alto sax. Needless to say he found ways to work around it, and ended up producing the uniquely magical sound he's famous for.

Though I've never stopped playing and performing with various combinations of musicians in the decade since Roxy last appeared together, I'm well aware that technology has moved on and there are new and easier ways to produce the unique sound which makes us authentically us. So, I set out to build the perfect rig which would enable me to manage quick guitar and effects changes during the live performance.

It's fifty years since I started with a Hiwatt amp and a Pete Cornish pedal board, and in all that time I've always embraced new guitar technology. I was determined to put together an up to date system and I duly ended up with a state-of-the-art pedal-board. My visit to the Stockholm pedal shop made me feel like a kid in a candy store, as only guitar nerds will understand. This enables my brilliant guitar tech and friend Lucas Polo to override what I select if needed and change the settings remotely

On Tour USA

offstage. It's a long way from the VCS3 which was especially designed for me after Eno left the band all those years ago, but it allowed me to reproduce the exact sound I was looking for. I shot some videos of the process which have turned out to be warmly appreciated by a dedicated band of fellow guitar lovers via my YouTube channel.

Since this tour might well have proven to be Roxy Music's last proper outing, I took along my '51 Telecaster, my black Les Paul, and of course the famous red Firebird. I also treated myself to a very nice red Gibson 335 to replace the one I'd had stolen many years ago.

By the time we finally assembled for full rehearsals in August, we were all physically and mentally in the right zone. Five decades after we'd first come together as young guys with big dreams and high hopes to match, here we were, all of us still standing and united under the Roxy banner, ready to entertain and give everyone a memorable evening. It felt good, and it sounded good too. I remember hearing Paul McCartney

Red Gibson 335, USA

say that the thing about The Beatles was that in the end they were just "a great little rock and roll band." Roxy has never been that, but there is undoubtedly something unique about our sound which can only be authentically reproduced when the four of us are at the heart of it. We felt it ourselves, and we were happy when music journalists reviewing the tour commented on the same thing. Over the years Bryan has brought together some brilliant musicians for his solo tours, but no-one except Roxy sounds exactly like Roxy.

The process of rehearsing and then touring with the band has given me a better understanding of who we are, and what each of us really does. I know that must seem an odd thing to say after so long working together, but maybe it's only with the passage of time, and having worked with some of the greatest musicians in the world, that these perspectives have fully made themselves known to me. Andy, for example, studied music at university and has a great knowledge of classical music, but also the great tradition of soul-sax playing. There are those amazing jazz licks coming from that horn and who else plays the oboe in rock? Paul Thompson is the perfect rock drummer from the John Bonham school and helps to keep us rocking. So important to the Roxy sound. Also, for many years I'd find myself becoming impatient with Bryan's apparently endless attention to detail. His Fine Arts background obliged him to tinker and fiddle way beyond the point where the vast majority of people would long since have settled. I now understand this is all about his need to make everything he does artistically beautiful and perfect. I tend to want to do things quickly and am not worried if they have a primitive edge, and what we've learned is that in Roxy opposites can attract. That's integral to what makes Roxy music special. Makes it us. Makes us it.

With the dates for the first gigs of the tour rapidly approaching, I reflected that these could well be the last of their kind. Whatever else I did, I wanted to enjoy them. If not, what was the point? I've sometimes been told that I can appear to be a bit isolated on stage, maybe even slightly impervious to the reaction of the crowd, and so I was determined that this wouldn't be the case this time around. The only reason the fans were paying their money and taking the trouble to come to these gigs was to see us perform and to enjoy themselves, so let's see if we could all do it together.

For some reason, maybe it was being 70 and feeling on top of my game, I think I probably enjoyed playing guitar with Roxy more on this tour than I 'd ever done before. I was able to rediscover the freedom I'd originally felt in the earliest days when we were making it all up as we went along, and before everything became so much more sophisticated and rehearsed. It was gratifying when my thoughts were confirmed by reviewers along the way, who kindly said many highly complementary things about my performance. It was a welcome reminder of all the joy that can be derived from this simple but beautiful thing called a guitar.

About ten years ago I developed a habit, before I go on stage, of visualisation. I find a quiet spot and then slowly run through in my mind every step of what lies ahead; from leaving the dressing room, walking on stage, checking my guitar, turning to the audience, absorbing the moment, and then striking the first chords and hearing them echo around the auditorium. When I visualised all that ahead of the gigs on this last tour, I envisaged myself picking up my Firebird, turning to the audience, and this time giving them a big wave.

Each night I'd come on stage to the intro music of *India* from the *Avalon* album, pick up my trusty cardinal red Gibson Firebird, plug in and wave hello to a crowd of ecstatic people. They all waved back and maybe it was my imagination, but I'm sure I felt one of the warmest bursts of affection we've ever experienced from a Roxy crowd. It's a moment to savour, like a long-awaited reunion with some of your best friends, most of whom you've known for well over half your life.

The 50th anniversary reunion tour ended up taking us from Toronto to L.A. and then back to play in front of huge crowds in Glasgow, Manchester, and London. Everywhere we played the audiences were warm and welcoming, and every bit as happy to see us after all this time as we were to see them.

They've been faithful, they've been patient, and they've turned out in their thousands to re-live the Roxy experience. A chance to revisit their youth maybe, to see if they can still squeeze into some of those outfits, they've been hanging on to all this time, and to join in singing and dancing to some of the songs they've grown up with. It's been a heartwarming experience to commune with them.

Roxy 50th Anniversary tour, 2022

Personally this 50th Anniversary 'victory lap' was about sharing it, not only with the fans, but with family and friends. It was great to have all six children joining us along the way and sharing in the fun.

I have mentioned previously that my life changed when Sharon and I had children: it changed for the better. Chloe, Charlie and Sophie bring great joy to my life, and I am immensely proud of all their achievements. I have navigated their ups and their downs and still do, and have always tried to be there for them, regardless of the inevitable choppy waters that beset every family. I was conscious that with my dad dying when I was fifteen, I had no role model of how to father them, especially as they moved into adulthood. As parents we do our best, and don't always get it right, but for me the unconditional love for them is always there ... tempered by some sort of objectivity when needed! When I fell for Claire, I knew that being part of her three children's lives might be a challenge for all concerned, but lucky for me Alex, Sarah and Izzy accepted and welcomed me from the get-go, they've always been a delight to be with and I love them dearly. I like to think that we have a mutual respect and although I'm not their dad, they have a great one in Colin, I am their Padrastro.

So, what does it all add up to? What are we to make of the phenomenon which is and has been Roxy? In the end it's a group of people who come together from time to time to make music. The process is a magical blending of our different experiences and influences through the years – it's the sum total of everything we were, are, and have achieved. It's about our families, our triumphs, our disappointments, and our losses too. It's about the break-ups and the make-ups. It's about creativity, originality, and an alchemy that cannot be explained. Something about Roxy has defied a neat definition and I think Eno has come the closest with his made up word *Scenius*: we were a part of a new wave of young artists creating our own scene in the early 70s. All this reinforces my belief that music has the power to bring people together and enrich people's lives: Hasta la victoria Siempre.

REVOLUCIÓN TO ROXY

274

ADDENDUM

Celebrating 50 Years of Roxy Music – Tour 2022

Far be it for me to blow my own trumpet but if these were the last performances of Roxy Music then I'll settle for this:

2022 Roxy Music Tour Quotes – Phil Manzanera

> Guitarist Phil Manzanera was fantastic, nailing solo after solo.

Just One More Concert – Toronto

> Everytime guitarist Phil Manzanera is unleashed for a solo is a highlight.

Next Toronto

> A particularly searing Manzanera solo.

Toronto Star – Toronto

> Phil Manzanera in particular was on fire turning out some scorching solos.

Washington Concert Addicts – Washington

❝ A mesmerising turn from Manzanera ... leading to a blistering solo.

Under The Radar – Washington

❝ The fans kept roaring as Manzanera shredded over Paul Thompson's drums.

Washington Post – Washington

❝ Bringing the real music dynamism was Manzanera and Mackay who can still solo and blow with magnum force.

Vintage Rock – New York

❝ Manzanera's guitar work as elegant as ever.

Brooklyn Vegan – New York

❝ (Manzanera's) explosive solos ... who also added filigree to quieter songs.

New York Times – New York

❝ Andy Mackay and Phil Manzanera's instrumental duets are stunning. Phil Manzanera is playing lead guitar as incisively as ever.

Brighton and Hove News – London

❝ Phil Manzanera snatches the limelight on several occasions with his string of blistering guitar solos.

i – New York

ADDENDUM

> Manzanera let loose on his whammy bar and delivered a torrent of guitar pyrotechnics. His shimmering leads skated effortlessly across many of the evening's arrangements.
>
> *Spin – LA*

> Manzanera's slashing power chords: I loved it when Manzanera and Mackay got cranking.
>
> *Rock + Roll Globe – Boston*

> It was Manzanera and Mackay who shined brightest, the latter by making his guitar make alien sounds sound so catchy that one of these days he'll attract life from another planet.
>
> *Riff Magazine – San Francisco*

> (In Every Dream Home A Heartache) … the highlight here was an absolutely manic guitar solo by Manzanera … one tends to forget just what a talented guitarist he is.
>
> *Best Classic Bands – LA*

> Phil Manzanera's coolly assured guitar god wailing.
>
> *NME – London*

> (In Ladytron) Phil Manzanera is pealing out rafter-rattling guitar sounds 50 years young with Manzanera and Mackay facing off, letting rip solos with equal amounts of ferocity and sleaze.
>
> *i News – London*

> Phil, was of an unsurpassed level last night.
>
> *Priptonaweird – Glasgow*

> Phil Manzanera takes the limelight on several occasions with his string of fabulous guitar solos.
>
> *All Music Magazine – Manchester*

> (Out of the Blue) Phil's guitar was electrifying.
>
> *Standard – London*

> Manzanera sliding through solos like a hot knife through butter. (In Every Dream Home a Hearrtache) the audience braced for Manzanera's thunderous, arresting guitar solo, with the might of the O2's sound system, it was a real violation of the eardrums and a welcomed one at that.
>
> *Far Out – London*

> … the guitarist, with an array of effect pedals at his feet, added echoing shards of sound to the needling beat of Bogus Man … Manzanera making masterful use of guitar distortion.
>
> *Financial Times – London*

> (Manzanera) who came alive with slashing chords and a vibrato-shaking squall … reminding us that he was the progenitor of noise guitar.
>
> His solo, which hummed with string bends and slides up the neck … Manzanera rang a fierce solo over cascading drum fills.
>
> *Arts Fuse – London*

ADDENDUM

> The only thing missing with Phil's performance were the "fly-eye" glasses and the long, dark hair.

Live Music News – Boston

> Manzanera and Mackay traded their first of many bristling solos.
> Manzanera lashed into the song's expansive outro, thrashing his guitar during a stratospheric solo infused with twang and snarl.
> Manzanera was in high spirits, radiating pride in his bandmates, playing with conviction and sending goodwill into the room.

Illinois Entertainment, Chicago

> (Manzanera) truly took the sound to another level … who knew the brilliance of Phil Manzanera and what he'd add, ditto Andy Mackay.

Lefetz.com. LA

> Phil Manzanera is one of rock's most under appreciated guitarists … he delivered big time.

TalkBass Philadelphia

> More often than not the real driver is the instrumental interplay between Manzanera's inventive guitar leads and Mackay's splendid sax and oboe solos.

Austin American Statesman – Austin

> Manzanera's creepy guitar lines.

The Guardian – London

Claire and Phil Dressing Room, O2, London

ADDENDUM

Phil, Chloe and Charlie, Manchester

REVOLUCIÓN TO ROXY

Wendy, Claire, me, Sarah, James, O2, London

Guy, Izzy, Christina, Claire and Phil, Boston

ADDENDUM

Sophie, Phil and Charlie

Alex, Claire, Phil, Sophie, Sabina and Charlie, San Francisco

THANKS

The writing of this book would not have been possible without two very important people, one already part of my life and the other a brand new friend.

Firstly, Claire, mi querida mujer, who is so literate, intelligent, loving and patient. She knows my stories like the back of her hand and has actually lived through many of my escapades. Claire has spent many hours helping me read through the chapters and correct any factual or tonal mistakes, and made me pay attention when my eyes glazed over with the arduous task of reliving my adventures. Thank you for getting me to the finishing line and making me understand why I was embarking on a memoir in the first place (see the preface).

It hasn't all been plain-sailing. After it had taken me about a month to draft the preface and the first chapter, I realized that writing wasn't going to come as naturally to me as creating new music, and I think I'd more or less shelved the project. Then my friends Misha Glenny and Kirsty Lang kindly read what I'd written and, while continuing to urge me to persevere, suggested the possibility of finding a writing collaborator. For a while I stubbornly believed that if I was going to do it, I should do it all myself, but then of course inevitably nothing got written. A couple of years went by and often, after reading and hearing my stories in media interviews, people would kindly tell me that I should write a book. One of them was the broadcast journalist, writer and chair of literary events Georgina Godwin, who then helpfully went on to suggest someone she had interviewed at various book festivals. That person was Stuart Prebble.

Obviously I immediately Googled him and was impressed by his illustrious broadcasting career, which included being a former CEO of

ITV. More relevant to me though, were the books he'd written, which included one on the sinking of the Belgrano called "Secrets of the Conqueror" and he'd also ghost-written a book by Parm Sandhu called "Black and Blue".

Claire and I were just in the process of reading Stuart's CV when my phone rang and the caller ID said "Steve". When I answered, a familiar-sounding voice said, "Hello Phil, it's Steve Mason here and I understand my brother's coming to see you about working on your memoir." Steve had been the promoter of the famous gig at the Greyhound pub in Croydon in May 1972 when Roxy supported Davie Bowie. He explained that his industry name was Mason, but his real name was Prebble, and that Stuart was his younger brother. What's more, Stuart had helped to put up the posters for that gig nearly fifty years earlier.

Stuart and I met up a few days later and I immediately warmed to this man from South London, who also plays guitar and, together with his wife Sam runs the TV production company Story vault Films, which produces 'Portrait Artist of the year' and 'Landscape Artist of the year'.

Stuart and I agreed that it would be fun to collaborate on my memoir and so the process began, taking a couple of years, with time off and breaks. Stuart would listen carefully as I randomly downloaded my various memories and anecdotes, taking detailed notes, and then turn them as if by magic into readable prose. The resulting narrative prompted Claire and I to spend many hours remembering more of whatever I'd forgotten, and adding in the details to complete the stories. Stuart has become a good friend, I'm eternally grateful to Stuart for taking on this task and doing such a great job.

Ramón de España deserves a big Gracias for the Spanish translation which is so important for me and Juan Puchades my publisher for Spain and Latin America.

PHOTO CREDITS

Most of the photos in this book come from our family collection and the more recent from ctacta.co.uk. Below are photo credits for all images where the photographer is known. All photographs are copyright as listed. Apologies to any photographer who is not credited. Omissions can be corrected in future editions of the book.

page 50; Jon Prew,

page 57; Kieron 'Spud' Murphy,

page 78; Baríon,

page 86; Jon Prew,

page 94; Richard Wallis,

page 106; Tony McGee,

page 111; Ton Hendiks,

page 112; illustrated by Mmario Guión Lapresovitz,

page 126; Domingo J Casas

page 142; Domingo J Casas

page 191; Mark Allen,

page 194; Mark Allen,

page 199; Polly Samson,

page 206; Brian Rasic,

page 237; Wilson Popenoe

Back cover photo by Matthew Becker

Polly Samson lyrics by kind permission of Polly Samson

INDEX

Page numbers in italics refer to photographs. Names of albums are shown in italics, and tracks/songs in quotation marks. Abbreviation: PM = Phil Manzanera.

6PM (PM) 212–13, *213*
10cc 99, 115
   see also Creme, Lol; Godley, Kevin
50 Minutes Later (PM) 213–14, *213*
88-Keys 224–5
801 (band) 50, 94–8, *94*, *95*, *96*, *98*, 185
801 Live (801) 50, *94*, 97

Abbey Road studios, London 48, 60, 72, 125, 202–3
aeroplanes
   BOAC Stratocruiser 6–7, *6*, *7*
   Bristol Britannia *24*, 25
African Gypsies, The *178*, 179
Afro-Celt Sound System 181
Agee, Tawatha 253
Air Studios, London 72, 171, *172*
air travel
   in/from Colombia 150-151, 153, 155
   to/from Cuba 6–7, 24–5, *24*
   Roxy Music tours 92–3
   solo trips to Caracas 37–8
'All Along the Watchtower' (Bob Dylan) 143–4, 146
'All the Young Dudes'
   (group performance) 258

'All You Need is Love'
   (group performance) 152
Allen, Tony 232
'Amazona' (Roxy Music) 81
Amigo, Vicente 139, 141
analogue versus digital recordings
   (blind test) 202
Anderson, Ian 182, 183
Anderson, Rusty 173–4
Argentina 169, 249–50, *250*
Ash, Carola 9–10
asthma (in childhood) 10
Astoria studio, Hampton 117, *118*, 201, 202
'Astrud' (PM) 212
Aterciopelados 175–6, *175*
Atlantic Studios, New York 106–7, *106*
'Avalon' (Roxy Music) 108–9, 253
Avalon (Roxy Music) 105, 108–9, 211, 271

Baier, Fred 101
Baker, Ginger 182–3
   see also Cream
Ballet Flamenco de Mario Maya, El (flamenco dance troupe) 140

Baloi, Gito 179
Barbados 115
'Barbudos' (Cuban military) *19*, 22–3, *23*
Barone, Joao 172
    see also Paralamas
Barranquilla, Colombia 165, 242, 246, 248
    see also Colombia
Barrett, Syd 48, 49
Basing Street Studios, London 103, 105
Batista, Fulgencio 8, 15, 18–19
Beatles 38, *38*, 47, 52, 60, 61, 73, 270
    'All You Need is Love'
        (group performance) 152
    Ian MacCormick/MacDonald's
        book about 41
    'Let It Be' 52
    see also Harrison, George; Lennon,
        John; McCartney, Paul
Beck, Jeff 139, 185
Benson, George 139
Bernardo, Sonia 249, *249*
Bessey, Keith 134–5
'Big Day' (PM) 88
Blackwell, Chris 64, 108
BOAC (airline) 5, 6, 10, 30, 45, 166
    Stratocruiser 6–7, *6*, *7*
'Bob (Medley),' The (Roxy Music) 72
Boddy, Mike 260
Bogotá, Colombia 153–4, *154*, *155*
    see also Colombia
Boman, Eric 85–6
'Boots of Spanish Leather ' (Bob Dylan)
    142–3, 146–7
Bosé, Miguel 141
Bowie, David *246*
    at Chicago airport 93
    death 245
    influence on Roxy Music 66
    performs at David Gilmour concert
        205–7, *206*
    Roxy Music supports 67–9, *69*
    'Ziggy Stardust' 64
Brando, Marlon 9

Brexit 239
Brieva, Lucho 246–7
Bristol Britannia (jet prop plane) *24*, 25
British Council 5, 164–6, *164*
broken leg (twice) 84, 106
Bruce, Jack
    in Cuba with PM 243–5, *244*, *245*
    funeral and tribute concert 182–3
    at Guitar Legends, Seville 139, 141,
        142, 144, *145*, 147
bug-eyed glasses 63, *63*
Bunbury, Enrique 121, 129–30, *129*,
    130, 213, 247
    see also Héroes del Silencio

Cale, John 73
Cali, Colombia (charity concert) 149–53
Canada 91–2, 271
'Can't Turn You Loose' (group
    performance) 147
Capri 169–71
Capri Digital studios, Capri 169, *170*,
    171
Caribbean 115, 241
Carin, John 203, 237
Carrack, Paul 105
Cartagena, Colombia 246–7, *247*, 248,
    248
    see also Colombia
Castro, Fidel 15, 20, 22, 132
Caught by the Heart (Tim Finn and PM)
    258–61, *259*
CCK arena, Buenos Aires 250, *250*
'Chance Meeting' (Roxy Music) 61
childhood and youth *3*, *4*
    asthma 10
    Clapham neighbourhood 3–4
    Cuba 5–8, *9*, 10–14, *11*, 16–18,
        20–5, *23*, 212, 213
    death of father 43–6
    dog 25
    dressing up *11*, 12, 38

INDEX

early musical influences 13–15, *13*, 33, 38, 41
first bands 40–3, *40*, *41*, *42*, 49–50
Hawaii 27–30, *29*, *30*
schools
    Clapham primary 4
    Cuba 10, 12
    Dulwich College 34–7, *34*, *35*, *36*, 39, 40–1, 45–6, 47, 48
    Hawaii 28
    Venezuela 32, 36–7
songs about 212, 213
temporary jobs 51, 55–6
university applications 48, 49, 51, 59
Venezuela 30–4, *31*, 37–8
see also family
children 108, 115, 118, 222, 272–3, *281*, *282*
Chiorboli, Dan 178, 182
Christmas gatherings 117
Christmas on Earth Continued (concert event) 49
'Church in the Wild' (Jay Z and Kanye West) 222–5
Circo Beat (Fito Páez) 172, *173*
Clapham, London 3–4
Clapton, Eric 139
clothes and costumes
    bug-eyed glasses 63, *63*
    David Bowie 66, 69
    double denim 59
    dressing up as a child *11*, 12, 38
    Firebird outfit *84*
    platform boots 84
    school cricket pullover *55*, 60, 69
    see also Roxy Music: sartorial style
Cocker, Joe 139, 141
Cohen, Benjamin 241
Cohen, John 241–2
Cohen family tree *240*, 241, *242*
Collins, Albert 138
Colombia 149–55, 165, 175, 241, 242, 246–8, *247*, *248*

'Comfortably Numb' (Pink Floyd) 206
Command Studios, London 60
Compass Point studio, Nassau 108, *108*, *109*
Cooper, Ray 139
Corroncho (PM and Lucho Brieva) 246–7
Country Life (Roxy Music) 85–6
Cray, Robert 139, *140*, 147
Cream 41, 182, 183
Creme, Lol 102–3, 210
    see also Godley and Creme
Cropper, Steve 139, 141, 147
Crosby, David 203, 206
Cuba
    flight to 5–7
    gangsters and glamour 8–10
    Grand Prix 15–18, *16*, *17*
    homes in 10–12, *11*, *15*, 24, 133–4, *134*
    Hotel Naciónal 8–9, *8*, *9*
    initial impressions 7–8
    Karl Marx theatre 135, 245, *245*
    music scene 13, 15
    rebels and revolution 15–25, *19*, 212, 213
    returns to in adulthood 131–5, 243–5, *244*, *245*
Cuban missile crisis 24
Cubillas, Pito 120–1

Dagworthy, Wendy 67, *84*
Dali, Salvador 78–9, *78*
Daltrey, Roger 149, 150, 152–3, 155
'Dance Away' (Roxy Music) 107
Dark Side of the Moon (Pink Floyd) 73, 202
David Gilmour, Live in Gdansk (David Gilmour) 207–8
Davies, Rhett 108, *109*
Davis, Paul 101
de Crescenzo, Eduardo 130

de Ville, Nick 63
'Desaparecido' (PM) 213
Diamond Head (PM) 88–9, *88*
Diddley, Bo 138
disco sound 107
Division Bell (Pink Floyd) 201, 202, 207, 215
Dos Margaritas (Paralamas) 172–3, *173*
Draco Rosa, Robi 173–5, *174*
Drag Alley Beach Mob 40, *40*
drugs raid by Canadian Mounties 91–2
Dulwich College 34–7, *34*, *35*, *36*, 39, 40–1, 45–6, 47, 48
Dylan, Bob *140*, 141–8, *142*, *145*

'East of Asteroid' (801) 185
Echeverri, Andrea 232
'Echoes' (Pink Floyd) 205, 207
Edmonds, Dave 147
EG Management 54, 57, 60, 93, 104, 113–14
'Eight Miles High' (Roxy Music) 107
employment (temporary jobs) 51, 55–6
Endless River, The (Pink Floyd) 215–19, *216*, *217*, 230
Eno, Brian
    in *6PM* 212–13
    with 801 94–7, *94*, *95*
    advice on moving on 237
    allure 67, 77
    in *Diamond Head* 88
    green credentials 253
    musical talent 97
    personality clash with Bryan Ferry 77–8, 81, 195
    with Quiet Sun 90
    with Roxy Music 53, 54, 56, *57*, 77, 80–1, *81*, 194–5
    style 67
    see also 801 (band); Roxy Music
Enriquez, Augusto 132

see also Grupo Moncada
'Entre Dos Tierras' (Héroes del Silencio) 126
Ertegun, Ahmet 107
exposes PM to wider music 114–16
Expression Records
    creation of 119–20
    signings 120–2

Fame, Georgie 203
family
    brother (Eugen) *3*, 5, *5*, 13, 28, *28*, 34, *36*, 43, 48, 123
    children 108, 115, 118, 222, 272–3, *281*, *282*
    father (Duncan) *see* Targett-Adams, Duncan
    father's sisters (Gigi and Gertrude) *see* Owen, Gigi (Mary); Targett-Adams, Gertrude ('Gerts')
    mother (Magdalena) *see* Targett-Adams, Magdalena (née Manzanera)
    mother's ancestry *240*, 241–2, *242*
    mother's family 5, 150–1, 152–4, *154*, *155*, 248
    paternal biological grandfather (Mr Sparano) 161
    paternal grandfather (Percy Targett-Adams) 159–60, 161–2
    sister (Rosemary) *3*, 5, *5*, 13, 28, *29*, 121, 122
Fangio, Juan Manuel 15, 17–18
feathered dancers *191*, 193
Fenwick, Mark 54, 93, 113
Ferry, Bryan
    ego in Roxy Music 78, 93, 108–11
    fine art degree 63, 65
    with The Gas Board 65
    guitar playing 76
    perfectionism 270

INDEX

personality clash with Brian Eno 77–8, 81, 195
PM meets 53
relationship with Jerry Hall 87, 93, 104
Rock and Roll Hall of Fame induction 252, 254
solo work 93, 103–4, 189–90
songwriting 73–6
see also Roxy Music
'Fidel' (PM) 212
Finn, Neil 210, *256*, 258
see also Split Enz
Finn, Tim 86, 105, 120, 210, 258–61, *259*, *260*, *261*
see also Split Enz
Firebird VII (PM) 184, 185
Fleetwood Mac 258
see also Nicks, Stevie
Flesh and Blood (Roxy Music) 105, 107–8
food and drink
Clapham 4
Cuba 10, 12
Hawaii 28
school (Dulwich College) 35
For Your Pleasure (Roxy Music) 72–3, 77, 78
Ford Zodiac (family car) 12, *12*
Forenzics (Forenzics) 258
'Forever Young' (Bob Dylan) 247
Franca (family friend) *12*, *13*, 16
Fricke, David 219
'Frontera' (PM) 89, 140

Gabriel, Peter 120
gadgets, love of 119
Gallery Studios, Queen's Park 193, 202
Gallery Studios, St Ann's Court 101–3, *101*, *102*, *103*, 105, 108, 116, 127–8, 168, *183*
Gas Board, The 65

Geldof, Bob 200
Ghost of Santiago, The (Tim Finn and PM) *260*, 261
Giddings, John 191
Gilmour, David *197*
in *6PM* 213
Astoria studio 117, *118*, 201, 202
in Colombia 149, 150, 152–3, 155
David Gilmour, Live in Gdansk 207–8
misses Guitar Legends concert 139
On An Island album and tour 200–7
personality clash with Roger Waters 116, 117
PM meets and is inspired by 48, 49
as PM's West Sussex neighbour 199–200
Rattle That Lock album and tour 235–7, *237*
at Ronnie Scott's club *184*, 185
Royal Festival Hall concerts 200, 201
see also Pink Floyd
Girl, Jose (Josefa Gómez) *130*
Glover, Martin 218
Godley, Kevin 99, 102–3, 210
Godley, Sue 99–100, 119
Godley and Creme 104–5
see also Creme, Lol; Godley, Kevin
golf 32
Gore, Martin 122
Graceland (Paul Simon) 179
Grand Prix, Cuba (1958) 15–18, *16*, *17*
Grant, Eddy 115, 116
'Great Day for Freedom, A' (Pink Floyd) 207
Greene, Graham: *Our Man in Havana* 166
Greyhound pub, Croydon 67–9, 120
Griot (storytelling tradition) 181
Grunwald, Eveline 85–6
Grupo Moncada 131–2, *132*, 134–5
'Guantanamera' (PM) 212
Guevara, Che 15, 18

Guitar Legends, Seville (1991) 137–48, *138*, *140*, *142*, *143*, *145*, *147*
guitar playing (PM)
   with The African Gypsies *178*
   with Bryan Ferry (solo work) 103–4, 189
   at charity concert in Colombia 149–52
   with David Gilmour 203–7, *204*, *206*, 225, 236–7, *237*
   deliberate technical limitations 97, 211
   early experimentation 32
   Firebird VII gigs 184–5
   first chords on mother's guitar 14
   with Forenzics 258
   with Godley and Creme 104–5
   Greenwich, Millennium concert 190
   with Grupo Moncada 131–2, 134–5
   at Guitar Legends, Seville 140–7, *140*, *142*, *145*
   with Héroes del Silencio *127*
   improvisational style 42
   at Jack Bruce's tribute concert 183
   La Notte della Taranta festival, Puglia 227–8, *234*, 235
   The Liberation Project 180–2, *181*
   with Paralamas 172
   with Robi Draco Rosa 174
   in Roxy Music 61–2, 74, 85, 87, 110, *191*, 192–5, 210, 253, 255–6, *257*, *258*, 261, *262*, *263*, 267–71, *268*, *269*, *272*, 275–9
   sampled by Jay Z and Kanye West 221–5
   for San Remo TV festival 130–1
   with Tim Finn 258–61, *259*, *260*, *261*
   WOMAD tour 178–80
   see also solo work
guitars
   Epiphone Flying V 260
   Fender Stratocaster 59, 227

Fender Telecaster 260, 269
Framus Lorelei 32
Gibson 335 *50*, 51, 53, 61
Gibson 335 (replacement) 269, *269*
Gibson Firebird VII 79–80, *79*, *84*, 260, 269, 271
Gibson Les Paul 139, 269
Gibson SG guitar (failed hire-purchase) 50–1
Hofner Galaxie (hire-purchase) 38–40, *39*
Michael Sanchez Vegas's *33*
mother's 13–14, *14*

Hall, Jerry 87, 93, 104
Hard Rock Cafe 62
Harris, Ronnie 191
Harrison, George 147
   see also Beatles
Hastings *159*, 160–1
Havana *see* Cuba
Hawaii 27–30, *29*, *30*
Hay Festival in Colombia 246, 247, *247*
Hayward, Charles 40–1, 90, *90*, 183–5, *183*, *184*, *185*, 209
Helpmann, Robert 163
Hendrix, Jimi 49, 52
'Herida, La' (Héroes del Silencio) 128
Héroes del Silencio 120–2, *121*, *122*, 125–9, *126*, *127*, *129*
   see also Bunbury, Enrique
Hoffman, Rany 256
Holland, Jools 203
Hollingsworth, Tony 137–8
homes
   Cuba (childhood) 10–12, *11*, *15*, 24, 133–4, *134*
   London (childhood) 3, 43
   London (with mother) 53
   Queen's Park, London 193
   St Ann's Court, Chertsey 99–101, *100*, 117, 193, 199

INDEX

Venezuela (childhood) 32
West Sussex 199, 258, 265–6
Hotei, Tomoyasu 249, *249*
hotel bill, unpaid (Colombia) 152–3
Hotel Naciónal, Cuba 132, 244, *244*
Hotel Naciónal, Havana 8–9, *8*, *9*
Hubbard, Neil 110
'Hymn' (PM) 213
Hynde, Chrissie 246–7

'In Every Dream Home a Heartache' (Roxy Music) 253, 255
'In the Midnight Hour' (Roxy Music) 107
'India' (Roxy Music) 271
Island Records studio, London 88–90
Italian opera company (in Hastings) *159*, 161
Italy 180, 182, 207
   La Notte della Taranta festival 227–35, *227*, *228*, *233*, *234*, *235*

Jackson, Andy 215, 218
Jagger, Mick 104
Japan 90, 249
Jarrett, Dave 50, 90, *90*
Jason, Neil 253
Jay Z and Kanye West: *Watch the Throne* *221*, 222–5
jazz 53, 184–5
'Jealous Guy' (Roxy Music) 110
Jethro Tull (Roxy Music supports) 71–2
Jewish heritage 239–42
Jobson, Eddie 88, 93, 105, 252
   see also Roxy Music
K Scope (PM) 210
   sampled in 'Church in the Wild' (Jay Z and Kanye West) 221–5
Karl Marx theatre, Cuba 135, 245, *245*
Karoli, Constanze 85–6
Killarney, Ireland 114, *115*
King, BB 138

King, Mark 182–3
Kirios Studios, Madrid 125–6, *126*
Knopfler, Mark 139
Kouyate, N'Faly 180–1

'Ladytron' (Roxy Music) 61–2
Laister, Wendy 267, *283*
Lansky, Meyer 9
Latin music
   Aterciopelados 175–6, *175*
   Caught by the Heart (Tim Finn and PM) 258–61, *259*
   Corroncho (PM and Lucho Brieva) 246–7
   Diamond Head (PM) 88–9, *88*
   Fito Páez 169–72, *172*, *173*
   The Ghost of Santiago (Tim Finn and PM) *260*, 261
   Paralamas 172–3, *173*
   roots in 2–3, 13–14, 119, 168, 211
   Southern Cross (PM) 211–12
   see also Rock en Español
le Bon, Simon 253–4
Lear, Amanda 78
Leigh, Vivien 163, *163*
Lennon, John 110
   see also Beatles
Lennox, Annie 247
'Let It Be' (Beatles) 52
'Let's Stick Together' (Bryan Ferry) 103, 104
Liberation Project, The 180–2, *181*
Liberation Project, The (The Liberation Project) 180
Ligabue, Luciano 232, 233–5, *233*
Lindsell, Charlie 32
'Livin' la Vida Loca' (Ricky Martin) 174
Loder, Kurt 211
Lomax, Alan 229, 232
'Louder than Words' (Pink Floyd) 218–19
'Love is the Drug' (Roxy Music) 87, 253

295

Lowinger, Rosa, *Tropicana Nights* 9

McCabe, Annie 160
McCartney, Linda 102, 115–16
McCartney, Paul 102, 115–16, 269–70
   see also Beatles
MacCormick, Bill
attends Ronnie Scott's with PM 184
   and *Diamond Head* 89
   exposes PM to wider music 49
   and *Firebird VII* 184
   importance of friendship 209
   inspired by Soft Machine 48–9
   involvement with PM's record label 120
   and *K Scope* 210
   with Matching Mole 52, 55
   with Pooh and the Ostrich Feather 40, 41
   in Quiet Sun 90, *90*
   and *Southern Cross* 211
   see also 801 (band); Quiet Sun
MacCormick/MacDonald, Ian
   death 41
   and *Diamond Head* 89
   inspired by Soft Machine 48–9
   and *K Scope* 210
   and *Mainstream* 90
   at *New Musical Express* 41
   on PM's guitar playing 42–3
   Revolution in the Head (book) 41
   at Roxy Music press conference 192
   and *Southern Cross* 211
   suggests band name 'Pooh and the Ostrich Feather' 41
   translates lyrics for Héroes del Silencio 126
   writes press release for Quiet Sun 51–2
   see also 801 (band)
McGrath, Raymond 100
McGuinn, Roger 139

Mackay, Andy
   and *6PM* 213
   catches up with PM in New York 104
   children 108, 115
   and *Diamond Head* 88
   distinctive sound 268, 270, 276
   and The Explorers 114–16, *115*
   and *Firebird VII* 185
   leaves Roxy Music with PM 112–13
   Rock and Roll Hall of Fame induction 252, 254
   and *Rock Follies* (TV) 105
   shared house with Bryan Ferry 53
   solo work 93
   see also Explorers, The; Roxy Music
McNichol, Carol 67
Mainstream (Quiet Sun) 90, *91*
Mal, Baaba 179
'Maldito' (Héroes del Silencio) 126
Manifesto (Roxy Music) 106–7, *112*
Manzanera, Capitán 242
Manzanera, Magdalena *see*
   Targett-Adams, Magdalena (née Manzanera)
'Mariposa Tecknicolor' (Fito Páez) 172
Marr, Johnny 120
marriages
   Claire 139, 158, 199
   Sharon 69, 80, 157, 193
Marsden, Bernie 183
Martin, George 72, 73
   Air Studios 72, 171, *172*
Martin, Ricky 174
Mason, Nick 117, 216–18
   see also Pink Floyd
Mason, Steve 69, 120
Massarik, Jack 185
Matching Mole 52, 55
May, Brian 138, 172, 255, 256
Mello, Joao 236, 249
Melody Maker (magazine) 49, 51–2, 52–3, *52*, 79–80
   see also Williams, Richard

INDEX

'Memphis Soul Stew' (Roxy Music audition piece) 65
Mental Notes (Split Enz) 105
Merchan, Chucho 149, 151–2, 153
Millennium concert, Greenwich 190
'Million Reasons Why, A' (PM) 211–12
Mingus, Charlie 184
'Miss Shapiro' (PM) 88
Momentary Lapse of Reason, A (Pink Floyd) 117–18
Moncada Manzanera Live at the Karl Marx (Grupo Moncada) 134–5, *135*
Monkman, Francis 95
    see also 801 (band)
Moon, Keith 102
'More Than This' (Roxy Music) 253
Mosquitos, Los 120
Moss, Stirling 15–16, *16*, 17, 18
Mozdzer, Leszek *183*, 184–5, *185*, 207
Mtukudzi, Oliver 'Tuku' 179
Muller, Kari-Ann 64
musical director roles (PM)
    Guitar Legends, Seville (1991) 137–48, *138*, *140*, *142*, *143*, *145*, *147*
    La Notte della Taranta festival, Puglia (2015) 227–35, *227*, *228*, *233*, *234*, *235*
    see also producing (PM)
Musician's Union 171–2

Naples 161, 162
Nash, Graham 203, 206
Nassau, Bahamas (Compass Point studio) 108, *108*, *109*
New York City 28
Nicks, Stevie 252, 255, 258
Norman-Taylor, Dominic 229
Notte della Taranta, La (festival) (Puglia) (2015) 227–35, *227*, *228*, *233*, *234*, *235*

'Nuestros Nombres' (Héroes del Silencio) 128

O'List, Dave 53–4
On An Island (David Gilmour) 184, 200–3, 230
'One Slip' (Pink Floyd) 118
O'Rourke, Steve 113–14, 115, 117, 118, 150, 151
'Out of the Blue' (Roxy Music) 85, 253
Owen, Gigi (Mary) 43, 158, 159
    tells PM about paternal family 158–62

paddle steamer *241*, 242
Páez, Fito 169–72, *172*, *173*
Palladino, Pino 139
Paralamas 172–3, *173*
Paul, Les 139
Peel, John 56, 64, 183
Pemberton, Mike 115
Phillips, Simon 95, 97, 139, 141, 142, 143, 210
    see also 801 (band)
Phiri, Ray *178*, 179
piano lessons 37
Pink Floyd
    band dynamics and tensions 116
    Dark Side of the Moon 73, 202
    Division Bell 201, 202, 207, 215
    The Endless River 215–19, *216*, *217*, 230
    gigs and tours 49, 120
    A Momentary Lapse of Reason 117–18
    PM writes for 117–18
    production techniques 61
    A Saucerful of Secrets 48
    see also Gilmour, David; Mason, Nick; Wright, Richard
Pipa de la Paz, La (Aterciopelados) 175–6, *175*

297

pirate ancestry 241
pizzica music 229, 230
   see also Notte della Taranta,
      La (festival) (Puglia)
Poland 185, 207
Polo, Lucas 249, 268–9
Pooh and the Ostrich Feather 41, *41*, *42*
Portuguese citizenship investigations
   239–42
'Prairie Rose' (Roxy Music) 85
Pratt, Guy 195, 203, 206, 237
Preisner, Zbigniew 292
Price, Antony 62–3, 66, 85, 107
Price, Bill 73
Price, Dave 54
Primitive Guitars (PM) 211
producing (PM) 167–76
   Aterciopelados 175–6, *175*
   David Gilmour (*Live in Gdansk*
      album) 207–8, *233*
   David Gilmour (*On an Island*)
      200–3
   David Gilmour (*Rattle That Lock*)
      235–6
   Fito Páez 169–72, *172*, *173*
   Héroes del Silencio 120–2, 125–9,
      125
   Los Mosquitos 120
   Paralamas 172–3, *173*
   Pink Floyd *(The Endless River)*
      215–19
   Robi Draco Rosa 173–5, *174*
   Split Enz 86, 105
   see also musical director roles (PM)
Punter, John 73
Puxley, Simon 76
'Pyjamarama' (Roxy Music) 76

Queen Elizabeth Hall, London 97
Quiet Sun 50–2, *51*, 89–90, *90*, *91*, 183

Rak Studios, London 192, 195
Ramone, Phil 139, 144
Rattle That Lock (David Gilmour)
   235–7, *237*
Rayner, Eddie 210, 258
   see also Split Enz
'Rayo De Bala' (PM) 213
Reading Festival 95, 97, *98*
record label (Expression Records) 180
   creation of 119–20
   signings 120–2
Ribeiro, Bi 172
   see also Paralamas
Richards, Keith 139, *140*, 141, 143–4,
   147
Ridge Farm studio, Surrey 105–6, *197*
Robertson, Robbie 147
Rock and Roll Hall of Fame, Roxy
   Music's induction 251–6, *254*,
   256, *257*, *258*
rock and roll music (PM discovers) 33
Rock en Español 168
   Enrique Bunbury 121, 129–30, *129*,
      130, 213, 247
   Héroes del Silencio 120–2, *121*, *122*,
      125–9, *126*, *127*, *129*
   Los Mosquitos 120
   Robi Draco Rosa 173–5, *174*
Rock Follies (TV) 105
Rolling Stone (magazine) 107, 111, *121*,
   211, 219
Rolls-Royce (Roxy Music metaphor)
   196–8, *196*
Ronnie Scott's Club 184–5, *184*, *185*
Rose, Chris 101
Rosen, Jeff 141, 144
Roxy (Roxy Music) 60–5
Roxy Music 60, 66, 75, 76
   1976 breaks up 93
   1978 reforms 104–5
   1982 breaks up 112
   2000 reforms 190–2
   album covers *112*

INDEX

Country Life 85–6
Roxy 63–4, 65
For Your Pleasure 78
band dynamics and tensions 53–4, 77–8, 108–12, 195
changing line-up 66, 81, *81*, 105, 252, 253, 254
critical reception 64, 107, 211, 270, 275–9
EG Management audition 54
fans 83–4, 270–1
finances
    album income 87–8
    gig income 69
    "tape lease" deal 57, 60
    World Tour 191, 192
gigs and tours
    50th anniversary tour (2022) 261, *262*, *263*, 266–79, *268*, *269*, *272*, *274*
    Australia (1970s) 80, 86
    Australia (1982) 211
    Britain (1970s) 57, 59–60, 67–9, *69*, *70*, 71, 80, 83–4
    Canada (1976) 91–2
    Europe (1970s) 80, 84
    New Zealand (1970s) 80
    punishing schedule 91, 92–3
    United States (1970s) 71–2, 80, 92–3
    United States (1981-1982) 111–12, *111*
    World Tour (2001-2006) *188*, 191, *191*, 192–3
guitar setup (2022 tour) 268–9
PM auditions with 52–3
PM joins 56–7
recording 55
    Avalon 105, 108, 211
    Country Life 85
    Flesh and Blood 105
    'Jealous Guy' 110
    latest attempt (aborted) 194–5

Manifesto 106–7
Roxy 60–2
technology and production techniques 61–2, 73, 74, 77
For Your Pleasure 72–3, 77
reflections on 196–8, 270, 273
Rock and Roll Hall of Fame induction 251–6, *254*, *256*, *257*, *258*
Rolls-Royce metaphor 196–8, *196*
sartorial style 59–60, 62–3, 66–7, *67*, *68*, 70, 84, *84*, 107
session musicians 108–9, 110
songwriting 73–6, 81, 85
sound 61–2, 70, 77, 107, 110, 254, 268, 270
stagecraft 62, 84, 193
TV appearances 67, 87, 93
    Top of the Pops 70, 193, *194*, 253–4
video ('Avalon') 109
see also Eno, Brian; Ferry, Bryan; Jobson, Eddie; Mackay, Andy; Thompson, Paul; *specific albums and tracks*
Rutherford, Angie 200
Rutherford, Mike 200

Saatchi, Phil 130
sampled guitar riff 221–5
Samson, Polly 150, 200, 202, 218–19, 235
San Remo TV festival, Italy 130–1
Sanchez Vegas, Michael 32
    father 33, 34, 43
    guitar *33*
Satriani, Joe 139
Saucerful of Secrets, A (Pink Floyd) 48
schools
    Clapham primary 4
    Cuba 10, 12

Dulwich College 34–7, *34*, *35*, *36*, 39, 40–1, 45–6, 47, 48
Hawaii 28
Venezuela 32, 36–7
Senderos de Traición (Héroes del Silencio) 126, *127*
Seville, Guitar Legends pre-event (1991) 137–48, *138*, *140*, *142*, *143*, *145*, *147*
'Shine On You Crazy Diamond' (Pink Floyd) 200
Simon, Franca *12*, *13*, *16*
Simon, Paul 179
Simonon, Paul 232, *233*
Simpson, Graham 65–6
Sinfield, Pete 60
Singers, Claire *280*, *281*, *282*, *283*
  children 273
  first meeting 139
  homes with 193, 199
  PR work 139, 200, 202, 203, 205, 236
  relationship and marriage to PM 158, 199
  vocals in 'Hymn' 213
singing (PM) 214, 256
Siren (Roxy Music) 87
Soft Machine 41, 48–9, 52
Solidarity Express (The Liberation Project) 182
solo work 209–14
  6PM 212–13, *213*
  50 Minutes Later 213–14, *213*
  concert in Cuba 243–5, *245*
  Diamond Head 88–9, *88*
  K Scope 210
    sampled by Jay Z and Kanye West 221–5
  Primitive Guitars 211
  The Sound of Blue 249–50, *249*
  Southern Cross 211–12
  Vozero 212, *213*
'Song for Europe, A' (Roxy Music) 81

songwriting (PM)
  with Charles Hayward (early years) 41
  with David Gilmour/Pink Floyd 117–18
  for Roxy Music 81, 85
  for solo albums 211–14
  with Tim Finn 258–61
Sound of Blue, The (PM) (album and tour) 249–50, *249*
South Africa 180, 182
Southern Cross (PM) 211–12
Spedding, Chris 103, 253
Spenner, Alan 105
Split Enz 86, *86*, 105
  see also Finn, Neil; Finn, Tim; Rayner, Eddie
sports
  Dulwich College 37, 117
  surfing, Hawaii 28–30
  tennis and water-skiing with Roger Waters 116–17
Squire, Chris 210
St Ann's Court, Chertsey 99–101, *100*, 117, 193, 199
  Gallery Studios 101–3, *101*, *102*, *103*, 105, 108, 116, 127–8, 168, *183*
Stavi, Yaron *183*, 184, 249, *249*
Stewart, Eric 115
Stranded (Roxy Music) 81
Strawberry Studio, Stockport 102–3
Sun Park studio, Surrey 210
'Sunshine of Your Love' (Jack Bruce/PM) 145–6, 245
surfing, Hawaii 28–30
Symbiosis 51
  see also Matching Mole

Tabernilla, General 11–12, 20, 22, 23
Targett-Adams, Duncan *12*, *16*, *29*, *36*
  acting work 162–3
  biological father 161

INDEX

BOAC work 5, 6, 10, 30
British Council work 5, 164–6, *164*
cars 12, 28
death 43–6
early memory of (Brighton trip) 4–5
golf 32
lifestyle in Havana 10–11, 12
lifestyle in Hawaii 28, 30
love of gadgets 119
marries Magdalena Manzanera 5, 165, *165*, 248
newspaper interview about fall of Batista 20–1, *21*
OBE citation *44*, 45, 166
settles guitar hire-purchase debt 39–40
song about ('Hymn') 213
Targett-Adams, Eugen *3*, 5, *5*, 13, 28, *28*, 34, *36*, 43, 48, 123
Targett-Adams, Gertrude ('Gerts') 43, 158, 159
Targett-Adams, Lizzie 159–62
Targett-Adams, Magdalena (née Manzanera) *5*, *12*, *15*, *16*
  after Duncan's death 45
  ancestry *240*, 241–2, *242*
  on the dangers of Colombia 149
  and fall of Batista 22, 23
  family 5, 123, 150–1, 152–4, *154*, *155*, 242, 248
  guitar 13–14, *14*
  illness and death 122–3
  marries Duncan Targett-Adams 5, 165, *165*, 248
  moves nearby 119
  pride in children 123
  song about ('Tuesday') 213
  supports PM's music 47–8, 50, 59, 65
Targett-Adams, Percy 159–60, 161–2
Targett-Adams, Rosemary *3*, 5, *5*, 13, 28, *29*, 121, 122
Targett-Adams, Sharon 69, 80, 118–19, 157, 193, 272

Taylor, John 253
'Technicolour UFO' (PM) 213–14
'Tema de Piluso' (Fito Páez) 172
'That's All I Know' (PM) 214
therapy 212
Thomas, Chris 73, 77, 85, 87, 194, 202
Thompson, Paul
  in *6PM* 213
  in *Corroncho* 247
  in *Diamond Head* 88
  in *K Scope* 210
  'perfect rock drummer' 270
  Rock and Roll Hall of Fame induction 252, 253
  with Roxy Music 54, 103, 105, 192, 266, 270
  solo work 93
  see also Roxy Music
Thompson, Richard 145–7, *145*
Thornton, Fonzi 253
'Tomorrow Never Knows' (801) 97
Top of the Pops (TV) 70, 193, *194*, 253–4
Tropicana Club, Havana 13
'Tuesday' (PM) 213
Tunnard, Christopher 100
TV appearances
  Guitar Legends, Seville (1991) 137–48, *138*, *140*, *142*, *143*, *145*, *147*
  with Roxy Music 67, 70, 87, 93, 193, *194*, 253–4
  San Remo TV festival 130–1

university applications 48, 49, 51, 59

Vagabundo (Robi Draco Rosa) 174, *174*
Vai, Steve 139
'Vampiro Bajo El Sol, El' (Paralamas) 172
Velvet Underground 41, 53, 61, 73

301

'Venceremos' (PM) 212
Venezuela 30–4, *31*, 37–8
Venice 207
Vianna, Herbert 172, 173
video for 'Avalon' (Roxy Music) 109
'Virginia Plain' (Roxy Music) 70, 192
Vozero (PM) 212, *213*

Waikiki beach, Hawaii 28–30, *30*, 89
Wakeman, Rick 139
Walsh, Joe 138
Watch the Throne (Jay Z and Kanye West) *221*, 222–5
Waters, Roger 116–17, 139
Watson, Lloyd 97
   see also 801 (band)
West Runton Pavilion, Cromer *96*, 97
Wetton, John 103, 210
Weyler, Javier 249
Williams, Richard 51–2, 54, 64, 98
'Wish You Were Here' (Pink Floyd) 205
WOMAD tour *177*, 178–80
Wraith, James 114
   see also Explorers, The

Wright, Richard 117, 200, 203, 205, 215, 219
Wyatt, Robert
   in *6PM* 213
   accident 89
   in *Corroncho* 247
   with David Gilmour 200, 206
   in *Diamond Head* 89
   PM is inspired by 48–9
   with Symbiosis 51
   visits Ronnie Scott's with PM 184
   see also Soft Machine

'Years of the Quiet Sun' (Quiet Sun) 51–2
'You Really Got Me' (801) 97
Youth (Martin Glover) 218

Zappa, Frank 105
Zenith radio 33, *33*
Ziegler, Robert 203
'Ziggy Stardust' (David Bowie) 64

DISCOGRAPHY

1972	Roxy Music	Roxy Music	Member of Attributed Artist, Guitar
1973	For Your Pleasure	Roxy Music	Member of Attributed Artist, Guitar
1973	Stranded	Roxy Music	Member of Attributed Artist, Guitar, Treatments, Composer
1973	These Foolish Things	Bryan Ferry	Guitar, Guitar (Electric)
1974	Country Life	Roxy Music	Producer, Member of Attributed Artist, Guitar, Drums, Composer
1974	Fear	John Cale	Main Personnel, Guitar, Slide Guitar, Executive Producer
1974	Here Come the Warm Jets	Brian Eno	Guest Artist, Main Personnel, Guitar, Composer
1974	In Search of Eddie Riff	Andy Mackay	Guest Artist, Guitar, Saxophone
1974	MusikLaden	Roxy Music	Composer
1974	Taking Tiger Mountain (By Strategy)	Brian Eno	Guest Artist, Arranger, Main Personnel, Guitar, Assistant Producer, Composer
1974	The End	Nico	Guitar, Guitar (Electric)
1975	Diamond Head	Phil Manzanera	Primary Artist, Producer, Vocals, Guitar, Tiple, Piano, Organ, Mellotron, Keyboards, Synthesizer Strings, Handclapping, Bass, Fuzz Guitar, Composer
1975	Mental Notes	Split Enz	Producer
1975	Ruth Is Stranger Than Richard	Robert Wyatt	Composer
1975	Siren	Roxy Music	Member of Attributed Artist, Guitar, Composer
1975	Slow Dazzle	John Cale	Main Personnel, Guitar
1976	801 Live	801	Liner Notes, Primary Artist, Vocals, Guitar, Composer
1976	Let's Stick Together	Bryan Ferry	Guitar

Year	Title	Artist	Credits
1976	Mainstream	Quiet Sun	Guitar, Guitar (Electric), Guitar (12 String Electric), Guitar (12 String), Piano, Fender Rhodes, Keyboards, Group Member, Composer
1976	Second Thoughts	Split Enz	Producer
1976	Viva!	Roxy Music	Guest Artist, Guitar, Group Member, Composer
1977	Before and After Science	Brian Eno	Guest Artist, Main Personnel, Guitar, Guitar (Rhythm)
1977	Dysrhythmia	Split Enz	Producer
1977	Greatest Hits	Roxy Music	Guitar, Composer
1977	In Your Mind	Bryan Ferry	Guitar, Musician
1977	Listen Now	801 / Phil Manzanera	Primary Artist, Producer, Vocals, Guitar, Piano, Keyboards, Organ (Hammond), Composer
1978	K-Scope	Phil Manzanera	Primary Artist, Producer, Liner Notes, Vocals, Guitar, Piano, Piano (Electric), Farfisa Organ, Keyboards, Synthesizer, Composer
1978	Resolving Contradictions	Andy Mackay	Guest Artist, Guitar
1979	Freeze Frame	Godley & Creme	Guitar, Composer, Producer
1979	Manifesto	Roxy Music	Guitar, Composer
1980	Caught in the Crossfire	John Wetton	Guitar
1980	Flesh + Blood	Roxy Music	Member of Attributed Artist, Guitar, Bass, Guitar (Rhythm), Lead, Composer
1980	Underwater Moonlight	The Soft Boys	Composer
1981	First 7 Albums [Box Set]	Roxy Music	Guitar
1981	Rock Bottom/Ruth Is Stranger Than Richard	Robert Wyatt	Composer
1981	Total Recall: A History, 1972-1982	Roxy Music	Composer
1982	Avalon	Roxy Music	Guitar, Group Member, Composer
1982	Enz of an Era	Split Enz	Producer
1982	First Edition [EG]		Performer, Composer, Primary Artist
1982	Primitive Guitars	Phil Manzanera	Primary Artist, Producer, Engineer, Mixing, Liner Notes, Vocals, Guitar, Keyboards, Composer
1983	Atlantic Years (1973-1980)	Roxy Music	Guitar, Composer

DISCOGRAPHY

1983	The High Road [Live EP]	Roxy Music	Guitar
1983	The High Road [Video]	Roxy Music	Guitar, Composer
1984	Steeltown	Big Country	Composer
1985	The Collection 1973-1984 [Concept]	Split Enz	Producer
1985	The Explorers	The Explorers	Producer, Composer, Guitar, Keyboards, Guitar (Synthesizer)
1986	Count Three & Pray	Berlin	Composer
1986	Miami Vice II		Composer
1986	More Blank Than Frank	Brian Eno	Guest Artist
1986	More Blank Than Frank (Desert Island Selection)	Brian Eno	Guest Artist, Producer, Guitar
1986	Park Hotel	Alice	Guitar
1986	Street Life: 20 Great Hits	Bryan Ferry / Roxy Music	Guitar, Composer
1987	A Momentary Lapse of Reason	Pink Floyd	Composer
1987	Angels in the Architecture		Producer, Performer, Composer, Primary Artist
1987	First (The Sound of Music)	Then Jerico	Composer
1987	Guitarissimo (1975-1982)	Phil Manzanera	Primary Artist, Producer, Compilation Producer, Guitar, Tiple, Harmonica, Piano, Synthesizer, Bass, Treatments, Composer
1987	History Never Repeats [Video]	Split Enz	Producer
1987	History Never Repeats: The Best of Split Enz	Split Enz	Producer
1987	King's Road, 1972-1980	John Wetton	Guest Artist, Guitar
1987	Learning to Fly	Pink Floyd	Composer
1987	One Slip	Pink Floyd	Composer
1987	One World	Phil Manzanera	Primary Artist, Producer, Composer, Arranger, Guitar, Keyboards
1987	Shore Leave	Yung Wu	Composer
1987	Wetton/Manzanera	Phil Manzanera / John Wetton	Primary Artist, Producer, Arranger, Member of Attributed Artist, Guitar, Keyboards, Composer
1988	Crack the Whip	Phil Manzanera	Primary Artist, Guitar
1988	Delicate Sound of Thunder	Pink Floyd	Composer

1988	Greetings from...Louisiana	Al Ferrier	Composer
1988	Guitar Speak		Producer, MIDI Guitar, Performer, Composer, Primary Artist
1988	Possessions	Ann Dejarnett	Composer
1989	Christmas	Andy Mackay / Phil Manzanera / The Players	Primary Artist, Producer, Guitar, Executive Producer
1989	Manzanera & MacKay	Andy Mackay / Phil Manzanera	Primary Artist, Producer, Guitar, Keyboards, Composer
1989	Museum	Mary My Hope	Composer
1989	Novice	Alain Bashung	Guest Artist
1989	Thing of Beauty	Volcano Suns	Composer
1989	Up in Smoke	Phil Manzanera	Primary Artist, Producer, Guitar
1990	Fire on the Moon	Dream Command	Composer
1990	Heart Still Beating	Roxy Music	Guitar, Composer
1990	Mato Grosso	Phil Manzanera	Primary Artist, Engineer, Mixing, Guitar (Acoustic), Guitar (Electric), Keyboards, Programming, Drum Programming, Performer, Composer
1990	Monster Is Bigger Than the Man	Mary My Hope	Composer
1990	Senderos de Traición	Héroes del Silencio	Dirigida, Realization, Mixing, Producer, Remix Engineer
1990	Southern Cross	Phil Manzanera	Primary Artist, Producer, Composer, Vocals, Guitar, Guitar (Electric), Tiple, Keyboards, Synthesizer, Guitar (Synthesizer), Guitar (Bass), Programming, Drum Programming, Bass, Effects
1990	Trashes the World	Alice Cooper	Composer
1991	Abracadabra	ABC	Guest Artist, Musician
1991	Boleros Hoy	Tania Libertad	Vocals, Primary Artist
1991	Delicate Sound: Live	Pink Floyd	Composer
1991	Mexico Voz Y Sentimiento, Vol. 2		Performer, Primary Artist
1992	La Carrera Panamerica	Pink Floyd	Composer
1992	Shine On	Pink Floyd	Composer
1992	Sounds of the Seventies: FM Rock, Vol. 3		Composer

DISCOGRAPHY

1992	Volume Five		Guitar
1993	1973-1979: Oddz & Enz	Split Enz	Producer
1993	Ambient, Vol. 1: A Brief History of Ambient		Producer, Performer
1993	Brazilian Contemporary Instrumental		Performer, Composer, Primary Artist
1993	El Espíritu del Vino	Héroes del Silencio	Mixing, Producer, Remix Engineer
1993	El Mar No Cesa	Héroes del Silencio	Mixing, Remix Engineer
1993	Eno Box II: Vocals	Brian Eno	Guitar, Guitar (Rhythm), Composer
1993	Hit the Ground Running, Pt. 1	Tim Finn	Guitar
1993	Live at the Borderline	Tim Finn	Guitar
1993	Live at the Karl Marx	Phil Manzanera	Primary Artist, Producer, Composer, Guitar, Vocals (Background)
1993	Revolution Ballroom [Single]	Nina Hagen	Producer
1994	Ambient, Vol. 2: Imaginary Landscapes		Producer, Performer, Composer, Primary Artist
1994	Dali's Car	Brian Eno	Guitar
1994	Jewel	Marcella Detroit	Guitar
1994	Mamouna	Bryan Ferry	Guest Artist, Guitar
1994	Oceano De Sol	Antonio Vega	Producer, Guitar, Conductor
1994	Que Bonito Es Casi Todo	La Lupita	Guest Artist
1994	Revolution Ballroom	Nina Hagen	Producer, Guitar, Guitar (12 String Acoustic), Drum Programming
1994	Seducing Down the Door: A Collection 1970-1990	John Cale	Guest Artist, Guitar
1995	Avalancha	Héroes del Silencio	Mixing, Remix Engineer
1995	Circo Beat (Beat Circus)	Fito Páez	Producer, Executive Producer
1995	Manzanera Collection	Phil Manzanera	Primary Artist, Producer, Guitar (Acoustic), Guitar (Electric), Tiple, Piano, Keyboards, Synthesizer, MIDI Guitar, Percussion, Programming, Vocals (Background), Bass, Composer
1995	Pile Up	Pansy Division	Composer

1995	So Bad	Nina Hagen	Producer
1995	Take a Chance	Wofford Band	Composer
1995	Thrill of It All	Roxy Music	Guitar, Treatments, Composer
1995	Walk You Home	Tim Finn	Guitar (Electric)
1995	Wasted [Volume]		Guitar (Electric)
1996	One Chord to Another	Sloan	Composer
1996	Space Daze 2000		Composer
1996	Supernatural Fairy Tales: The Progressive Rock Era		Guitar
1996	The Island Years	John Cale	Guest Artist, Guitar, Slide Guitar, Executive Producer
1996	To Cry You a Song: A Collection of Tull Tales		Guitar, Primary Artist
1996	Vagabundo	Robi Rosa	Guest Artist, Producer, Director, Guitar
1997	9 Songs of Ecstasy	New London Consort / Philip Pickett / Pilgrimage	Guest Artist, Guitar (Electric)
1997	A Million Reasons Why	Phil Manzanera	Primary Artist, Arranger, Vocals, Guitar, Guitar (Electric), Tiple, Cello, Keyboards, Guica, Composer
1997	Euforia	Fito Páez	Producer
1997	La Pipa de la Paz	Aterciopelados	Guest Artist, Producer, Guitar
1997	Live at the Palace	The Explorers	Guitar
1997	Nowhere		Composer
1997	Radical Sonora	Bunbury / Enrique Bunbury	Producer, Guitar, Sampling
1997	Shleep	Robert Wyatt	Guest Artist, Main Personnel, Guitar
1997	Spellbound: The Very Best of Split Enz	Split Enz	Producer
1997	The Best of Then Jerico	Then Jerico	Composer
1997	This Is Space [Box Set]		Composer
1997	When the Red King Comes	Elf Power	Composer
1997	Wizard's Convention, Vol. 2	Eddie Hardin	Guest Artist, Guitar
1998	1998 Latin Grammy Nominees		Producer

DISCOGRAPHY

1998	A Nice Nightmare [Sony Special Products]	Alice Cooper	Composer
1998	Brazil Classics: Beleza Tropical, Vol. 2		Producer
1998	Live at Manchester University	801 / Phil Manzanera	Primary Artist, Guitar, Composer
1998	Live at Rainbow Music	Roxy Music	Guitar, Composer
1998	Outlandos D'Americas: A Rock en Español Tribute to the Police		Producer
1998	Rarezas	Héroes del Silencio	Producer, Director
1998	The Classic Years	Nico	Guest Artist, Guitar
1998	Trance Remixes: A Momentary Lapse of Reason	Pink Floyd	Composer
1998	Velvet Goldmine		Composer
1999	As Time Goes By	Bryan Ferry	Guitar
1999	Electronica Classix		Composer
1999	Jazz Spectrum: Real Jazz for Real People		Composer
1999	Nowomova: Wasted Lands	Phil Manzanera	Primary Artist, Producer, Composer, Guitar (Acoustic), Guitar (Electric), MIDI Guitar, Drum Programming, Guitar (Electroacoustic)
1999	Other Enz: Split Enz & Beyond	Split Enz	Guitar, Composer, Primary Artist
1999	Tribute to the Titans		Guitar
2000	1, 2, 3, Let's Dance		Producer
2000	Minage	Mónica Naranjo	Guitar
2000	Pequeño Cabaret Ambulante	Enrique Bunbury	Interpretation
2000	Soupsongs Live: The Music of Robert Wyatt		Guest Artist, Guitar (Electric), Composer
2000	Top Latino 2000 [12 Tracks]		Producer
2000	With a Song in My Heart	Caterina Valente	Composer
2001	Anthology	John Wetton	Guest Artist, Producer, Guitar, Keyboards

Year	Title	Artist	Role
2001	Canciones 1984-1996: The Best of Héroes del Silencio	Héroes del Silencio	Producer, Mixing, Remixing, Realization, Mezcla, Remix Engineer
2001	Classic Electronica		Guitar, Composer
2001	Concerto	Roxy Music	Engineer, Musician, Group Member, Composer
2001	Ediciones del Milenio	Héroes del Silencio	Dirigida, Realization
2001	El Jinete	Enrique Bunbury	Producer
2001	Libertad del Alma	Robi Rosa	Producer
2001	Live @ Hull	801	Primary Artist, Guitar, Composer
2001	Manzanera Archives: Rare One	Phil Manzanera	Primary Artist
2001	Musicos Poetas y Locos, Vol. 1		Director
2001	Ping Pong Bitches [EP]	Ping Pong Bitches	Guitar
2001	The Best of Roxy Music	Roxy Music	Musician, Composer
2001	Under Cover	Big Country	Composer
2001	Vintage	Roxy Music	Composer
2001	Vozero	Phil Manzanera	Primary Artist, Producer, Main Personnel, Vocals, Guitar, Guitar (Electric), Spanish Guitar, Piano, Synthesizer, Loops, Vocals (Background), Composer
2001	Xavier Cugat with José Luis Moneró: 1946-1948	Xavier Cugat	Composer
2002	Canterbury Tales: Nuggets from the Psychedelic Underground		Primary Artist
2002	Evolucion	Aterciopelados	Producer
2002	Goddess of Love	Bryan Ferry	Guitar
2002	Ladytron	Roxy Music	Musician, Composer
2002	Latino	801 / Phil Manzanera	Primary Artist, Producer, Vocals, Guitar, Percussion, Vocals (Background), Vox Organ, Composer
2002	Live at Manchester	801	Primary Artist, Guitar, Composer
2002	Live at the Apollo [Warner DVD]	Roxy Music	Composer
2002	Loose Screw	Pretenders	Producer, Translation, Vocal Producer

DISCOGRAPHY

2002	Reflection	Roxy Music	Guitar, Composer
2002	Singles Collection: The Mercury Tears	Big Country	Composer
2002	Solo Para Mi	Augusto / Augusto / Jose Augusto	Producer, Guitar, Percussion, Concept
2002	Stay Young 1979-1982	INXS	Composer
2002	The Complete Explorers	The Explorers / Andy Mackay / Phil Manzanera	Primary Artist, Liner Notes, Guitar (Synthesizer), Composer
2003	Cuckooland	Robert Wyatt	Guest Artist, Vocals
2003	Live	Roxy Music	Guitar, Composer
2003	Ringodom or Proctor	Head of Femur	Composer
2004	6pm	Phil Manzanera	Primary Artist, Producer, Main Personnel, Vocals, Guitar, Guitar (Acoustic), Guitar (Electric), Piano, Organ, Keyboards, Synthesizer, Drum Programming, Organ (Hammond), Composer
2004	Antología Audiovisual	Héroes del Silencio	Remixing, Dirigida, Realization, Mezcla
2004	Brian Eno's Taking Tiger Mountain by Strategy	Doug Hilsinger	Composer
2004	Como Me Acuerdo	Robi Rosa	Producer, Audio Production, Guitar
2004	Early Years/Avalon	Roxy Music	Composer
2004	His Greatest Misses	Robert Wyatt	Main Personnel, Guitar
2004	Inside Roxy Music 1972-1974: The Ultimate Critical Review	Roxy Music	Group Member
2004	Le Maquis Presents: Residence 3		Composer
2004	Night in Old Town	Susan & the Surftones	Composer
2004	The Collection [EMI]	Roxy Music	Composer
2004	The Platinum Collection	Bryan Ferry / Roxy Music	Guitar, Composer
2004	This Is Music		Producer, Composer, Primary Artist
2004	Universal Es Antonio Vega	Antonio Vega Tallés / Antonio Vega	Conductor

Year	Title	Artist	Role
2005	50 Minutes Later	Phil Manzanera	Primary Artist, Producer, Main Personnel, Vocals, Guitar, Guitar (Electric), Keyboards, Composer
2005	Colección Privada	Mónica Naranjo	Producer
2005	Lo Mejor de Antonio Vega: Autorretratos	Antonio Vega	Conductor
2005	Miami Vice: The Ultimate Collection		Composer
2005	The Strat Pack: Live In Concert		Group Member, Primary Artist
2006	Arnold Layne	David Gilmour	Vocals, Guitar
2006	Canciones 1996-2006	Bunbury / Enrique Bunbury	Guest Artist, Producer, Guitar
2006	Girl Monster		Composer
2006	On an Island	David Gilmour	Producer, Engineer, Audio Production, Main Personnel, Piano, Keyboards
2006	Smile	David Gilmour	Producer
2006	Thrill of It All: A Visual History 1972-1982	Roxy Music	Composer
2007	Comicopera	Robert Wyatt	Main Personnel, Guitar
2007	Era Vulgaris	Queens of the Stone Age	Composer
2007	Los Angeles	Michaela Melián	Composer
2007	Make It Wit Chu	Queens of the Stone Age	Composer
2007	Oh by the Way	Pink Floyd	Composer
2007	Remember That Night: Live at the Royal Albert Hall	David Gilmour	Vocals, Guitar
2007	The Art of Chill 4	The Orb	Assistant Producer
2007	The Unfairground	Kevin Ayers	Main Personnel, Performer
2008	Celebrations	Sterling International	Composer
2008	Classic Rock [EMI]		Composer
2008	El Hombre Delgado Que No Flaqueará Jamás	Enrique Bunbury	Producer

DISCOGRAPHY

2008	Everything That Happens Will Happen Today	David Byrne / Brian Eno	Guitar, Guitar (Resonator)
2008	Firebird VII	Phil Manzanera	Primary Artist
2008	Live at the Apollo	Roxy Music	Composer
2008	Live in Gdansk	David Gilmour	Producer, Mixing, Audio Production, Main Personnel, Vocals, Guitar, Guitars
2008	Modernity Killed Every Night	The Wolfmen	Composer
2008	Playlist: 70's Pop		Guitar
2008	Playlist: Driving		Guitar
2008	Sunshine of Your Love [Live]	Jack Bruce / Bob Dylan / Phil Manzanera / Keith Richards	Primary Artist
2008	The Coolest Songs in the World, Vol. 6		Composer
2008	The Music 1972-2008	Phil Manzanera	Primary Artist, Vocals, Quotation Author, Composer
2008	This Is 1972		Guitar
2008	This Is 1974		Guitar
2008	This Is 1980		Guitar
2008	Tour 2007	Héroes del Silencio	Guitar
2008	Where Were You: 1980		Composer
2009	Corroncho	Corroncho	Producer, Primary Artist, Vocals, Guitar, Composer
2009	Good Evening	Nite Jewel	Composer
2009	The Best of the Pretenders/ Break Up the Concrete	Pretenders	Introduction
2010	Olympia	Bryan Ferry	Additional Production, Composer, Guest Artist, Guitar
2011	Discovery	Pink Floyd	Composer
2011	Guitar Gods, Vol. 1	Steve Lukather / Phil Manzanera / Brian May	Primary Artist
2011	Hechizo: Tributo a Heroes Del Silencio/Bunbury		Primary Artist
2011	Siren/Manifesto/Flesh and Blood/Avalon	Roxy Music	Composer

Year	Title	Artist	Credits
2011	Watch the Throne	Jay-Z / Kanye West	Composer, Composer / Lyricist
2012	A Spoonful of Time	Nektar	Composer
2012	Another Music	Hopewell	Composer
2012	Nth Entities	Anna Le / Phil Manzanera	Primary Artist, Producer, Photography, Liner Notes, Guitar, Harmonica, Piano, Keyboards, Bass, Digital Effects, Composer, Piano (Grand), Synthesizer Strings
2012	The Complete Studio Recordings	Roxy Music	Primary Artist, Guitar, Treatments, Composer
2013	Cover Art	The Next Collective	Composer
2013	Excitement at Your Feet: The Tommy Keene Covers Album	Tommy Keene	Composer
2014	Different Every Time	Robert Wyatt	Composer, Guitar, Primary Artist, Producer
2014	Europa	Holly Johnson	Guitar
2014	Las 100 Mejores Canciones del Pop Español, Vol. 3		Guitar, Producer
2014	Las Clasicas del Rock Pop en Español, Vol. 2		Producer
2014	Love Child	FosseyTango	Featured Artist, Guitar
2014	Silver Rails	Jack Bruce	Guitar
2014	The Endless River	Pink Floyd	Producer
2015	Rattle That Lock	David Gilmour	Producer, Guitar (Acoustic), Keyboards, Organ (Hammond)
2015	Sinfonía Del Rock		Producer
2015	The Sound of Blue	Phil Manzanera	Primary Artist, Composer
2016	Archivos, Vol. 2: Duetos	Bunbury / Enrique Bunbury	Primary Artist
2017	Live at the Curious Arts Festival	Phil Manzanera	Primary Artist, Producer, Vocals, Guitar, Composer
2017	Live in Japan	Phil Manzanera	Primary Artist, Producer, Vocals, Guitar, Group Member, Composer
2017	Wonderland: The Essential Big Country	Big Country	Composer
2018	Canciones 1987-2017	Bunbury	Producer

DISCOGRAPHY

Year	Title	Artist	Role
2018	Vagabundo 22	Draco Rosa	Producer
2019	The Later Years 1987-2019	Pink Floyd	Composer
2019	The Later Years 1987-2019 [Highlights]	Pink Floyd	Composer
2020	Law of Attraction	Mike Casey	Composer
2020	Roxymphony	Andy Mackay / Phil Manzanera	Primary Artist
2020	Sympathy for the Devil: Live at the Royal Albert Hall, 1974	Bryan Ferry	Guitar
2021	Caught by the Heart	Tim Finn / Phil Manzanera	Primary Artist
2021	Film Music: Europa	Brian Eno	Assistant Producer, Guitar
2021	Film Music: Voices & Words	Brian Eno	Assistant Producer, Guitar
2021	Oh! You Pretty Things: Glam Queens & Street Urchins 1970-1976		Composer, Primary Artist
2022	Olympia Remixes	Bryan Ferry	Composer, Guitar, Producer
2022	The Ghost of Santiago	Tim Finn / Phil Manzanera	Primary Artist
2023	AM/PM	Manzanera Mackay	Primary Artist, Guitar, Keyboards
2023	50 Years of Music	Phil Manzanera	Primary Artist, Producer, Guitar

It's the jacket what did it # jacket!

Milton Keynes UK
Ingram Content Group UK Ltd.
UKHW050222280324
440095UK00001B/7